AF709372

AMERICAN ACCOUNTING ASSOCIATION

The By-Laws of the American Accounting Association state that the first purpose of the Association shall be "to initiate, encourage, and sponsor research in accounting and to publish or aid in the publication of the results of research." In harmony with this objective, the publication of the Studies in Accounting Research is aimed at encouraging and publishing research. This series is an outgrowth of the research program initiated by the Association in 1965. Under this program research projects and authors are selected by the Director of Research, who is assisted by a Research Advisory Committee.

When the project is commissioned, the author is allowed maximum freedom in conducting research. The author is solely responsible for the procedures followed and the research conclusions.

This project was commissioned by B. E. Cushing during his term as Director of Research and was overviewed by S. Sunder and N. Dopuch during their terms as Directors of Research. The Research Advisory Committee for this project consisted of:

D. S. Dhaliwal	University of Arizona
T. J. Frecka	University of Notre Dame
R. W. Holthausen	University of Pennsylvania
W. E. Ricks	Rosenberg Institutional Equity Management

Library of Congress Catalog Card Number 92-074726
ISBN 0-86539-078-9
Printed in the United States of America

Market Microstructure and Capital Market Information Content Research

By

Philip Brown, Greg Clinch, and George Foster

Philip Brown is KPMG Peat Marwick Professor of Accounting, University of Western Australia, Greg Clinch is Associate Professor of Management, Australian Graduate School of Management, University of New South Wales, and George Foster is Paul L. and Phyllis Wattis Professor of Management, Graduate School of Business, Stanford University.

American Accounting Association
1992

TABLE OF CONTENTS

PREFACE

Financial support for this monograph came from the American Accounting Association, University of New South Wales, University of Pennsylvania, Stanford University and University of Western Australia. B. E. Cushing, S. Sunder, and N. Dopuch, in their role as successive Directors of Research for the American Accounting Association, provided important support and encouragement.

This monograph benefitted from the constructive criticism of many individuals. Our advisory committee and reviewers consisted of:

- W. M. Cready, Texas A & M University
- D. S. Dhaliwal, University of Arizona
- T. J. Frecka, University of Notre Dame
- R. W. Holthausen, University of Pennsylvania
- M. C. Lee, University of Michigan
- W. E. Ricks, Rosenberg Institutional Equity Management

Seminars where our research was discussed included: University of Alberta, University of Arkansas, University of Arizona, CUNY-Baruch College, University of Colorado at Boulder, Glasgow University, University of Illinois at Urbana-Champaign, McGill University, University of Michigan, University of Nebraska, University of New South Wales, Rice University, San Francisco State University, University of Southern California, Stanford University, Texas Christian University, University of Washington, and University of Waterloo. Presentations were also made at the American Accounting Association's Annual Meeting and Doctoral Consortium, at the First Australian Finance and Banking Conference, and the Second International Conference on Asian - Pacific Financial Markets. Comments from individuals at these seminars and presentations provided valuable input into many aspects of the research reported in this monograph. Many individuals provided detailed input outside of seminars and presentations. We especially would like to thank M. Blume, C. Bronfman, R. Bowen, P. Jain, A. Kleidon, T. McInish, M. McNichols, R. Schwartz, D. Shores, T. Shevlin, and R. Wood.

Important details on the NYSE institutional infrastructure were obtained from interviews with officials of Dow Jones, Francis Emory Fitch, the New York Stocks Exchange, selected brokerage firms and selected specialist firms. We thank these officials for their time and willingness to share their institutional knowledge and insight.

The research assistance of A. Dravid, M. Gupta, B. Pearson, L. Sjoblom and D. Then, and the programming assistance of P. Vowles, are greatly appreciated.

Jeannette Ochoa and Lu Yujuico helped prepare the many revisions of this manuscript. We thank them for their endless patience and for the care, skill and humor with which they handled the manuscript.

Chapter 1
Introduction and Summary

1.1: Objectives of Research

Capital market information content research occupies a center-stage position in the accounting and finance literature. A growing trend in this research is the use of intraday data as a key element of the experimental design. This monograph has two related objectives:

- explore and illustrate how the growing body of knowledge about market microstructure can (a) provide new insights into how the capital market reacts to information releases, and (b) strengthen the design of information content studies using intraday data.
- extend the literature on the information content of earnings releases.

This chapter summarizes the major findings related to each of these two objectives. The sample examined is 100 companies listed on the New York Stock Exchange (NYSE) in the 1980 to 1985 period.[1] These companies are drawn from a broad cross-section of 20 industries from the extractive, manufacturing and service sectors of the economy.

1.2: Information Content Research and Market Microstructure

The market microstructure literature "focuses on the details of the trading process. The major elements of this process include the generation and dissemination of information, the arrival of orders, and the rules, institutions, and other design features of a market that determine how orders are transformed into trades" (Schwartz [1988, p. 168]).[2]

Market microstructure studies of the NYSE highlight the role played by trading floor operators. The results in this monograph are consistent with floor operators moving quickly once an earnings release appears on the Broadtape.[3] Significant increased security return variability occurs on the very

---

[1] The rate of change in capital markets has been sizable since the mid-1970s—see Schwartz [1988, 1991]. For this reason results in the 1980 to 1985 period may not readily generalize to other periods. For example, since 1985 there has been an increase in programmed trading which would have implications for the analysis of a trading volume series at the time of information releases.

[2] An early use of the "market microstructure" terminology is Garman [1976].

[3] Schwartz [1991] notes that "NYSE members who operate on the trading floor include:

- *Specialists*...supply immediacy to the market by providing two-way quotes in the absence of other trading interest.
- *Commission-House Brokers*...employed by the brokerage houses, commission-house or floor brokers link the brokerage houses with the specialist posts.
- *Two-Dollar Brokers*...perform the same functions as the commission-house brokers but are not employed by a brokerage house.
- *Competitive Traders*...deal for their own accounts.
- *Registered Competitive Market Makers*...deal for their own accounts—can be called upon by a floor official to aid a specialist firm by adding liquidity to the market at times of particular stress" (pp. 24-25).

Lee, Mucklow and Ready [1991] report evidence that specialists increase the bid-ask spread and reduce the depth of their quotations at the time of earnings releases.

first transaction after the earnings release. Security analysts and trading floor operators interviewed indicated that the first trade after an information release is often made by commission-house brokers operating on their own (firm's) account. Trading floor operators put a premium on responding quickly to earnings releases on the Broadtape. Being part of the NYSE infrastructure, they are able to trade rapidly in response to new information releases. (The advent of electronic-order-routing systems, such as SuperDOT, means that a set of players outside the NYSE infrastructure can now also trade rapidly in response to new information releases.)

Chapter 4 reports that systematic intraday patterns exist in nonearnings release periods in all four of the financial series we examine—mean security returns, security return variability, trading frequency, and trading volume.[4] Two examples of these intraday patterns are:

- the first transaction of the day has over four times the number of shares traded than other transactions during the day and has the highest security return variability of any transaction during the day.
- the last minute of trading has a spiked increase in the number of transactions vis-a-vis the number of transactions in prior trading minutes of the day.

Chapter 5 illustrates alternative ways to recognize these systematic intraday patterns, including: (i) separately examining subsamples in which the regularities may have different implications, and (ii) using a comparison portfolio that is constructed to control for these intraday patterns.

Because earnings releases cluster by time of the day, failure to incorporate intraday trading patterns into the research design can lead to misleading inferences about the information content of earnings releases. For example, Cready [1988] reports an increase in shares traded per transaction at the time of earnings releases based on an analysis of daily trading volume and the daily number of transactions. Focusing on the first transaction subsequent to an earnings release, we likewise find an increase in shares traded per transaction for our full sample of earnings releases. However, this increase is most marked in the subsample with earnings releases made outside trading hours. The first transaction of each day is conducted with an auction trading regime in which many overnight orders may be batched into a single transaction. An increase in shares traded for the opening transaction subsequent to an earnings release may be due to:

(a) an increase in the number of shares per overnight order,
(b) an increase in the number of overnight orders batched into the opening transaction, or
(c) a combination of (a) and (b).

[4] Many of the patterns documented in Chapter 4 have been reported elsewhere in the literature—see Appendix A. The trading frequency series patterns have been less fully documented elsewhere vis-a-vis other series we examine (such as the security return variability series).

Given the current NYSE institutional arrangements, it is not possible to assess from transaction data the relative importance of (a), (b) and (c) for earnings releases made outside trading hours. When we examine earnings releases made in the 10.30 A.M. to 3.30 P.M. trading period, there is not a statistically significant change in shares traded for the first transaction subsequent to an earnings release.

1.3: Information Content of Earnings Releases

Chapter 5 presents a comprehensive analysis of the behavior of four financial series (security return variability, trading frequency, trading volume, and mean security returns) at the time of earnings releases. Both transaction time and calendar time modes of analysis are employed:

- transaction time—the most granular unit of analysis we use is each individual transaction. Observations are sequenced according to the number of transactions prior to and subsequent to an information release.[5]
- calendar time—the most granular unit of analysis we use is a calendar minute. Observations are sequenced according to the number of minutes (in trading time) prior to and subsequent to an information release.[6]

Chapters 4 and 5 highlight the differences in results in transaction time vis-a-vis calendar time. For example, Chapter 5 reports for the full sample that security return variability is significantly different from a control group (at the .05 level) for the first transaction subsequent to an earnings release but not for any of the next sixty transactions. The security return variability series in transaction time shows a highly spiked increase at the time of an earnings release. In contrast, this same series in calendar time shows a more smoothed pattern of increased variability—29 out of the first 30 trading minutes from the minute of the earnings release show significantly different security return variability. As discussed in Chapter 4, this difference between transaction time and calendar time is explained by the "smoothing" phenomenon where calendar time analysis aggregates results across firms which do not trade in each calendar unit time employed.

Of the four financial series we examine, trading frequency is the least analyzed one in the existing literature.[7] Chapter 5 reports that immediately

---

[5] A refinement of the transaction time approach reported in this monograph would be to examine changes in bid-ask spreads or the depth of specialist's quotations in between successive transactions—see Lee, Mucklow and Ready [1991]. The results we report are based on the most granular unit of analysis for the transaction series, but not the most granular unit of analysis for a combination of capital market series (such as a transaction series and a bid-ask spread series).

[6] The ISSM data base described in Appendix B reports the minute and second of each transaction. Thus, the most granular calendar time unit of analysis in the ISSM data base is a calendar second. This data base was not available for the full 1980 to 1985 period covered in this research.

[7] The most detailed evidence on trading frequency is Woodruff and Senchak [1988]. They report trading frequency ratios for the first half hour, second half hour, second hour and third hour subsequent to an earnings release.

prior to the minute of the earnings release there is a reduction in trading frequency. This is consistent with the earnings release time being relatively predictable and market participants reducing the frequency of their trading immediately prior to the release. Once an earnings release appears on the Broadtape, there is a significant increase in trading frequency that extends over the 22 subsequent transactions. The average time from transaction -1 (last transaction prior to the earnings release) to transaction 0 (first transaction subsequent to the release) is 39.76 minutes (compared to 40.69 minutes in a control group). A breakdown of the time between transactions -1 and 0 shows a marked pattern not documented in the prior literature:

Average Times	Earnings Release Sample	Control Group Sample
• Transaction -1 to earnings release	25.54 min.	20.93 min.
• Earnings release to transaction 0	14.22 min.	19.76 min.

This marked pattern of reduced trading frequency prior to and then increased trading frequency for the first transaction after the earnings release is a new result. It illustrates the importance market participants place on the earnings release.

Prior studies have documented a sizable increase in trading volume per calendar time period at the time of an earnings release. Chapter 5 reports the new finding that this increase is primarily due to an increase in trading frequency rather than an increase in the number of shares traded per transaction. One explanation is that each investor does not (on average) increase the size of his trading order at the time of an earnings release, but that there is a higher proportion of total investors trading. An alternative explanation is that investors do increase their average trading order size, but that it shows up in terms of more transactions per time unit rather than more shares per transaction. One possibility consistent with this alternative explanation is that specialists increase their debundling of incoming orders at the time of earnings releases. Specialists interviewed discounted this explanation.[8]

1.4: Implications for Design of Information Content Studies

The following considerations are appropriate when using intraday data in information content studies:

1. The more granular the unit of analysis in information content research, the greater the importance of explicitly incorporating market microstructure considerations into the research design. The available capital market data bases permit a highly granular unit of analysis—trading seconds with the ISSM data base and trading minutes with the Fitch data base. With this level

[8] Yet another explanation is that a subset of investors (informed traders) reduce their intended increase in purchase order size to mask their purchase behavior from other investors—see Kyle [1985] and also the analysis in Admati and Pfleiderer [1988, 1989].

of granularity, market microstructure effects can exceed information effects by several orders of magnitude.

Market microstructure is heterogeneous in its effect. Chapter 4 provides guidance on intraday heterogeneity for four financial variables. The literature on market microstructure is rapidly expanding and continuing to add to the already widespread evidence of intraday heterogeneity—see, for example, McInish and Wood [1991b] on intraday patterns in bid-ask spreads. Alternative approaches to incorporating market microstructure in the research design include:

(a) separately examining subsamples in which the regularities may have different implications, and

(b) using a comparison portfolio that is constructed to control for intraday patterns.

Both approaches aim to retain the full set of information releases, in contrast to the approach in some prior information content studies of excluding observations believed to be nonhomogeneous.

The most common exclusion approach is to exclude all earnings releases made outside trading hours—see Appendix B. For our sample, this would exclude approximately 29 percent of the sample. As firms self select their earnings release time, it is unlikely that this subsample is a random one. For example, the largest 10 percent of firms (based on market capitalization) and the 10 percent most actively traded firms are more likely to release their earnings outside trading hours (vis-a-vis the smallest/least actively traded 10 percent or the full sample):

	Firm Size		**Trading Frequency**		
	Smallest 10%	**Largest 10%**	**Least Traded 10%**	**Most Traded 10%**	**Full Sample**
Outside trading hours	30.3%	40.5%	27.5%	43.1%	29.0%
During trading hours	69.7	59.5	72.5	56.9	71.0

Excluding all earnings releases made outside trading hours will result in a disproportionate number of the releases of large firms/more actively traded firms being excluded from a study.

2. The causes of intraday heterogeneity in financial variables are not well understood—see Appendix A. While a control group approach may significantly reduce the effect of market microstructure factors, it likely will not eliminate them. Market microstructure patterns appear to be most marked at the start and end of trading. This monograph partitions earnings releases made during trading hours into two subsamples: (a) those made in the first thirty minutes and last thirty minutes of trading, and (b) those made between 10.30 A.M. and 3.30 P.M. The motivation for this partition is to obtain subsamples in which the effect of microstructure differs. Analysis of the plots in Chapter 4 leads to the conclusion that the 10.30 A.M. to 3.30 P.M. earnings

release subsample is less affected by market microsctructure factors vis-a-vis the subsample with releases at the start/end of trading (and the subsample with releases made outside of trading hours).

There is nothing magical about our 10.30 A.M. and 3.30 P.M. cutoffs for the subsample we examine. Structural change in capital markets (such as the increase in the number of transactions per day since 1985) may well cause the start of day/end of day patterns to occur in periods shorter than the first thirty/last thirty minutes of trading in more recent time periods. Nevertheless, the researcher is still well advised to avoid the assumption that information releases made within trading hours are homogeneous as regards the effects of market microstructure.

3. Calendar time and transaction time can each provide its own insights to a capital market researcher. For example, a transaction time approach provides insight into how individuals who are better able to react rapidly to a Broadtape release (such as a floor trader) are able to exploit information in that release. In contrast, calendar time can provide insight into the returns available to an investor who has calendar time restrictions in his ability to make a trading decision (such as seeking approval from an investment head of department for large transactions).

Research studies that form calendar-time subpartitions within trading hours have an inherent interpretation problem. The first transaction of each trading day does not occur at the same fixed calendar time for all stocks or for the same company over different trading days. The result is that the first transaction effect is comingled with any information effect of interest across different calendar time subpartitions. Moreover, this comingling occurs in a non-randomized way. There are systematic patterns in which stocks have opening transactions close to the start of trading and those which have sizable delays e.g., stocks of larger companies trade, on average, closer to the start of trading than do stocks of smaller companies. (One approach to avoiding this comingling problem is first to use transaction time data to separate out the opening transaction and then to partition the remaining transactions on a calendar-time subpartition basis.)

The smoothing phenomenon likely with a calendar time approach is most marked when a highly granular calendar time unit is used as the basic unit of analysis and when the sample includes many infrequently traded securities.[9] Not all capital market variables are affected by this smoothing phenomenon in calendar time. For example, the trading frequency variable we examine in Chapters 4 and 5 is unaffected by smoothing since its focus is on one of the causes of smoothing.

4. The research infrastructure required to manage a capital market information content study using intraday data is much larger than one using daily, weekly or monthly data. At a data handling level, there is a dramatic increase

[9] This assumes that capital market changes are transaction driven rather than calendar driven.

in the number of observations with intraday data bases. There is also the challenging task of incorporating market microstructure issues into the research design. For example, given the high rate of change in capital market trading structures and regulations, it is likely that our understanding of the causes of specific intraday patterns will lag our knowledge of their existence. The development of control portfolios requires an awareness of ongoing developments in the market microstructure literature.

Researchers should always pose the question of whether and how intraday data can add a new dimension to probing the research question under investigation in an information content study. Chapter 2 provides further discussion of this issue.

Chapter 2
Information Content Research and Market Microstructure

An increasing number of information content studies are using intraday capital market data pertaining to variables such as security returns, security return variability, bid-ask spreads and their depth, trading frequency and trading volume. The behavior of these variables can be significantly influenced by market microstructure. Indeed, in some cases the systematic patterns induced by market microstructure are several orders of magnitude larger than the effect associated with many information releases. This chapter (1) examines areas where intraday capital market data is expanding and extending the issues addressed by past information content studies, (2) outlines research directions in the market microstructure literature and how they relate to intraday data analysis, and (3) notes several caveats that should be considered when deciding on the type of data to use in an information content research project.

2.1: Insights Available with Intraday Information Content Research

The vast majority of published information content studies use daily, weekly or monthly capital market data. The use of intraday data can both expand and extend the issues examined in prior information content studies in various ways:

1. Intraday data can provide greater insight into how individual participants change their behavior at the time of information releases. The market microstructure literature highlights the role of trading floor operators in the setting of security prices. Intraday data can provide insight into the speed with which floor operators respond to information releases. Since trading often takes place very rapidly, daily data in most cases cannot capture how floor operators and others change their behavior at the time of information releases.

The results in Chapter 5 of this monograph are consistent with the frequency of trading being below normal immediately prior to, and above normal immediately subsequent to, the *minute* of the earnings release on the Broadtape. The rapid response to earnings releases can come from several sources. Trading floor operators and security analysts interviewed believed that part of the rapid response was due to commission-house brokers[1] op-

[1] Commission-house brokers are "employed by brokerage houses". They "link the brokerage houses with the specialists posts" on the trading floor. They either execute orders "with the specialist, with each other or cross the trades. A cross trade occurs when the broker has both a buy and a sell order of the same size and completes the trade. All floor trades must be reported to and approved by the specialist" Schwartz [1991, p. 24].

erating on their firm's account. For example, one security analyst interviewed reported that his first response to a Broadtape earnings release (often within 1 minute) was to contact his firm's commission-house broker who then traded on the firm's account. A second source of the rapid response is investors who can gain quick access to the specialist via an electronic order routing system. (In 1976 the NYSE developed DOT and it has subsequently been expanded and upgraded.)

Lee, Mucklow and Ready [1991] document how earnings releases are associated with increases in the bid-ask spreads that specialists quote and the decreases in depth of the quotation in the half-hour prior to and the half-hour subsequent to the release. This behavior is consistent with specialists "protecting themselves against informed traders either by quoting a wider spread or by quoting less depth" (p. 1). These authors provide stronger evidence of this phenomenon than the mixed results in prior studies that relied on daily data.

The behavior of the trade size variable (number of shares traded per transaction) can also be used to make inferences about the behavior of individual classes of investors assuming that trade size can be used as a proxy for investor class. Cready [1988] and Lee [1991a] both adopt this approach.

Current theoretical research has made limited progress in modeling how individual market participants might react to information releases at the market microstructure level. One benefit of the existing intraday information content research is that it can help identify aspects of market participants' behavior that is of interest to theoretical modelling.

2. Intraday data can provide greater insight into the path and speed of adjustment of capital market variables to information releases. Where the capital market reacts to information in less than one calendar day, daily data will not capture the path of adjustment.[2] Moreover, use of daily data may mask differences across financial variables in their speed of adjustment if the adjustment in one or more series occurs in less than one trading day. This monograph reports sizable differences across financial series in their path of adjustment. For example, Chapter 5 reports that security return variability exhibits abnormal behavior for only 1 transaction following an earnings release while the trading frequency variable exhibits abnormal behavior for 22 transactions following an earnings release. The median number of transactions per day for the companies in our sample ranges from 25 in 1981 and 1985 to 30 in 1983. Use of daily data would mask this difference between the security return variability and the trading frequency variables for many firms in our sample.

Information about the intraday path of adjustment is relevant to investors who use information about unexpected earnings in their investment de-

[2] Lee [1991b] expresses this observation as follows: "one important commentary from the intraday literature is that the market reaction to news is a process, not an instantaneous event. There is an adjustment period, following the news release, during which the information is disseminated and processed by market participants" (p. 4).

cisions. Consider an investment fund that makes purchase/sell decisions based on the difference between the security price and an internally generated "value estimate" computed (in part) using accounting earnings. Assume there are two approaches to implementing this strategy:

(a) make the comparison at the end of each day based on the end-of-day security price and the end-of-day "value estimate."

(b) make the comparison on an intraday basis whenever there is a change in the current security price or the "value estimate."

The more rapid the speed of adjustment of security prices to earnings releases, the greater the benefits foregone by adopting strategy (a) over (b). The results in Chapter 5 document a very rapid adjustment of security prices to the Broadtape earnings release. These results underline the importance of investment managers placing a premium on the speed with which they make decisions based on newly-released earnings reports.

Other intraday studies reinforce the importance of reacting quickly to information releases once they are placed in the public domain. Barclay and Litzenberger [1988] conclude the following in relation to announcements of new equity issues: "this pattern suggests the existence of profit opportunities for floor traders who have very low transaction costs and are able to act within the first 15 minutes following the public announcement" (p. 86). Holthausen, Leftwich and Mayers [1990] examine "how quickly prices attain new equilibrium levels after large-block transactions". They report that "prices adjust within at most three trades, with most of the adjustment occurring in the first trade" (p. 71).

3. Intraday data can provide potentially more accurate measures of the information content of information releases. The more granular the smallest unit of analysis used to measure information content, the greater the ability to exclude transactions or time periods that are unaffected by the information release of concern but are affected by other releases or empirical regularities. Consider, for example, Company XYZ with two announcements in one calendar day:

- 10:42 A.M. Secondary offering of 10 percent of the stock outstanding by senior managers.
- 2:38 P.M. Earnings release of $1.00 for the quarter that is 20 percent above that forecast by Value Line.

Assume each announcement is fully impounded into XYZ's security price within five transactions after each earnings release and that XYZ averages 10 transactions per hour in periods with no information release and 20 transactions per hour after an earnings release. Using daily data, the estimate of the information content of the earnings release will also incorporate the effect of the secondary offering (which could well be sufficiently negative to more that offset any good news associated with the earnings release). In contrast, use of intraday transaction data will facilitate measurement of the information content of the earnings release independent of the secondary offering release. Other things being equal, the faster the speed of adjustment to an information release and the greater the number of non-simultaneous information cues affecting a firm per trading day, the greater the advantage of intraday data over daily data in measuring the information content of a given release. Other things, however, are not always equal. The use of intraday data rather than daily data increases the importance of market microstructure phenomena relative to information-related phenomena. One purpose of this monograph is to increase our awareness of market microstructure phenomena so that the potential of intraday data to yield more accurate measures of information content is more likely to be achieved.[3]

Over time, information content researchers have been conducting experiments which are increasingly more sensitive to measurement error. Early research examined whether a given class of information release (such as earnings) for a broad sample of firms had information content. Information content was tested relative to an hypothesized benchmark of zero change in a financial series—see Ball and Brown [1968] and Beaver [1968]. Recent research is asking more demanding questions, such as:

(a) what are the determinants of differences across firms, across releases, or over time in the information content of releases?

(b) what is the incremental information content of cash flow numbers over earnings numbers?

(c) what is the response coefficient between the sign and magnitude of unexpected earnings and security returns?

Many studies on (a), (b) and (c) have reported relatively low explanatory power in regression analysis—see Lev [1989]. Measurement errors in unexpected earnings or security returns reduce this explanatory power. If a short event window is employed, use of intraday data may increase explanatory power because it has the potential to reduce the mismeasurement of security returns in at least two ways: (a) reduction of the confounding events problem, and (b) better ability to identify heterogeneity across firms, across releases, or over time in the event period used to measure information content. While intraday data may increase the mismeasurement of unexpected earnings (and thereby reduce explanatory power), it is possible that the efficiency lost because of the greater error in unexpected earnings is less than the efficiency gained because of less error in the security returns variable.

4. Intraday data can provide greater insight into the effectiveness of regulatory procedures relating to information transmission. Government and private-sector regulatory bodies are concerned with the enforcement of insider

---

[3] Mucklow [1991] documents that "as the size of the event window is decreased, the noise in the returns created by the market microstructure factors ... becomes more pronounced". However, she finds that "if the price reaction to an event occurs quickly, the increased statistical power from examining event windows shorter than one day is substantial" (p. i).

trading laws and other regulations governing information dissemination. Security price movements prior to major information releases have been used as evidence of possible violations of existing insider trading laws or regulations. Intraday data facilitate a more refined examination of the pre-release and post-release behavior of capital market variables. While the existence of abnormal behavior immediately prior to a release does not conclusively document leakage of the release, it does increase its likelihood.

The stock price movement of Dayton Hudson on June 23, 1987 illustrates the additional insights intraday data provides regulators vis-a-vis daily data.[4] Dayton Hudson opened at $54. At 9:45 A.M., the Dow Jones Broadtape reported that Stone Inc., a Cincinnati "private investment company", was offering $70 cash per share. Trading in Dayton Hudson was halted at 9:53 A.M. At 11:35 A.M. trading resumed on the NYSE, and a block of 655,000 shares traded at $59. At 12:40 P.M., the Broadtape reported that "circumstances surrounding the offer remain cloudy." At 3:30 P.M. the Broadtape indicated that the offer was a fabrication of Paul David Herrlinger. A lawyer for Herrlinger was reported to have said—"David is not feeling right. He is a man who made a mistake." The stock closed at 53-1/8 on the 23rd, down 7/8 on the day. The daily price change of -1.6 percent substantially masks the roller-coaster nature of Dayton Hudson's intraday stock prices. The events of that day prompted an investigation by the Securities and Exchange Commission.

5. Intraday data can provide greater insight into how institutional differences in trading mechanisms affect the way information is processed by the capital market. For example, does a market operating in a continuous mode result in information being impounded in security prices more rapidly than in a market operating in a batch mode? A second example would be whether the existence of market makers (such as specialists) reduces the variability of security returns at the time of information releases vis-a-vis a regime with an automated exchange (such as the Toronto Stock Exchange) where market makers have no formal role.

2.2: Market Microstructure Research Directions

Since the mid-1970s there has been a sizable increase in research on market microstructure. Two important factors underlying this increase are:[5]

- the high degree of "competitive, technological, and regulatory change" occurring in capital markets, and
- the divergence between the predictions of "classical price theory" and the observed behavior of capital markets.

The following research directions are illustrative of the diversity of issues being examined in this literature:

---

[4] *Business Week* July 6, 1987 provides details of the June 23 events surrounding Dayton Hudson.

[5] Excellent discussion of these factors is in Cohen, Maier, Schwartz and Whitcomb [1986] and Schwartz [1988, 1991]. This section draws heavily on those sources.

(i) Descriptive and comparative analysis of alternative institutional trading mechanisms. For example, Cohen et. al. [1986, Chapter 2] summarize differences across 15 trading markets (Amsterdam, Brussels, Frankfurt, Hong Kong, London, Luxembourg, Montreal, NYSE, Paris, Sydney, Tel-Aviv, Tokyo, Toronto, Vienna and Zurich). Two major differences noted include:

- whether the market operates in a batch mode (orders are collected and then crossed as a single transaction) or in a continuous mode (trades occur whenever two orders cross), and
- whether a dealer system exists (where "an intermediary 'makes the market' by satisfying the ultimate customer's order from the intermediary's own account") or an auction system exists ("where [brokers] act as agents for the ultimate customers"). (Cohen et. al. [1986, p.19]).

These and other institutional differences have the potential to influence the design of capital market information content studies and the inferences that can be drawn from them. For example, inferences about the impact of information releases on the size of transactions made by individual investors can more reliably be made in continuous markets than in batch markets. In batch markets, orders are aggregated with the result that individual transactions do not represent the orders of individual investors. (In practice, a continuous market and an auction market are best viewed as ends of a spectrum. For example, the NYSE has elements of both markets.)

(ii) Analysis of the effect of specific events or of specific regulations. The October 1987 crash on world equity markets led to an explosion of market microstructure studies on its causes and of suggested responses to reduce the likelihood of it being repeated. For example, Kleidon [1990] examines explanations for the "S & P index and futures contracts diverging [at the time of the Crash] by an amount which apparently greatly exceeded arbitrage based bounds" (p. 1). His conclusion was that much of this divergence was illusory—"the execution of stale limit buy orders given the high volume and NYSE market mechanisms resulted in unprecedented stale prices in the cash index" (p. i). The use of intraday data was an essential component of Kleidon's empirical research. Roll [1988] provides a review of the Kleidon findings and numerous other studies related to the October 1987 crash.

One proposal frequently mentioned in the post-1987 crash debate was the adoption of circuit breakers—a halt in trading when a preset change in an index occurs in a given period. McMillan [1990] examines how the introduction of circuit breakers affects the intraday price discovery process. The conclusion was that "circuit breakers impaired price discovery" (p. 27). He noted that it was unresolved whether circuit breakers reduced market volatility, in part due to our limited understanding of factors affecting volatility when trading is resumed.

(iii) Analysis of changes in the role of key groups. A major change in equity markets since the late 1980s is the growing importance of program trading.

Studies on the effect of program trading on intraday volatility of the market index illustrate market microstructure research in this area. Neal [1990] reports that "for stocks intensively involved in program trading, a typical amount of these trades can increase the intraday volatility by three to five percent of the daily volatility" (p. 1). Harris, Sofianos and Shapiro [1990] likewise report that program trading and volatility are positively correlated for a data base of all "NYSE trades and quotes in June 1989 for the NYSE S&P 500 stocks" (p. 7).

Capital market information content studies including data from the late 1980s onwards will reflect the increasing role of program trading. Research such as Neal [1990] and Harris, Sofianos and Shapiro [1990] provide a useful benchmark on how program trading, in general, is affecting trading volume and stock return variability. One use of such a benchmark is in the design of significance tests probing whether information releases are associated with increased trading volume or security return variability.

(iv) Role played by market makers (dealers and specialists) on organized exchanges. The services that market makers provide include: "(1) supply of immediacy, (2) price stabilization, (3) price discovery, and (4) services of an auctioneer who brings order and fairness to a market" (Schwartz [1988, p. 388]).

Research has included both theoretical modeling and empirical analysis. Madhavan and Smidt [1991] model "the effects of transaction costs, specialist inventory control, and asymmetric information." They note that the "estimated model provides strong support for the existence of information asymmetries, as perceived by the market maker" (p. 37). Stoll [1989] and Petersen and Umlauf [1990] illustrate empirical research on specialist behavior. Stoll [1989] finds that "serial covariances of returns calculated from NASDAQ transactions data are negative and strongly negatively associated with the square of quoted [bid-ask] spreads" (p. 132). Petersen and Umlauf [1990] examine the intraday quote-setting behavior of specialists for 119 NYSE stocks. They report that "the behavior of the specialist appears extremely rich, particularly in comparison to the picture portrayed by the existing literature on market making" (p. 2). Revisions in the midpoint of the specialist's quoted spreads were found to depend on transaction volumes, contemporaneous changes in market indices, and the time elapsed between quote revisions.

Research on market makers is directly relevant to information content research that examines the effect of information releases on bid-ask spreads (such as Lee, Mucklow and Ready [1991]). It is also relevant when making inferences from transaction data. For example, one role of a specialist is to maintain price stability. This role can result in new information being incorporated into security prices in a less rapid manner than in a market operating without specialists.

Morse and Mucklow [1991] examine autocorrelations of daily returns, based on daily closing prices, for high-priced securities (defined as a price greater than or equal to $40). High-priced securities are less affected by bid-ask spreads or price discreteness (trading only in one-eighths) than are low-priced securities. They conclude that "autocorrelations of daily returns for high-price stocks are generally significantly positive.... The results are consistent with the hypothesis that either the specialist is intentionally smoothing the closing price to create an orderly market or prices are consistently underreacting to new information" (p. i).

(v) Analysis of institutional factors affecting closing transaction prices. Closing transaction prices play a key role in many information content studies using daily data. One research direction is to analyze the balance between buy orders and sell orders, especially for orders at the end of each trading period. For example, Lease, Masulis and Page [1991] report that "at a seasoned public offering of common stock, purchase orders are diverted from the secondary market to the temporary primary market.... We document a significant downward shift in the average location of the closing transaction price relative to the closing bid and ask quotes on the public offering date of seasoned common stock offers, indicating an excess of sell orders in the secondary market" (p. 14). These authors argue that prior studies, which have ignored this market microstructure phenomenon, have overstated the negative event date impact of public offerings. Porter [1989] also reports systematic patterns in bid-ask spreads on the last trade of the day for stocks listed on the U.S. and on the Canadian exchanges. He reports that "systematic patterns in the probability of a trade at the ask may explain 20 percent of the Canadian and U.S. day-of-the-week and most of the U.S. 'U' shaped intraday effects" (p. i).

Research on closing transaction prices has implications for the inferences drawn from information content studies. For example, a sample of information releases made during trading hours is less affected by problems associated with the measurement of closing transaction prices than is a sample of releases made outside trading hours. (See Chapter 5 for discussion of how an event time analysis will diversify closing transaction prices across different time units for information releases made during trading hours vis-a-vis those made outside trading hours.)

(vi) Descriptive analysis of intraday properties of capital market variables. Appendix A reviews studies that have documented systematic intraday patterns in both transaction time and calendar time. Examples of the findings summarized in Appendix A are:

- the first transaction on each trading day has sizably higher mean trading volume than subsequent transactions.
- the last transaction on each trading day has a positive mean return.
- security return variability is higher during the first 30 minutes relative to subsequent trading minutes in the same day.
- the last trading minute of each trading day has a positive mean return.

These systematic patterns are found in periods both with and without observable information releases occurring. An active area of market microstructure research is the development and testing of models/hypotheses that could explain these observed systematic patterns. Progress in this area has been relatively slow. Most progress to date has been in documenting how proposed models/hypotheses are (at best) only partial explanations for observed patterns.

Overview

While there are many unresolved issues remaining in market microstructure research, the advances made in our knowledge of systematic intraday patterns in capital market variables are sizable. Because of these advances, researchers are now able to design experiments that have a greater likelihood of reliable inferences being drawn about whether and how information releases are associated with intraday changes in capital market variables.

2.3: Caveats Appropriate to Intraday Research

Intraday data, while offering additional insights over daily data in several areas, are not without their limitations. The following factors should be considered when deciding on the type of data to use in an information content research project:

1. The question being addressed. Where the issue being addressed does not require a highly granular mode of analysis, the use of intraday data is unlikely to meet a cost-benefit test. For example, the benefits of using intraday data are likely to be small in cross-sectional valuation studies of the association between security prices and alternative accounting earnings series and other variables (such as in Barth [1991]). The results in valuation research typically are less sensitive to the exact time of information releases than they are to the use of "reliable" measures of the independent variables.

2. Ability to precisely determine when the information release of interest is placed in the public domain. The earnings releases examined in this monograph are reported on a minute by minute basis on the Broadtape. Where the timing of an information release cannot be determined this precisely, there are fewer gains from using a transaction-by-transaction data base.[6] For ex-

---

[6] Note that the nonavailability of an intraday release time does not imply there is no gain from using intraday data. The conventional approach is to identify the information release time (on the Broadtape, Reuters or a similar source) and then examine the behavior of capital market variables surrounding this release time. An alternative approach is to examine the behavior of capital market variables and infer that there is a higher likelihood of information releases occurring when there is abnormal behavior observed in the variables examined. Both approaches are capable of providing insights and each is subject to its own limitations. For example, the conventional approach does not enable the researcher to eliminate the possibility that any abnormal behavior is due to: (a) information releases not being examined, (b) market microstructure factors, or (c) random fluctuation. The alternative approach likewise does not eliminate the possibility that the observed abnormal behavior is not informationally driven—it could be due to, say, (b) or (c) above.

ample, it is frequently possible to identify the day but not the hour or minute of information releases made by small regional firms. Similarly, for other information releases (such as an annual report), it is typically possible to identify only the day of its public release (but not when on that day).

3. Frequency of intraday changes in the variable(s) of interest. The fewer the number of intraday observations per day, the less likely that an intraday mode of analysis will yield results not observable in daily data. Note, however, that capital market variables should not be viewed in isolation from each other. For example, stocks that have only a small number of transactions on a given day may have changes occurring in the bid-ask spread between successive transactions. The result is that a myopic focus on only one variable may understate the richness of the intraday observations available to track the path of adjustment of the capital market to information releases. The analysis in Lee, Mucklow and Ready [1991] illustrates how the bid-ask series can be analyzed. An extension of the research reported in this monograph would be to combine the Lee et. al. approach with the transaction-by-transaction approach we conduct.

4. The level of measurement error in the observations used in the research. Our understanding of the systematic patterns in intraday variables that have been documented is far from complete. Moreover, there is a high likelihood that other systematic patterns exist that have not been fully documented. The result is that efforts to design control groups and significance tests are likely to introduce their own source of measurement error into an experiment. This problem always exists in empirical research, but may well be accentuated with intraday data due to the significance of market microstructure factors—see Mucklow [1991].

5. The computer resources and skills available. Transaction level studies can demand access to large computing budgets and a high level of computing skills.

2.4: Summary

The results in Chapters 5 and 6 of this monograph highlight systematic patterns in financial variables that are not observable with daily data. However, the extra cost of dealing with intraday data bases is not small. Researchers should always consider whether the extra investment required to incorporate intraday data into an experiment is cost-effective in terms of addressing new issues not amenable to reliable testing with say daily data or by increasing the reliability of inferences drawn from existing information content studies.

Chapter 3
Sample Selection, Data Bases and the Earnings Release Environment

This chapter presents descriptive information on the sample of firms examined and on the institutional environment in which earnings releases are placed in the public domain.

3.1: Sample Selection

The sample comprises 100 companies from 20 industries. Four steps were used in the selection process:[1]

Step 1: Using the 1984 edition of *Ward's Directory of 51,000 Largest U.S. Corporations*, select all 4 digit SIC code industries with at most 20 publicly held companies. The SIC codings in *Ward's Directory* follow those of Standard and Poor's in their data bases (including the Compustat Tape). This step resulted in 458 industries surviving. The limit of 20 per industry was set to enable examination of a broad cross-section of industries, given a limit on the number of companies that can be analyzed in the research. Intraday data bases are larger than daily bases by many orders of magnitude. Computer limitations place constraints on the number of companies that can be analyzed in any one project using intraday data.

Step 2: Eliminate industries where the common stock of the major companies are not publicly traded. Let n denote the number of companies with publicly traded common stock in an industry. The algorithm used to eliminate industries is:

(i) if $n \geq 4$, delete industry if the common stock of the top 4 (using 1984 sales) are not traded,

(ii) if $n=3$, delete industry if top 3 are not traded, and

(iii) if $n=2$, delete industry if top 2 are not traded.

Fifty-eight industries survived this requirement; 27 industries with $n \geq 4$; 9 with $n=3$; and 22 with $n=2$.

Step 3: Eliminate industries where the common stock of the major companies are not traded on the New York Stock Exchange (NYSE). The algorithm used to eliminate industries is:

(i) if $n \geq 3$, delete industry if the common stock of the top 3 (using 1984 sales) are not traded on the NYSE, and

(ii) if $n=2$, delete industry if top 2 are not traded on the NYSE.

---

[1] The sample selection was initially developed for this monograph to extend the study to information transfers between earnings releasing companies and other companies in the same industry. Subsequently it was decided to confine the monograph to information content issues using intraday data for earnings releasing companies.

This step resulted in 21 industries surviving.

Steps 2 and 3 are designed to select industries where a relatively high percentage of "industry sales" are made by the companies included in machine-readable data bases.

Step 4: Eliminate industries in which membership changes result in reductions such that the industry would not pass through Steps 1 to 3 in each year. Back years of *Ward's Directory* were used in Step 4, resulting in 20 industries surviving.

Exhibit 3-1 lists the 20 industries and the number of companies with common stock traded on the NYSE in each industry for each year of the 1980-1985 period. The total number of companies is 100. There is a maximum of 97 in 1980 and a minimum of 85 in 1985. Individual companies enter or leave the sample for a diverse set of reasons, e.g., changes in industry membership, bankruptcies, and mergers. Appendix C lists the 100 companies in the sample with details of the first and last year with NYSE common stock return data available. The industries to be examined include a broad cross-section from the extractive, manufacturing, transportation and financial sectors of the economy.

3.2: Data Bases

Information from capital market, earnings announcement release time, and earnings forecast data bases is used in the research:

A. Capital Market Information

- *Francis Emory Fitch*—reports the security price, trading volume, and time of day (to the calendar minute) of each transaction for the 100 NYSE stocks in our sample for the January 1, 1980 to September 26, 1985 period. During this period the NYSE was consistently open for six hours of trading (from 10.00 A.M. to 4.00 P.M.) each trading day. Fitch officials indicated in interviews that they receive the data from the NYSE, transfer it ("as is") to their own tapes, and then sell it to their customers (primarily brokerage houses). The Fitch time stamp (minute of trade) is that provided by the NYSE to Fitch.
- *Center for Research on Security Prices* (CRSP)—reports daily security returns, prices, and dividends for the 100 NYSE stocks for the January 1, 1980 to September 26, 1985 period.

The Fitch data are used for all intraday analysis in Chapters 4 to 6. The CRSP data are used to deflate the earnings forecast errors of companies and to partition companies into different size portfolios (based on market capitalization).

Exhibit 3-2 presents summary statistics on the average number of transactions per trading day for the sample examined in this monograph. There is a broad cross-section of trading frequency in the sample. For example, the range per trading day in 1985 is from 3 transactions (Puerto Rican Cement) to 266 transactions (General Motors).[2]

B. Earnings Announcement Release Time Information

The Broadtape (Dow Jones News Retrieval Service) is the source of the earnings announcement release time. This source reports the day, hour and minute that an earnings release becomes available on computer terminals located on the floor of the NYSE. We use the minute of the first Broadtape item that reports the earnings or EPS for the most recently ended quarter/year for the company in question. Many sites outside the NYSE (e.g., brokerage houses) also access the Broadtape on an instantaneous basis. This source, available in machine readable form from 1980 onwards, operates from approximately 7:45 A.M. to 6:45 P.M. on each trading day. (The earliest and latest earnings release time stamps for our sample are 8:06 A.M. and 6:31 P.M. respectively.)

The Broadtape release time was located by an on-line search of the Broadtape data base. Two other sources of earnings release dates are:

- *Standard and Poor's Compustat Tape,* which reports the day "on which quarterly earnings per share are first publicly reported in the various news media (such as the Wall Street Journal or the Dow Jones News Service)" [Industrial Compustat, 1980, p. 80].
- *The Wall Street Journal Index,* which reports the day that an earnings release is reported in The Wall Street Journal.

A comparison of the three earnings release sources revealed the following (using the Broadtape, each day is defined from 4:01 P.M. of the prior trading day to 4:00 P.M. of that day; that is, any announcement after the close of trading is coded as occurring on the next trading day):

- the Broadtape date *preceded* the Compustat date by 1 trading day 67.7 percent of the time, by 2 trading days 3.6 percent and by 3 days 1.6 percent.
- the Broadtape date *preceded* the Wall Street Journal Index date by 1 trading day 91.8 percent of the time, by 2 trading days 2.3 percent, and by 3 trading days 0.9 percent.

Compustat *precedes* the Broadtape date by at least 1 trading day 1.9 percent of the time while the Wall Street Journal Index *precedes* the Broadtape date by at least 1 trading day 0.6 percent of the time. Explanations for these delays in the Broadtape source include delays by Dow Jones in putting the company release on its service, errors in one or more of our data bases, or errors in our search of the data bases (such as not locating the first Broadtape release and then calling the second release the initial disclosure time).

---

[2] Cready and Ramanan [1991] randomly sample 25,000 daily observations of firms listed on the NYSE in the April 1, 1980 to September 30, 1984 period. The mean number of transactions in the lowest and highest trading frequency deciles is 10.1 and 102.9 transactions respectively. In 1984, the .1 and .9 deciles for our sample are 8 and 92 transactions respectively.

C. Earnings Forecast and Reported EPS Information

The Value Line Investment Survey is the source of one quarter ahead earnings forecasts for 95 of the 100 firms in our sample. For those five firms in our sample not covered by Value Line, the Institutional Brokers Estimate Systems (IBES) of Lynch, Jones and Ryan was used as the source of one quarter ahead earnings forecasts. The EPS reported on the Broadtape is used as the actual EPS figure.

3.3: Earnings Release Patterns

Exhibit 3-3 and Figure 3-1 present distribution statistics on the Broadtape announcement times for earnings releases. Trading hours during the January 1980 to September 1985 period were from 10:00 A.M. to 4:00 P.M. Observable patterns include:

1. The majority of earnings releases on the Broadtape are made during trading hours:

	MON.	TUES.	WED.	THURS.	FRI.	ALL
Before Trading Hours	13.9%	19.7%	17.5%	19.9%	16.5%	17.9%
During Trading Hours	71.6	72.1	72.3	70.8	65.4	71.1
After Trading Hours	14.5	8.2	10.2	9.3	18.1	11.0
	100.0	100.0	100.0	100.0	100.0	100.0

Approximately 29 percent of the announcements made each week occur outside trading hours. These announcements will be separately analyzed in several sections of Chapters 5 and 6.

Within each trading day, the distribution of earnings announcements is not uniform. The three hours with the highest number of earnings releases are 10:00-10:59 (16.6 percent), 9:00-9:59 (15.6 percent) and 11:00-11:59 (15.1 percent). Figure 3-2 presents the number of announcements per 15 minute time period from 8 A.M. to 7 P.M.

Start and end of trading day patterns are highlighted in subsequent chapters of this monograph. Trading commenced at 10:00 A.M. and ended at 4:00 P.M. in the time-period examined. Exhibit 3-4 presents data on earnings release patterns in this time period. The closing ten minutes of trading has less than one-third the frequency of earnings releases than does the opening ten minutes of trading. The last hour of trading has the lowest number of earnings releases of any hour during trading (and either the hour immediately before or immediately after trading).

2. The percentages of earnings releases reported each day of the week on the Broadtape are (this source does not operate on non-trading days):

Trading Day	% of Weekly Earnings Releases
Monday	17.3%
Tuesday	22.4
Wednesday	22.2
Thursday	28.1
Friday	10.0
	100.0%

Days with the lowest percentages of announcements in each week are Friday and Monday. Figure 3-2 presents summary data on daily earnings release patterns. Friday has the highest percentage of daily announcements made outside trading hours. It also has the highest percentage of each day's announcements made after the end of trading.

3. The largest 10 percent of firms (based on market capitalization) and the 10 percent most actively traded firms are more likely to release their earnings outside of trading hours than the remaining 90 percent of the sample. The following percentages relate to the firm size and trading frequency deciles reported in chapter 4:

FIRM SIZE DECILES			TRADING FREQUENCY DECILES		
DECILE	**% OUTSIDE**	**%DURING**	**DECILE**	**% OUTSIDE**	**% DURING**
1 (Smallest)	30.3%	69.7%	1 (Least Traded)	27.5%	72.5%
2	25.5	74.5	2	16.9	83.1
3	19.8	80.2	3	23.4	76.6
4	35.2	64.8	4	29.3	70.7
5	30.2	69.8	5	28.6	71.4
6	38.5	71.5	6	28.5	71.5
7	29.5	70.5	7	32.5	67.5
8	22.8	77.2	8	32.2	67.8
9	17.6	82.4	9	27.7	72.3
10 (Largest)	40.5	59.5	10 (Most Traded)	43.1	56.9

4. Industries differ in their mean reporting lags. A reporting lag is the time from the end of a fiscal period (quarter, year, etc.) to the public release of the financial results of that fiscal period. Summary statistics for reporting lags (in calendar time) for the 100 firms in the sample are in Exhibit 3-5. The day of the Broadtape earnings release is used as the public release date of earnings. The mean reporting lags for the first, second and third fiscal quarters are 22.6, 23.6, and 23.6 calendar days respectively; for the fourth fiscal quarter the lag is 34.9 calendar days.

Systematic earnings release patterns exist in the sample when it is partitioned by (a) a proxy for the earnings forecast error associated with the release, and (b) the time of release. The proxy we use for the earnings forecast error is:

$$\frac{\text{Actual EPS} - \text{Value Line Forecast of EPS}}{\text{Security Price at Start of Calendar Year}}$$

The most recent Value Line EPS forecast issued prior to the release date is used in our computations. Exhibit 3-6 presents distribution data for the earnings forecast error of releases made in:

- the pre-trading hours (Panel A)
- during trading hours (Panel B)
- after trading hours (Panel C).

The median earnings forecast error for each partition in Exhibit 3-6 is:

	Monday	Tuesday	Wednesday	Thursday	Friday	All Days
Pre-Trading	.0003	.0000	–.0004	.0005	–.0017	.0000
During Trading	.0000	–.0005	–.0005	–.0007	–.0021	–.0006
After Trading	–.0022	–.0005	–.0006	–.0027	–.0051	–.0025

Earnings releases made after trading has finished for the day consistently have a negative median forecast error. The most striking pattern in Exhibit 3-6 is the high percentage of earnings releases, made after trading hours on Fridays, which have a negative forecast error; more than 80 percent are negative for this group. This finding is consistent with that reported in Patell and Wolfson [1982] and Damodaran [1989].

3.4: Institutional Aspects Associated with Earnings Releases

Key players in the institutional environment place a premium on releasing or responding to earnings releases in a "very fast" way. The following examples, drawn from interviews with officials from Dow-Jones and brokerage/investment banking companies, illustrate this observation.

A. Dow Jones' Broadtape

Companies either (a) personally phone, telex, or fax their earnings press releases to Dow Jones, or (b) provide their releases to an intermediary who wires it simultaneously to major news organizations (including Dow Jones or Reuters). Once an earnings report is received by Dow Jones, it is edited and typically split into two Broadtape releases:

- *Broadtape Release #1:* Release of the "bottom line" earnings/EPS figure. This release can also include extraordinary or nonrecurring items if they are very significant. For larger or more widely followed companies, this release is done "within seconds" of its receipt by Dow Jones. For smaller or less widely followed companies, the timing of this release will depend on the level of traffic in other news. When Dow Jones is inundated with incoming news releases, those considered less newsworthy are put at the back of the queue.
- *Broadtape Release #2:* Release of a more detailed report outlining the major points in the company's press release (e.g., components of earnings and verbal statements). The delay between Broadtape Release #1 and the more detailed Release #2 is variable (up to one day) depending on the news content of the company release, the importance of the company, and the rate of traffic in other news on that day.

Exhibit 3-7 illustrates Release #1 and Release #2 for Evans Products. All the analysis in Chapters 4 to 6 use Broadtape Release #1 time as the source of the earnings release time. An extension of this study would be to examine the information content of Broadtape Release #2. Note, however, security analysts, investors, etc. may access the content of Broadtape Release #2 prior to its release time on the Broadtape (via telexes, faxes, etc. directly from the company). There is not a uniform period (in either calendar or transaction time) between Broadtape Releases #1 and #2 for all earnings releases in the sample.[3]

B. Brokerage/Investment Banking Companies

Interviews were conducted with security analysts and floor trade operators to gain insight into the speed with which earnings release information is acted upon. The following details, from a security analyst covering telecommunication stocks, illustrate the high priority he gives to reacting quickly to each earnings release:

> Firms we follow have relatively predictable earnings release patterns. We are in close contact with personnel from each company and call them prior to the expected release date to confirm the likely release date for the forthcoming announcement. Almost all companies will provide the likely release date with some also providing the likely release hour.
>
> At the start of each trading day, an information sheet is made available to internal analysts, traders, etc. that outlines for those firms with earnings releases expected within the next week:
>
> - the expected release date (and time).
> - the most recent analyst EPS forecast.
> - the actual EPS for the comparable quarter/year for the most recent year.
> - general comments about factors of special interest in the forthcoming release.
>
> The brokerage firm's trader knows an earnings release is forthcoming and typically reduces the number of trades until the release is made.
>
> On the day the earnings release is expected an assistant to the analyst continuously monitors the Broadtape. As soon as the first earnings release appears on the Broadtape, the analyst compares it with the forecast and immediately makes a phone call to a commission-house broker. This can be done within one minute of the earnings release appearing on the Broadtape. The broker purchases/sells if the release is viewed by the analyst as good news/bad news. While the security analyst has a detailed model underlying the EPS forecast, this first-pass reaction typically is restricted to the difference between the actual EPS and the forecast EPS. If the Broadtape release includes additional information (such as significant nonoperating components of EPS) these are also considered. The broker purchases/sells shares on the brokerage firm's account rather than for any client of the brokerage firm.

[3] Reuters is an additional news service that carries corporate news on a "real-time" basis. Like Dow Jones, Reuters views the speed (and accuracy) with which news releases are put on its service as of paramount importance.

The analyst/analyst's assistant then transmits (by fax, or phone) details of the first Broadtape earnings release to the internal salesforce of the brokerage firm. He may also contact major clients of the brokerage firm directly, but in most cases this task is done by the salesforce. Major clients can be contacted by the analyst or salesperson within five minutes of the Broadtape release time. (In many cases the analyst believed this call was redundant as the major client will already have observed the release on the Broadtape.)

The next earnings information item for the analyst to examine will be either (a) the full press release from the company or its intermediary (often no later than 15 minutes after the Broadtape), or (b) the more detailed release on the Broadtape. This information is processed and may lead to further purchases/sales by the brokerage firm's broker on the trading floor and further communications with the salesforce and major clients.

Within 1 hour of receiving the company's full press release, the analyst prepares a 1 to 2 page summary and analysis for it. This summary and analysis is relayed to internal salespeople and traders. Where the press release contains highly significant information, an internal conference call is held to discuss its content.

Other analysts reported that a similar set of events surrounding earnings releases occurred at their firms, especially for larger or widely followed companies. There was a consistent belief across analysts interviewed that a sizable part of any increased trading activity immediately following a Broadtape earnings release was due to trading by commission-house brokers.

3.5: Summary

The conclusions drawn in this monograph strictly apply only to the 100 companies examined. However, these companies are drawn from a broad cross-section of industries in the extractive, manufacturing, transportation and financial sectors of the economy. Moreover, where our analysis overlaps that conducted elsewhere in the market microstructure literature, we find similar results to those previously reported (see Chapter 4 and Appendix A).

Approximately 29 percent of the earnings releases examined in this monograph are made outside trading hours. Chapter 4 documents systematic start of day and end of day patterns in capital market variables. These patterns require explicit recognition in the experimental design used in Chapters 5 and 6 to examine the information content of earnings releases made outside trading hours.

Key institutional players in the environment in which earnings are publicly released highlight the importance of reacting to earnings releases in a very rapid manner. The results in Chapters 5 and 6 indicate that the market responds in the very first transaction subsequent to an earnings release.

EXHIBIT 3-1
INDUSTRY BREAKDOWN OF SAMPLE: 1980-1985

4-DIGIT INDUSTRY SIC CODE	INDUSTRY NAME	1980	1981	1982	1983	1984	1985
1011	IRON ORES	2	2	2	2	2	2
1044	SILVER ORES	2	3	3	3	3	3
2032	CANNED SPECIALITIES	2	2	2	2	2	2
2041	FLOUR/GRAIN MILLING	5	5	3	3	3	3
2043	CEREAL BREAKFAST FOOD	2	2	3	3	3	3
2046	CORN WET MILLING	2	2	2	2	2	2
2111	CIGARETTES	4	3	3	3	3	3
2421	SAWMILLS	7	7	7	7	7	7
2621	PAPER MILLS	13	13	11	11	11	10
3011	TIRES & INNER TUBES	9	9	9	9	8	8
3221	GLASS CONTAINERS	6	6	5	5	5	5
3241	CEMENT	8	7	5	5	5	5
3621	MOTOR & GENERATOR	7	7	7	7	7	7
3634	ELECTRICAL HOUSEWARES	2	3	3	3	3	3
3673	TRANSMITTING TUBES	2	2	2	2	2	2
3711	MOTOR VEHICLES	5	4	4	4	4	4
3721	AIRCRAFT	10	9	8	8	8	8
4712	FREIGHT FORWARDING	3	3	3	3	3	3
4953	REFUSE SYSTEMS	3	3	3	3	3	2
6411	INSURANCE AGENTS	3	3	3	3	3	3
TOTAL SAMPLE		97	95	88	88	87	85

EXHIBIT 3-2
SUMMARY OF AVERAGE NUMBER OF TRANSACTIONS PER DAY

A. Distribution Data, By Year

Distribution Statistic	1980	1981	1982	1983	1984	1985
Minimum	3	2	2	5	5	3
.1 Decile	8	8	8	10	8	9
.2 Decile	11	11	12	15	11	15
.3 Decile	14	15	16	18	15	18
.4 Decile	22	21	20	23	20	18
.5 Decile	29	25	26	30	28	25
.6 Decile	35	30	35	36	36	36
.7 Decile	47	46	43	50	43	44
.8 Decile	74	53	59	67	53	59
.9 Decile	90	70	87	123	92	65
Maximum	281	246	242	306	257	266
Number of Stocks	97	95	88	88	87	85

B. Five Least and Most Actively Transacted Stocks, 1980 and 1985

1980	Average # of Transactions	1985	Average # of Transactions
Puerto Rican Cement	3	Puerto Rican Cement	3
Alpha Portland	4	Giant Portland	6
Mohawk Rubber	5	Pope and Talbot	7
Brockway	6	Baldor Electric	7
Giant Portland	7	National Presto	8
•	•	•	•
•	•	•	•
•	•	•	•
General Electric	139	Chrysler	185
Ford Motor	179	R.J. Reynolds	197
Chrysler	222	Ford Motor	238
General Motors	252	General Electric	245
Boeing	281	General Motors	266

EXHIBIT 3-3
DISTRIBUTION STATISTICS ON BROADTAPE ANNOUNCEMENT TIMES FOR EARNINGS RELEASES

	MONDAY	TUESDAY	WEDNESDAY	THURSDAY	FRIDAY	ALL
8:00-8:59	1.9%	2.3%	2.3%	2.2%	3.6%	2.3%
9:00-9:59	12.1	17.4	15.2	17.7	12.9	15.6
10:00-10:59	13.9	17.7	17.8	18.9	9.3	16.6
11:00-11:59	13.3	16.7	17.3	12.6	16.4	15.1
12:00-12:59	14.2	11.6	13.9	11.0	12.4	12.5
1:00-1:59	13.9	11.2	9.7	13.3	9.3	11.7
2:00-2:59	9.2	9.2	7.2	9.5	11.3	9.0
3:00-4:00	7.1	5.7	6.4	5.5	6.7	6.2
4:01-4:59	11.5	6.4	6.7	5.1	11.9	7.5
5:00-5:59	2.1	1.6	2.8	3.1	5.2	2.7
6:00-6:59	0.9	0.2	0.7	1.1	1.0	0.8
	100.0%	100.0%	100.0%	100.0%	100.0%	100.0%
N	338	436	433	549	194	1950

EXHIBIT 3-4
START-OF-DAY AND END-OF-DAY EARNINGS RELEASE ANNOUNCEMENT PATTERNS

BEFORE TRADING		LAST 30 MINUTES OF TRADING	
Time	**%**	**Time**	**%**
Start to 9.50 A.M.	14.95%	3.31 to 3.51 P.M.	2.10%
9.51 A.M.	0.26	3.52P.M.	0.26
9.52	0.41	3.53	0.05
9.53	0.46	3.54	0.15
9.54	0.31	3.55	0.05
9.55	0.36	3.56	0.10
9.56	0.26	3.57	0.05
9.57	0.26	3.58	0.05
9.58	0.36	3.59	0.15
9.59	0.31	4.00	0.05
	17.94		3.01

FIRST 30 MINUTES OF TRADING		AFTER TRADING	
Time	**%**	**Time**	**%**
10.00 A.M.	0.05	4.01	0.21
10.01	0.26	4.02	0.31
10.02	0.46	4.03	0.36
10.03	0.36	4.04	0.21
10.04	0.46	4.05	0.21
10.05	0.36	4.06	0.05
10.06	0.21	4.07	0.05
10.07	0.67	4.08	0.36
10.08	0.56	4.09	0.05
10.09	0.26	4.10	0.15
10.10 to 10.29 A.M.	5.64	4.11 to End	9.03
	9.29		10.99

EXHIBIT 3-5
REPORTING LAGS FOR EARNINGS RELEASES : 1980-1985*

SAMPLE/STATISTIC	FISCAL QUARTER 1	FISCAL QUARTER 2	FISCAL QUARTER 3	FISCAL QUARTER 4
PANEL A.: AGGREGATE				
SAMPLE MEAN	22.4	24.1	23.5	35.0
.1 decile	13.0	15.0	14.0	23.0
.3 decile	18.0	19.0	19.0	28.0
.5 decile	22.0	23.0	22.0	32.0
.7 decile	25.0	26.0	26.0	39.0
.9 decile	33.0	33.0	33.0	51.0
PANEL B: INDUSTRY MEANS				
1011 IRON ORES	28.3	29.6	29.2	30.0
1044 SILVER ORES	27.6	30.4	28.8	43.6
2032 CANNED SPECIALITIES	21.4	19.3	21.9	42.4
2041 FLOUR/GRAIN MILLING	19.1	20.4	22.3	32.6
2043 CEREAL/BREAK. FOOD	26.2	25.6	27.1	45.3
2046 CORN WET MILLING	17.3	16.8	18.8	26.8
2111 CIGARETTES	20.3	20.6	19.4	31.4
2421 SAWMILLS	18.7	25.5	19.6	29.1
2621 PAPER MILLS	17.7	19.6	18.4	26.9
3011 TIRES	18.0	21.6	20.7	38.6
3221 GLASS CONTAINERS	20.8	21.7	22.8	32.4
3241 CEMENT	25.8	26.3	27.4	34.6
3621 MOTOR & GENERATOR	21.1	21.8	23.7	33.6
3634 ELECTRICAL HOUSEWARES	28.6	28.7	27.6	48.2
3673 TRANSMITTING TUBES	24.6	22.8	24.3	35.4
3711 MOTOR VEHICLES	24.2	33.4	26.8	42.4
3721 AIRCRAFT	24.9	26.7	25.5	34.0
4712 FREIGHT FORWARDING	29.5	30.9	31.5	41.4
4953 REFUSE SYSTEMS	23.9	21.9	23.8	46.5
6411 INSURANCE AGENTS	28.7	28.0	28.5	32.9

*Reporting lag is measured as the average number of calendar days from the end of a fiscal quarter to the day the earnings for that quarter are reported on the Broadtape.

EXHIBIT 3-6
EARNINGS FORECAST ERRORS PARTITIONED BY TIME OF DAY AND DAY OF WEEK: DECILES OF DISTRIBUTION AND AVERAGE FORECAST ERROR*

	MONDAY	TUESDAY	WEDNESDAY	THURSDAY	FRIDAY	ALL DAYS
A. PRE-TRADING						
DECILES .1	-.0044	-.0172	-.0388	-.0083	-.0728	-.0149
.2	-.0020	-.0081	-.0127	-.0036	-.0023	-.0052
.3	-.0014	-.0028	-.0051	-.0018	-.0104	-.0022
.4	.0000	-.0007	-.0022	-.0002	-.0055	-.0007
.5	.0003	.0000	-.0004	.0005	-.0017	.0000
.6	.0018	.0003	-.0002	.0013	-.0007	.0006
.7	.0038	.0014	.0007	.0021	.0003	.0017
.8	.0054	.0034	.0026	.0042	.0030	.0039
.9	.0073	.0069	.0060	.0085	.0069	.0078
Average	-.0004	-.0037	-.0159	-.0040	.0033	-.0055
B. DURING-TRADING						
DECILES .1	-.0136	-.0152	-.0155	-.0147	-.0281	-.0151
.2	-.0064	-.0087	-.0089	-.0082	-.0116	-.0082
.3	-.0035	-.0051	-.0044	-.0039	-.0070	-.0043
.4	-.0012	-.0019	-.0020	-.0021	-.0044	-.0019
.5	.0000	-.0005	-.0005	-.0007	-.0021	-.0006
.6	.0010	.0003	.0002	.0004	-.0009	.0004
.7	.0022	.0016	.0014	.0015	.0009	.0017
.8	.0042	.0028	.0036	.0041	.0036	.0036
.9	.0087	.0066	.0100	.0074	.0077	.0084
Average	-.0020	-.0042	-.0034	-.0022	-.0087	-.0035
C. AFTER-TRADING						
DECILES .1	-.0331	-.0553	-.0428	-.0353	-.0711	-.0363
.2	-.0155	-.0108	-.0142	-.0235	-.0407	-.0155
.3	-.0057	-.0064	-.0100	-.0133	-.0282	-.0071
.4	-.0039	-.0033	-.0042	-.0043	-.0082	-.0042
.5	-.0022	-.0005	-.0006	-.0027	-.0051	-.0025
.6	.0006	.0007	.0000	.0000	-.0032	.0000
.7	.0045	.0015	.0007	.0012	-.0025	.0015
.8	.0075	.0059	.0039	.0019	-.0008	.0047
.9	.0151	.0143	.0122	.0041	.0027	.0146
Average	-.0021	-.0061	-.0113	-.0180	-.0388	-.0144

*Earnings forecast error computed as (Actual EPS – Value Line Forecast of EPS)/Security Price at Start of Year.

EXHIBIT 3-7
ILLUSTRATION OF BROADTAPE RELEASES
FOR FOURTH QUARTER 1979 EARNINGS OF EVANS PRODUCTS

Release #1: 3.01 P.M. on 01/21/80

EVANS PRODUCTS CO 4TH QTR NET $1.22 A SHR VS OPER NET $1.0
01/21/80

NET $16.3 MILLION VS OPERATING NET $14 MILLION
IN THE YEAR AGO 4TH QUARTER AN EXTRAORDINARY GAIN OF $341 000 MADE FINAL NET $14.4 MILLION OR $1.03.

REVENUE $392.5 MILLION VS $318.1 MILLION.

YEAR NET $62.4 MILLION OR $4.65 VS OPERATING NET $52.9 MILLION OR $3.76.

AN EXTRAORDINARY GAIN IN 1978 MADE FINAL NET $54.2 MILLION
OR $3.85.
3 01 PM

Release #2: 3.26 P.M. on 01/21/80

EVANS PDTS CO EARNINGS
01/21/80
EVANS PRODUCTS CO REVENUES FOR THE 1979 YEAR WERE $1.5
BILLION VS $1.2 BILLION.

IN 1978 THE EXTRAORDINARY GAINS IN BOTH THE QUARTER AND
YEAR RESULTED MAINLY FROM CANADIAN TAX BENEFITS.

MONFORD A. ORLOFF CHAIRMAN AND CHIEF EXECUTIVE SAID THAT WHILE HIGHER INTEREST RATES AND UNFAVORABLE MARKET CONDITIONS IN THE FOREST PRODUCT INDUSTRY WILL ADVERSELY AFFECT EARNINGS EARLY IN THE YEAR THE COMPANY CONTINUES TO LOOK FOR 1980 TO BE ANOTHER RECORD YEAR UNLESS THE NATION EXPERIENCES A DEEPER OR MORE PROLONGED RECESSION THAN EVANS ANTICIPATES.

THE COMPANY ADDED THAT ALTHOUGH THE IMPACT OF THE EXPECTED DECLINE IN HOUSING STARTS WILL UNFAVORABLY AFFECT LUMBER AND PLYWOOD OPERATIONS THE OUTLOOK IS PROMISING FOR THE COMPANY'S TWO MAJOR BUSINESSES - BUILDING MATERIALS RETAILING AND TRANSPORTATION EQUIPMENT LEASING AND MANUFACTURING AS WELL AS STEEL CASTINGS.
3 26 PM

FIGURE 3-1
FREQUENCY OF EARNINGS ANNOUNCEMENTS BY TRADING DAY OF THE WEEK

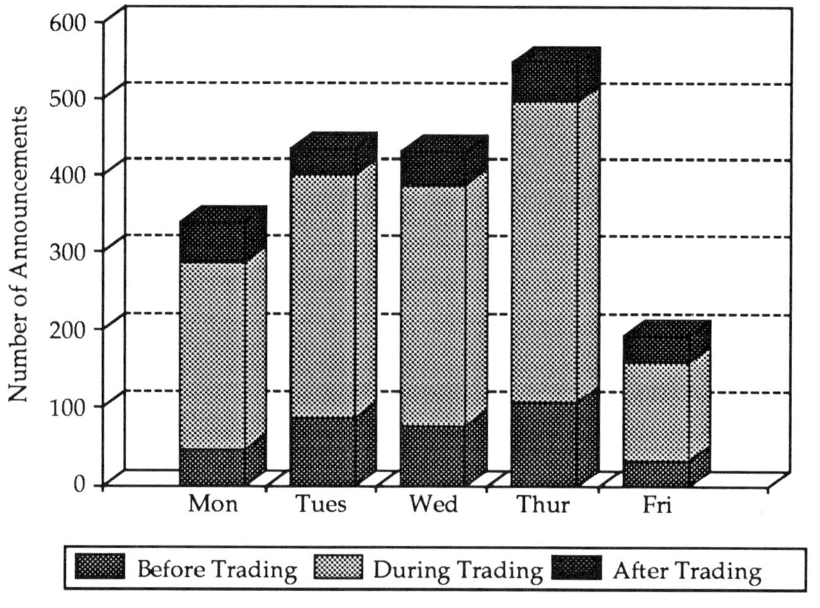

FIGURE 3-2
FREQUENCY OF EARNINGS ANNOUNCEMENTS FOR SUCCESSIVE FIFTEEN MINUTE PERIODS FROM 8 A.M. TO 7 P.M.

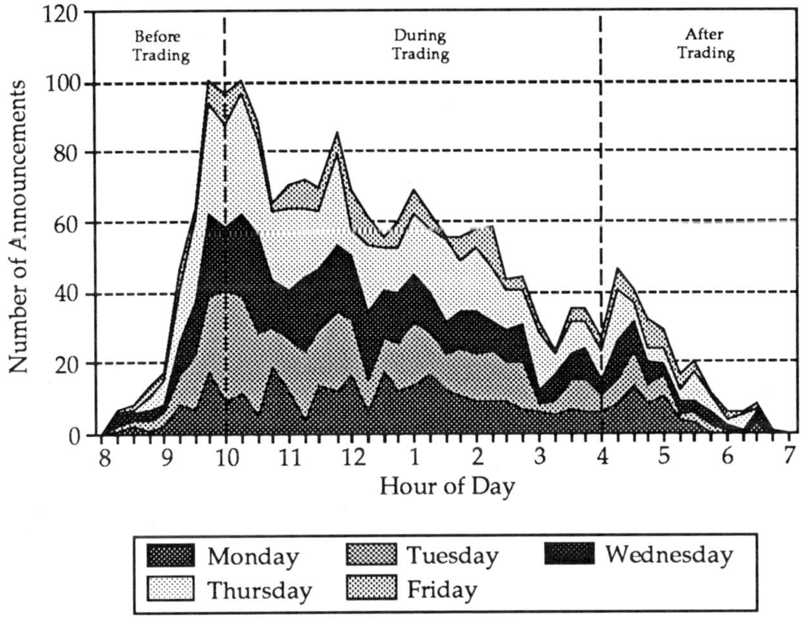

Chapter 4
Intraday Properties of Capital Market Variables

4.1: Introduction

This chapter describes key institutional features of the NYSE and then examines the intraday behavior of four capital market variables—mean security returns, variability of security returns, trading frequency, and trading volume. Each variable exhibits sizable heterogeneity in its intraday behavior. The nature and magnitude of this heterogeneity guides the experimental design used in Chapters 5 and 6.

Two modes of analysis are presented in this chapter:

- transaction time—the smallest unit of analysis we use is each individual transaction. Observations are sequenced according to the number of transactions prior to and subsequent to an information release.
- calendar time—the smallest unit of analysis we use is a calendar minute. (The Fitch data base used in this study reports individual transactions by calendar minute.) Observations are sequenced according to the number of minutes (in trading time) prior to and subsequent to an information release.

In transaction time, each security need not have the same number of observation units (transactions) per trading day. In calendar time, each security will have the same number of observation units (e.g., calendar minutes) per trading day. Calendar time in this study is defined as the calendar time during which the NYSE is open for trading (10:00 A.M. to 4:00 P.M. in the time period studied).

The focus of Sections 4.3 and 4.4 of this chapter is on intraday properties of our sample of firms over the 1980 to 1985 period. We use a consistent presentation format for each variable to highlight why the observed intraday properties are pivotal to the experimental design used in Chapters 5 and 6. Many of the intraday properties we report for the mean security returns, variability of security returns, and trading volume variables have been documented elsewhere. The trading frequency variable has not been extensively examined previously. Appendix A contains an overview of prior research including an annotated bibliography of key papers.[1]

[1] There are several reasons for presenting Chapter 4 results for all four financial variables rather than relying on prior studies and reporting in Chapter 4 only the missing gaps in the literature: (i) our approach provides a cohesive link between Chapter 4 and the Chapters 5 and 6 information content results, and (ii) prior studies have examined different samples and different time periods and hence may not apply to our sample/time period (especially due to the relatively high rate of change in institutional features of the NYSE).

4.2: Market Microstructure on NYSE

The NYSE can be described as a continuous trading market with dealer, order book, and auction features.[2] It is continuous since trades can be made at any time during the trading day as long as a counterpart offer exists at a suitable price. Exceptions occur on resumption of trading at the beginning of a trading day, or following a halt in trading. In these situations, trading resembles an ordinary (double) auction, with market clearing prices being determined by contemporaneous buy and sell demand.

Trading for an individual security is organized around a specialist who performs several functions:

1. By recording and executing limit orders for the security, the specialist acts as a broker's broker (i.e., an agent of the broker through which the order originated). A limit order specifies the price and quantity of shares to be bought or sold, possibly with additional directions attached. Thus limit orders are not intended for immediate execution. Rather they create a "pool" of available trades against which market orders may be executed. A market order is an order for immediate execution at the best available price.

   The specialist also acts as a broker in certain circumstances by holding and executing market orders for floor traders/brokers. This typically occurs when trading in the particular security is relatively quiet.

2. The specialist trades on his/her own account. In particular, the specialist stands ready to meet an incoming order (at the stated bid or ask price) if no matching position is provided by recorded limit orders or by floor traders. According to specialists interviewed, they participate in approximately twenty percent of transactions in this way, although this varies across securities and across trading circumstances.

3. The specialist has an affirmative obligation to ensure a fair and orderly market in the security. This obligation is reflected in various NYSE regulations concerning the circumstances under which specialists are expected to trade (or are prohibited from trading).

Overall, the structure of the market is designed to direct trading orders to a single location (the specialist post) in order to promote market liquidity. Requirements governing specialists' behavior are intended to enhance this liquidity.

A. Auction and Dealer Trading Regimes

While the NYSE operates as a continuous market in trading hours, the opening trade each day (and any resumptions of trading following a halt) occurs using an auction trading regime, whereas subsequent trades occur using a dealer regime.

---

[2] The following description draws on (a) interviews with NYSE officials, specialists, and traders, (b) published material by the NYSE (such as annual editions of the New York Stock Exchange, *Fact Book*), and (c) other description and analysis of the NYSE (such as Schwartz [1988, 1991]).

First trade of the day (auction regime)

The specialist aggregates ("batches") all orders that have accumulated prior to the opening, including expressions of interest from floor traders/brokers for trades at particular price levels. The specialist then begins trade at a price which best clears the market. This often involves the specialist buying or selling on his/her own account. Schwartz [1988, p. 454] gives the following description for the opening trade in CBS on March 1, 1985:

> On March 1, 1985, the New York Stock Exchange's trading floor opened at 10.00 A.M.; the market for CBS opened at 10:30:02. At the opening trade, 171,500 shares of CBS common changed hands at a price of 86. The opening trade comprised all crossing orders from (a) the limit order book, (b) the trading crowd on the floor, and (c) orders delivered to the specialist's post by the Opening Automated Report System.

This example illustrates how the opening trade brings together many orders into a single transaction.

Subsequent trades (dealer regime)

A typical trade on the NYSE proceeds with a market order arriving at the specialist's post where it is matched against either a limit order on the specialist's records, the specialist's own account, a corresponding order held by a floor trader/broker, or some combination of these three. As a result, a single order sent to the NYSE can be joined with other orders to form a single transaction. Alternatively, a single order can span several trades. This means that the observed history of transactions recorded on the NYSE need not reflect the flow of orders into the market.

The majority of transactions are transacted on the floor of the NYSE. Block trades, however, are typically transacted in the so-called "upstairs market":

> [The upstairs market] is the network of trading desks that can communicate with each other and with institutional investors by means of electronic display systems and the telephone. In their bilaterial negotiations, the upstairs traders use floor information, whatever other knowledge they can gather of market conditions, their detailed knowledge of their institutional clients' holdings and likely trading interests, and a good deal of strategy as they play the negotiation game... Trades negotiated in the upstairs market are generally taken to the [NYSE floor] to be executed. Schwartz [1988, pp. 26-33]

The NYSE definition of a block trade is a transaction involving 10,000 or more shares. This definition is an administrative one[3]. Specialists and other par-

[3] Choe, McInish and Wood [1991a] use two alternative definitions of a block trade: "a trade of more than 20,000 shares with a dollar value of more than either $1 million or, alternatively, $3 million. This block identification criterion is arbitrary, but there is no definitive rule for defining a 'large' transaction. Although the NYSE uses a 10,000 share criterion to identify blocks, many firms do not consider a 10,000 share transaction to be a 'true' block. The $1 million and $3 million secondary classification rules are used because the 20,000 share level may be too small" (p. 4).

ties interviewed indicated that while many trades larger than 10,000 shares were transacted in the upstairs market, there was not an automatic cutoff between those transactions made on the floor vis-a-vis those made in the "upstairs market". For example, in large, actively traded companies (such as General Motors) trades larger than 10,000 shares are frequently brought to the floor through a floor trader.

The NYSE *Fact Book* (annual editions) reports the following summary data for the 1980-1985 period:

Year	Total Number of Transactions With 10,000 or More Shares Traded	Total Shares Traded in Large Block Transactions (000s)	Percent of Total NYSE Reported Volume	Percent of all Transactions
1980	133,597	3,311,132	29.2%	1.03%
1981	145,564	3,771,442	31.8	1.24
1982	254,707	6,742,481	41.0	2.02
1983	363,415	9,842,080	45.6	2.41
1984	433,427	11,492,091	49.8	3.35
1985	539,039	14,222,272	51.7	3.68

Block trades are not distributed randomly throughout each trading day. In particular, the first trade of each day (conducted under the auction regime) contains a higher than average proportion of block trades.

B. Institutional Factors Affecting Reported Transaction Series

The intraday data base used in this research is developed by Francis Emory Fitch. Fitch reports the security price, trading volume, and time of day (to the calendar minute) of each transaction. The data also provide various codes used to identify trading halts, trades out of sequence, corrections, etc. Fitch officials indicated in interviews that they receive the data from the NYSE, transfer the data ("as is") to their own tapes, and then sell the tapes to their customers. The Fitch time stamp per transaction is that provided by the NYSE to Fitch.

The following caveats are appropriate when interpreting the Fitch transaction data (including the time-stamp and sequencing):[4]

(i) Only recorded transactions on the NYSE are included in the Fitch data base. This restriction can exclude several classes of transactions. For stocks listed on multiple exchanges (for example, the NYSE and the London Stock Exchange) non-NYSE transactions are excluded. Transactions made outside organized exchanges are also excluded. An example is a transaction in which ownership in shares is passed without the involvement of any NYSE associated person. For instance, large transactions at the time of acquisitions need

[4] Bronfman [1991b] provides an insightful discussion of institutional issues that are important to consider when making inferences from intraday transaction data on the NYSE.

not be made via the NYSE. Transactions on private electronic trading systems (such as *Instinet*) are also not included in the Fitch data base.

(ii) The time-stamp on each transaction may not always be an accurate reflection of when the relevant parties agreed on the sale. Consider transactions made "on the main floor" of the exchange. Clerks ("recorders") on the exchange record transactions on cards and these cards are then entered into a reader. In days of high trading volume, there may be some delay in the entering of these cards into the reader. For instance, on October 19, 1987 delays in entering of cards of over one hour occurred (Kleidon [1990]). Specialists interviewed indicated that delays of less than one minute occurred in the vast majority of cases. (Technological change occurring since 1985 is resulting in many trades being automatically executed, reducing the potential time lag between the trade and its time stamp.)[5]

As a second example, consider block sales. Harris [1990, p. 19] describes this market as follows:

> Block trade initiators may have a block dealer or a block broker organize liquidity for their trades... Block dealers execute trades for their own inventory. They charge a bid/ask spread and/or a commission to compensate them for the costs and risks associated with their trading. Block brokers contact likely contra-parties to their trade and stake their reputations on their assurances to them that the trade is not especially risky. They are compensated for their expenses by the commissions they charge the block initiator... Block sells are about four times more common than block buys.

Some block trades occur on the floor while others are arranged in the "upstairs market" and then reported to the floor for entry into the card reader. When sales from the "upstairs market" are folded in with transactions made on the main floor, it is not always possible to enter them in the exact time and sequence in which transactions were consummated on the main floor and consummated in the "upstairs market". (This can arise even if the floor times are entered in sequence.)

(iii) There need not be a one-to-one correspondence between the number of individual orders placed with specialists and the number of recorded transactions on the NYSE. Both batching and splitting up of orders can occur, and on both the buying and selling sides. For example, an incoming market order might be batched with other (simultaneous) market orders or the specialist's own account and traded against limit orders, the specialist, or market orders held by floor traders/brokers. Alternatively, a single incoming market order might be split up into several trades (at different prices) if offsetting limit or other orders are not available to cover the entire order at one price.

---

[5] Lee and Ready [1991] report that "trades transacted under unusual settlement conditions or reported out of sequence are identified with special condition codes [in the ISSM data base]. Such trades have traditionally been a small proportion of total trading volume" (p. 6).

The first transaction of the day, operated under an auction trading regime, typically has batching on both the buying and selling sides. Subsequent transactions, operated under a dealer trading regime, may have batching (or splitting of orders) on one or both sides. No systematic evidence is known concerning the extent of batching and splitting in this way on the NYSE.

(iv) The sequence in which transactions are made need not be the same as the order in which trading orders are received. In some cases, investors give instructions that govern the time at which the transaction is to be made. Three orders listed by Schwartz [1988, pp. 47-8] are:

> At the opening: The *at the opening* instruction... directs the order to be executed only at the opening; any unfilled portion of the order that remains after the opening is to be cancelled.
>
> Market-on-Close: The order is to be executed as close to the market closing as possible.
>
> Limit or Market-on-Close: The *limit or market-on-close* order is placed as a limit order, but if it does not execute during the trading day, it is to be executed as a market order as near to the close as possible.

The potential effect of these orders is to induce a clustering of transactions at the open and the close of the day.

In addition, it is common for floor traders/brokers to "work" many of the orders they receive. This means that they will split the orders according to how they gauge prevailing market conditions in order to achieve a better trading outcome than if the entire order were traded in a single transaction. Floor traders/brokers also will leave some of their orders with the specialist to match against subsequent incoming orders. This enables the orders to be "worked" without the brokers/trader's presence. Typically this is done when the market is relatively quiet and does not require the broker/trader's attention.

In each of these cases the sequence of recorded transactions need not accurately reflect the underlying sequence of order arrival (to brokers/traders).

(v) Several trading protocol rules can affect the sequencing with which incoming orders are processed. Schwartz [1988, pp. 48-9] illustrates the rules operating on the NYSE. The primary rule is that the highest bid and the lowest ask are executed first. The secondary rules determine the priority of multiple orders at the same price; there are three rules, *priority, parity and price*, which together tend to result in larger orders being transacted before smaller ones when the transaction price is unchanged from the previous trade.

The Fitch data base used in this research reports transaction data but not bid-ask spread data. The following sections of this chapter present intraday properties of these data in both transaction time and calendar time. Ongoing research in market microstructure is also examining intraday properties of bid-ask spreads. Appendix A of this monograph notes that many of the intraday properties observed with transaction data are also observed with bid-ask spread data. Appendix B describes the ISSM data base which includes bid-ask spread data as well as transaction data and discusses information content studies that analyze these data on an intraday basis.

4.3: Transaction Time Analysis

Transaction time takes the individual transaction as its smallest unit of analysis. Observations are sequenced according to the number of transactions prior to and subsequent to an information release.

A. Transaction Time Series Examined

Four transaction time series are examined in this section:

- **Mean Security Returns.** Mean security returns per transaction.
- **Variability of Security Returns.** Mean of the absolute value of each security return (from transaction t-1 to transaction t).
- **Trading Frequency.** Time between transactions—average time (in minutes of trading time) since the previous trade.
- **Trading Volume.** Average number of shares traded per transaction (in hundreds): numerator is the number of shares traded; denominator is 100 times the number of transactions.

B. Systematic Intraday Patterns

Figures 4-1 to 4-4 plot mean patterns for each of the first ten transactions and for each of the last ten transactions of the day.[6] The patterns noted in these figures cover the 1980 to 1985 period and include firms that differ markedly in firm size and trading frequency. Summary results are also reported for three sub-partitions of the sample:

a. *Time-period.* Year by year partitions for each of the 1980 to 1985 calendar years.
b. *Firm size.* At the start of each year, firms are ranked on market capitalization and placed into one of five portfolios (I = smallest, . . ., V = largest). This ranking is repeated each year.
c. *Trading frequency.* At the start of each year, firms are ranked on the average number of transactions per day (computed for each stock as the number of transactions for the year divided by the number of days the stock is listed that year). This ranking is repeated each year.

Grouping firms by firm size is not independent of a grouping by trading frequency. Pearson correlations between the log of firm size and the log of trad-

[6] For firms with less than 20 transactions in a trading day, a subset of observations will be included in both the first 10 transactions and the last 10 transactions. Where firms have less than 10 transactions in a trading day, these transactions are included in the computation of Figures 4-1 to 4-4. Missing observations are excluded from the numerator and the denominator when computing the mean values reported in Figures 4-1 to 4-4. Tables of the data underlying the figures presented in this chapter are available from the authors.

ing frequency each year range from a low of .53 (1981 and 1984) to a high of .63 (1985).

Mean Security Returns

The systematic patterns observed in Figure 4-1 include:

(i) negative mean returns for the first nine transactions on Mondays, and positive mean returns for the first three transactions on Tuesdays through Fridays.

(ii) a positive mean return for the last transaction on each trading day of the week.

Both patterns (i) and (ii) have been extensively documented in the literature—see Appendix A.

A negative mean return for the first transaction on Monday occurs in five of the six years examined (it is positive in 1980). A positive mean return for the first transaction on Tuesday through Friday occurs in 18 of the 24 yearly partitions (four trading days times six years), for 19 of the 20 firm size partitions (four trading days times five firm-size partitions), and for 17 of the 20 trading frequency partitions (four trading days times five trading frequency partitions). The mean return for the last transaction of the day is positive in all 30 time period observations, for all 25 firm size observations, and for 24 of the 25 trading frequency observations.

Variability of Security Returns

The most marked intraday pattern in Figure 4-2 is the high variability of the first transaction vis-a-vis the next nine transactions or the last ten transactions of the day. This pattern is observed for each year of the 1980-1985 period, for each firm size partition, and for each trading frequency partition.

An additional pattern observed in the sub-partition data is an inverse relationship between firm size and the variability of security returns. As an example, the mean absolute value of percent security returns for the first and second transactions of each trading day is:

	Firm-Size Partitions				
	(Smallest) I	II	III	IV	(Largest) V
1st Transaction	.87	.76	.62	.55	.49
2nd Transaction	.53	.44	.32	.27	.18

Smaller firms have higher variability than larger firms in their security returns of each trading day. This pattern is observed for all of the five trading days.

Trading Frequency

Figure 4-3 shows that the time between successive transactions is higher for the first transaction than for the subsequent transactions plotted. This pattern implies a longer average time between the last transaction on the prior trading day and the first transaction on the next trading day vis-a-vis the time between subsequent successive transactions. All computations underlying Figure 4-3 focus only on trading minutes; the time from 3.59.00 P.M. of one trading day to 10.01.59 the next trading day is treated as three trading minutes (3.59.00 to 4.00.00; 10.00.00 to 10.00.59; 10.01.00 to 10.01.59) in the same way that the time from 10.01.00 to 10.03.59 on the same day is treated as three trading minutes.

Marked differences exist across the five trading frequency partitions in the time (trading minutes) between transactions. Mean values of this variable for the first ten transactions across the five trading frequency partitions are:

	Trading Frequency Partition					
Transaction	**(Least Traded) I**	**II**	**III**	**IV**	**(Most Traded) V**	**All**
1st	97.6	40.4	20.3	12.9	8.8	35.9
2nd	51.1	28.1	15.7	9.7	4.6	21.5
3rd	45.7	26.6	14.4	8.3	3.9	19.2
4th	41.6	26.1	14.0	8.0	3.6	17.8
5th	39.4	26.5	14.5	8.0	3.5	17.2
6th	36.8	25.7	14.4	8.1	3.6	16.2
7th	33.7	25.7	15.1	8.3	3.5	15.5
8th	30.3	24.3	15.0	8.3	3.5	14.4
9th	28.6	23.6	15.5	8.6	3.5	13.9
10th	27.0	22.3	15.2	8.7	3.6	13.1

The least frequently traded quintile (I) has an average time between transaction over seven times that for the most frequently traded quintile, for each of the first ten transactions.

Trading Volume

The trading volume variable reported in this subsection is the mean number of shares traded per transaction. The inferences reported here are the same as those drawn from the following two trading volume proxies we also examined—mean $value of shares traded per transaction, and mean number of shares traded per transaction divided by the number of shares outstanding.

Figure 4-4 shows that the mean number of shares traded in the first transaction of each trading day is dramatically larger than for any of the next nine transactions. This pattern is observed in each of the six calendar years and for each of the five firm size categories examined. Note that under the NYSE institutional arrangements, the first transaction of the day is conducted using an auction regime; it is an aggregation of individual orders that have been placed before the start of the trading session.

The pattern observed in Figure 4-4 is not consistently observed for all five trading frequency sub-partitions. The mean number of shares traded (in thousands) for the first transaction across the five trading frequency partitions is:

I	II	III	IV	V
0.891	1.449	2.876	4.758	15.136

The ratio of the mean number of shares traded for the first transaction to the mean number of shares traded for the second to tenth transaction of each trading day is:

	Trading Frequency Partition					
Transaction	**(Least Traded) I**	**II**	**III**	**IV**	**(Most Traded) V**	**All**
1st/2nd	1.07	1.47	2.18	3.33	7.17	3.75
1st/3rd	1.04	1.49	2.18	3.86	10.04	4.24
1st/4th	1.08	1.54	2.13	3.45	10.19	4.16
1st/5th	1.01	1.44	2.10	3.57	10.39	4.09
1st/6th	0.95	1.49	2.21	3.71	9.62	4.06
1st/7th	0.97	1.48	2.13	3.58	9.43	3.95
1st/8th	0.99	1.52	2.19	3.71	9.72	4.04
1st/9th	0.98	1.44	2.28	3.64	9.76	4.00
1st/10th	0.99	1.41	2.37	3.73	10.02	4.05

Across the highest four trading frequency partitions, the first transaction has a larger number of shares traded than any of the next nine transactions. The first transaction is over seven times the size of any of the next nine transactions for the highest trading frequency partition. In contrast, the first transaction of the day for the lowest trading frequency partition has a similar size to each of the next nine transactions. One explanation for this result is that stocks in the lowest trading frequency partition have minimal overnight orders which results in minimal batching for the first transaction.

Block trades (institutionally defined by the NYSE as transactions with 10,000 or more shares traded) are concentrated in the more highly traded partitions for the first transaction of the day. The percentage of total trades that are block trades for selected transactions at the start and end of the day are:

	Trading Frequency Partition					
Transaction	**(Least Traded) I**	**II**	**III**	**IV**	**(Most Traded) V**	**All**
1st	2.35%	2.01%	5.49%	10.23%	40.14%	11.78%
2nd	2.17	1.63	2.48	2.75	4.69	2.57
3rd	2.21	1.60	2.53	2.20	2.78	2.07
•						
•						
•						
3rd Last	1.10	1.44	2.41	1.81	2.55	1.88
2nd Last	1.10	1.43	2.45	2.14	3.18	2.07
Last	0.92	1.48	2.15	2.30	4.43	2.26

Approximately 40 percent of all first transactions in the highest trading frequency partition have volumes of 10,000 or more shares traded.

C. Serial Correlation Evidence

The appropriate significance test to use in an experiment is contingent, in part, on the distributional properties of the data being examined. Chapters 5 and 6 use an empirical based significance test developed from data of the sample of firms we examine. The serial correlation evidence in this section (and Section 4.4D) supports our use of empirical-based distributions rather than a parametic approach assuming independently and identically distributed data.

Exhibit 4-1 presents cross-sectional evidence for the first four autocorrelation coefficients (r_1, r_2, r_3 and r_4) of each of the four transaction time series examined in Figures 4-1 to 4-4. For the mean security returns series, results are reported for:

(a) the full set of transaction data, and

(b) the subset of transactions with non-zero returns.[7]

The (b) series differs from (a) by excluding all transactions with zero returns. Approximately 57 percent of all transactions in the data base have zero returns. Both the (a) and (b) mean security returns transaction series have negative first order autocorrelations for over 90 percent of the distribution. This result has been frequently documented in the literature—see Appendix A. The negative autocorrelation evidence is most marked in the mean return series based on non-zero return observations.

Both the variability of security returns (excluding zero returns) series and the trading frequency series exhibit statistically significant evidence of positive autocorrelation. The .1 decile of the distribution for r_1 is positive for both these series. High variability in security returns is more likely to be followed by high variability in the next non-zero transaction, than by low variability. A reduction in the time between successive transactions is more likely to be followed by reduced time until the next transaction, than by an increase in the time to the next transaction. The trading volume variable in Exhibit 4-1 exhibits little evidence of serial correlation over successive transactions (or over lags of two, three or four transactions). High trading volume on one transaction does not increase or decrease the likelihood of high trading volume on the next transaction.

The autocorrelation evidence in Exhibit 4-1 for the security return series is based on the sign and magnitude of each observation. An alternative approach is a decision tree format, which is based on the sign of successive observations. Results are in Exhibit 4-2. This approach probes the reversal phenomenon, which is of specific interest to the Niederhoffer and Osborne

[7] One motivation for including the (b) series is to provide a comparison with prior studies that have examined transaction returns computed on successive price changes—see Patell and Wolfson [1984] and Jennings and Starks [1985].

[1966] hypothesis about the role of the specialist on the NYSE (see Appendix A). Several patterns are apparent in Exhibit 4-2. First, more than half the transactions (57.2 percent) take place at an unchanged price. Second, given a sequence of two successive price changes of the same sign, a reversal in the sign of the next transaction is more likely than a continuation. For example, conditional probabilities, based on the data underlying Exhibit 4-2, are:

Reversals		Continuations	
Pr(−|++)	= .575	Pr(+|++)	= .161
Pr(+|−−)	= .576	Pr(−|−−)	= .158

Prior research has documented similar evidence of price reversals—see Appendix A.

4.4: Calendar Time Analysis

Calendar time analysis takes a calendar unit of time—such as a minute or an hour—as its unit of analysis. Observations are sequenced according to the number of (say) minutes prior to and subsequent to an information release.

The analysis in this monograph aligns calendar time in trading time minutes. During the time period studied (1980-1985) the NYSE was open for trading between 10 A.M. and 4.P.M. Thus, there are 361 trading minutes per trading day. The motivation for this definition of calendar time is that it is only during trading periods that successive changes in capital market variables can be observed.[8]

A. Smoothing Patterns with Calendar Time

Smoothing patterns can result when each observation unit in calendar time does not include a transaction. Consider an analysis of the number of shares traded per transaction in both transaction time and calendar time. Assume:

- five securities are being examined,
- each security has one and only one transaction in the first five trading minutes of the day (10:00 to 10:04), and
- each security trades at a different calendar time minute.

The number of shares traded per security and the time of each transaction is:

Security	Time of Transaction	Number of Shares Traded
AA	10:00	5,460
BB	10:01	3,765
CC	10:02	7,280
DD	10:03	4,340
EE	10:04	5,625

[8] By using the closing price on trading day -1 and the opening price on trading day 0, one can compute a single price change covering the non-trading time period—see French and Roll [1986].

In transaction time, all securities are aligned at transaction 1 with a mean trading volume of 5,294 shares traded per transaction. All the trading volume effect will be reflected in the first transaction time observation unit. In calendar time, the results are (assuming a trading minute is the unit of analysis):

Event Time	Mean Shares Traded Per Transaction: No Trades Excluded From Denominator	Mean Shares Traded Per Transaction: No Trades Included In Denominator
1	5,460	1,092
2	3,765	753
3	7,280	1,456
4	4,340	868
5	5,625	1,125

Calendar time shows trading volume being smoothed over the first five observation units of the trading day.

Smoothing of capital market variables will be most marked when the smallest unit of calendar time is used as the unit of analysis and when stocks are traded infrequently. Consider the effect of using different calendar time periods as the smallest unit of analysis. Assume there are 30 transactions per trading day (the median number of transactions per trading day in 1983).

Smallest Calendar Time Unit of Analysis	Average Number of Transactions Per Unit of Time
1 minute	0.08
15 minutes	1.25
30 minutes	2.50
60 minutes	5.00
361 minutes	30.00

With 30 transactions per trading day and a minute as the smallest unit of analysis, there would be a transaction (on average) only every 12 minutes. Approximately 11 out of every 12 trading minutes would have no transaction. In contrast, with 60 minutes as the calendar time unit of analysis, there would be five transactions (on average) every time unit of analysis.

A trading minute is the basic unit of calendar time in much of the analysis in this monograph. The smoothing phenomenon discussed in this section is an important consideration when interpreting the calendar time results we present.

B. Calendar Time Series Examined

Five calendar time series, covering four areas, are examined:

- **Mean Security Returns**. Mean security returns per minute (%).
- **Variability of Security Returns**. Mean of the absolute value of each security return per minute (from the last transaction in or before minute t-1 to the last transaction in minute t).

- **Trading Frequency.** Mean number of transactions per minute (in 10ths)—numerator is 10 times the number of transactions executed during this trading minute; denominator is the number of firms in the sample listed on the NYSE in that minute.

Trading Volume.

- Mean number of shares traded per transaction per minute (in hundreds, for transactions that occurred in that minute)—numerator is the number of shares traded in that minute; denominator is 100 times the number of transactions that took place in that minute.
- Mean number of shares traded per firm per minute (in hundreds, for transactions that occurred in that minute)—numerator is the total number of shares traded for all transactions recorded in the same minute; denominator is 100 times the number for firms with one or more transactions in that minute.

The motivation for including two trading volume series is to highlight how calendar time can show smoothed patterns of series that in transaction time have a spiked pattern.

C. Systematic Intraday Patterns

Figures 4-5 to 4-9 report calendar time intraday patterns for each of the above series. Each figure reports results for (a) the six one hour trading periods per day, and (b) the first 5 trading minutes (10:00 to 10:04) and the last 5 trading minutes (3:55 to 4:00) of each trading day. (Note that the scale for the hour-by-hour patterns in Figures 4-6 to 4-8 is different from that for the minute-by-minute patterns.)

Mean Security Returns

Figure 4-5 reports results for the mean security returns series based on actual transactions. Where no transaction occurs in the time period examined, the observation is excluded from both the numerator and the denominator in the mean return calculation. When computing calendar time returns, transactions must have occurred in both of the adjacent time periods. Observations with no transaction in either or both of the adjacent time periods are omitted from the computations. Results were also computed with no trade observations recorded as a zero return in the numerator and a single observation in the denominator. The inferences outlined in this chapter were not affected by this alternative way of computing returns.

Hourly patterns in the data evident in Figure 4-5 are:

(i) positive mean returns for the last hour of trading on all five trading days.

(ii) positive mean returns for the first hour of trading on Tuesdays through Fridays.

(iii) negative mean returns for the first hour of trading on Mondays.

Patterns (i) and (ii) are consistently found across all three subpartitions (year, firm size, and trading frequency). Pattern (iii) is observed for each year of the 1980 to 1985 period, for each of the five firm size partitions, and for four of the five trading frequency partitions. (The least traded frequency partition has a positive mean return for the first hour of trading on Mondays.)

The most marked start or end of day pattern in Figure 4-5 is the consistently positive mean return for the last trading minute. It is observed for all 30 data points in the yearly partitions (5 days times 6 years), for all 25 data points in the firm size partitions (5 days times 5 firm size partitions), and for 24 of the 25 data points in the trading frequency partitions (5 days times 5 trading frequency partitions).

Variability of Security Returns

Figure 4-6 reports intraday patterns for the variability of security returns series (the mean of the absolute value of each security return). The start of each trading day has the highest period of variability. Returns in the first trading minute and the first trading hour are more variable than returns at other times of the day. The middle hours of the trading day are the periods with lowest security return variability. These patterns are found for each year in the 1980-85 period, across all five firm size partitions, and across all five trading frequency partitions.

Trading Frequency

Trading frequency is measured in Figure 4-7 as the mean number of transactions per unit of calendar time. The first plot in Figure 4-7 reports the average number of transactions per trading hour. There is a U-shaped pattern in hourly trading frequency; the opening and closing hours have higher numbers of transactions per hour than do hours in the middle of the trading period. The U-shaped pattern is observed for each year of the 1980-85 period, and for each trading frequency partition. The difference across trading hours in their trading frequency means that the "smoothing effect" found in calendar time vis-a-vis transaction time will be strongest in the middle of the trading day (where trading frequency is lowest).

Figure 4-7 also reports the mean number of transactions per calendar minute for the first five and last five trading minutes (using a different scale than for the hourly series). The most marked pattern in Figure 4-7 is the dramatic increase in trading frequency in the last minute of trading vis-a-vis the prior four trading minutes or any of the first five trading minutes. This pattern is found in each year. It is most marked for the largest 20 percent of the firms (by size) and the largest 20 percent of the firms (by trading frequency).

Mean trading frequency statistics for the second-last and last trading minutes for the five firm size (I = smallest) and the five trading frequency (I = least traded) partitions are:

	I	II	III	IV	V	ALL
Firm Size						
Second Last Minute	.11	.13	.17	.19	.34	.19
Last Minute	.25	.29	.39	.42	.73	.42
Trading Frequency						
Second Last Minute	.04	.07	.13	.21	.48	.19
Last Minute	.11	.20	.34	.48	.94	.42

As discussed in Section 4.2, "Market-on-Close" and "Limit or Market-on-Close" orders will result in trades occurring near the end of the trading day.

Trading Volume

The two trading volume variables reported in this subsection are the mean number of shares traded per transaction (in Figure 4-8) and the mean number of shares traded per calendar time unit (in Figure 4-9).

MEAN NUMBER OF SHARES TRADED PER TRANSACTION: One pattern in Figure 4-8 is the high level of this variable in each of the first five minutes of trading vis-a-vis the average for any of the six hourly trading periods. One explanation for this result is the smoothing pattern inherent in a calendar time analysis when the basic time unit is small relative to the time between transactions. Figure 4-4 shows that the number of shares traded for the first transaction of the day is approximately 4 times larger than for the next nine transactions. When this first transaction is spread over different calendar minutes, the calendar time results will smooth this first transaction pattern over several calendar time minutes.

Larger firms and firms with more actively traded securities have the greatest increase in the number of shares traded per transaction in the first minute of trading, relative to the average size in the first trading hour. The ratio of (a) the mean number of shares traded per transaction in the first minute to (b) the mean per minute for the first trading hour for each firm size partition (I = smallest 20 percent) and for each trading frequency partition (I = least traded 20 percent) is:

	I	II	III	IV	V	ALL
Firm Size	1.82	2.08	1.88	1.95	2.98	2.14
Trading Frequency	1.03	1.11	1.20	1.87	3.90	2.14

The ratio is greatest for the largest 20 percent of observations by firm size and for the 20 percent with the highest trading frequency.

MEAN NUMBER OF SHARES TRADED PER CALENDAR TIME UNIT: The marked patterns in Figure 4-9 are:

i. the U-shaped pattern in hourly values, with the opening hour having the highest value.

ii. the increase in the average number of shares traded per firm in the last trading minute.

Both patterns are observed for all six calendar years, for all firm-size partitions, and for all trading frequency partitions.

The mean number of shares traded per calendar time unit in Figure 4-9 is a composite of the mean number of transactions per calendar time unit (Figure 4-7) and the mean number of shares traded per transaction (Figure 4-8). Patterns observed in Figure 4-9 can be predicted from the patterns in the underlying variables in Figures 4-7 and 4-8.

The inferences drawn from the mean number of shares traded per calendar time unit in Figure 4-9 are the same as those drawn from the following two trading volume proxies we also examined—mean $ value of shares traded per calendar time unit and the mean number of shares traded per calendar time unit divided by the number of shares outstanding.

D. Serial Correlation Evidence

Exhibit 4-3 reports serial correlation evidence for the mean security return series. Eight different calendar time holding periods are examined: 1 minute, 5 minutes, 10 minutes, 15 minutes, 1 hour, 2 hours, 4 hours, and 1 day. One limitation of examining serial correlations for a calendar time series (especially for shorter holding periods) is the high percentage of zero returns. Exhibit 3-2 reports that the median number of transactions per trading day ranges from 25 (1981 and 1985) to 30 (1983). This implies that when calendar returns are measured on a minute by minute basis, the minimum median number of trading minutes with no transaction (and hence zero return) is over 90 percent of the sample. Moreover, even when a transaction does occur, there is a zero return more than 57 percent of the time.

Exhibit 4-3 reports cross-sectional statistics. Serial correlations are computed for each firm in the sample and the cross-sectional distribution statistic is then computed. Results for the first (r_1), second (r_2), third (r_3) and fourth (r_4) order autocorrelations are reported. Several patterns are found in the cross-section data. First, negative autocorrelations are more frequently observed in Exhibit 4-3 than are positive autocorrelations. Second, shorter holding periods exhibit more evidence of a negatively skewed distribution. Third, the first order autocorrelation exhibits the strongest evidence of negative skewness, especially for holding periods up to 60 minutes.

4.5: Summary

Both the transaction time and the calendar time series examined in this chapter exhibit systematic patterns in their intraday properties. These systematic patterns in many cases are found at the start of each trading day or the end of each trading day.

Four different dimensions of intraday behavior have been examined—mean security returns, variability of security returns, trading frequency, and trading volume. These four dimensions, while not independent, show sufficient differences in their behavior to warrant separate analysis in subsequent research in this monograph.

The sample of firms examined differs markedly in their trading frequencies. The median number of daily transactions per company is 28; the range is from 2 to 306 transactions per day. Even the most frequently traded security averages less than 1 transaction per trading minute. This non-trading phenomenon creates the potential for transaction time and calendar time modes of analysis to differ in their intraday properties. Chapters 5 and 6 show that these differences are important when designing intraday information content research and when drawing inferences from that research.

EXHIBIT 4-1
TRANSACTION TIME ANALYSIS: DISTRIBUTION STATISTICS OF AUTOCORRELATION COEFFICIENTS FOR SELECTED TRANSACTION TIME SERIES

	DISTRIBUTION STATISTIC			
SERIES	**Mean**	**.1 Decile**	**.5 Decile**	**.9 Decile**
Mean Security Returns (incl. zero returns)				
r_1	–.18	–.33	–.18	–.05
r_2	–.02	–.05	–.02	.02
r_3	.01	–.02	.01	.03
r_4	.01	–.02	.01	.03
Mean Security Returns (excl. zero returns)				
r_1	–.30	–.57	–.29	–.08
r_2	.17	.04	.12	.37
r_3	–.07	–.25	–.03	.04
r_4	.08	.00	.04	.18
Variability of Security Returns (incl. zero returns)				
r_1	.00	.00	.00	.01
r_2	.00	.00	.00	.01
r_3	.00	.00	.00	.00
r_4	.00	.00	.00	.00
Variability of Security Returns (excl. zero returns)				
r_1	.23	.10	.20	.37
r_2	.16	.05	.12	.31
r_3	.14	.04	.10	.30
r_4	.14	.03	.09	.28
Trading Frequency				
r_1	.10	.04	.10	.17
r_2	.12	.06	.11	.12
r_3	.10	.04	.09	.16
r_4	.10	.04	.10	.16
Trading Volume				
r_1	.05	.01	.03	.19
r_2	.02	.00	.01	.05
r_3	.02	.00	.01	.05
r_4	.01	.00	.01	.03

EXHIBIT 4-2
TIME SERIES RELATIONSHIP BETWEEN SIGN OF PRICE CHANGE FROM FOUR SUCCESSIVE TRANSACTIONS

RETURN BASED ON TRANSACTIONS T-3 AND T-2 | **RETURN BASED ON TRANSACTIONS T-2 AND T-1** | **RETURN BASED ON TRANSACTIONS T-1 AND T** | **SEQUENCE OF SIGNS**

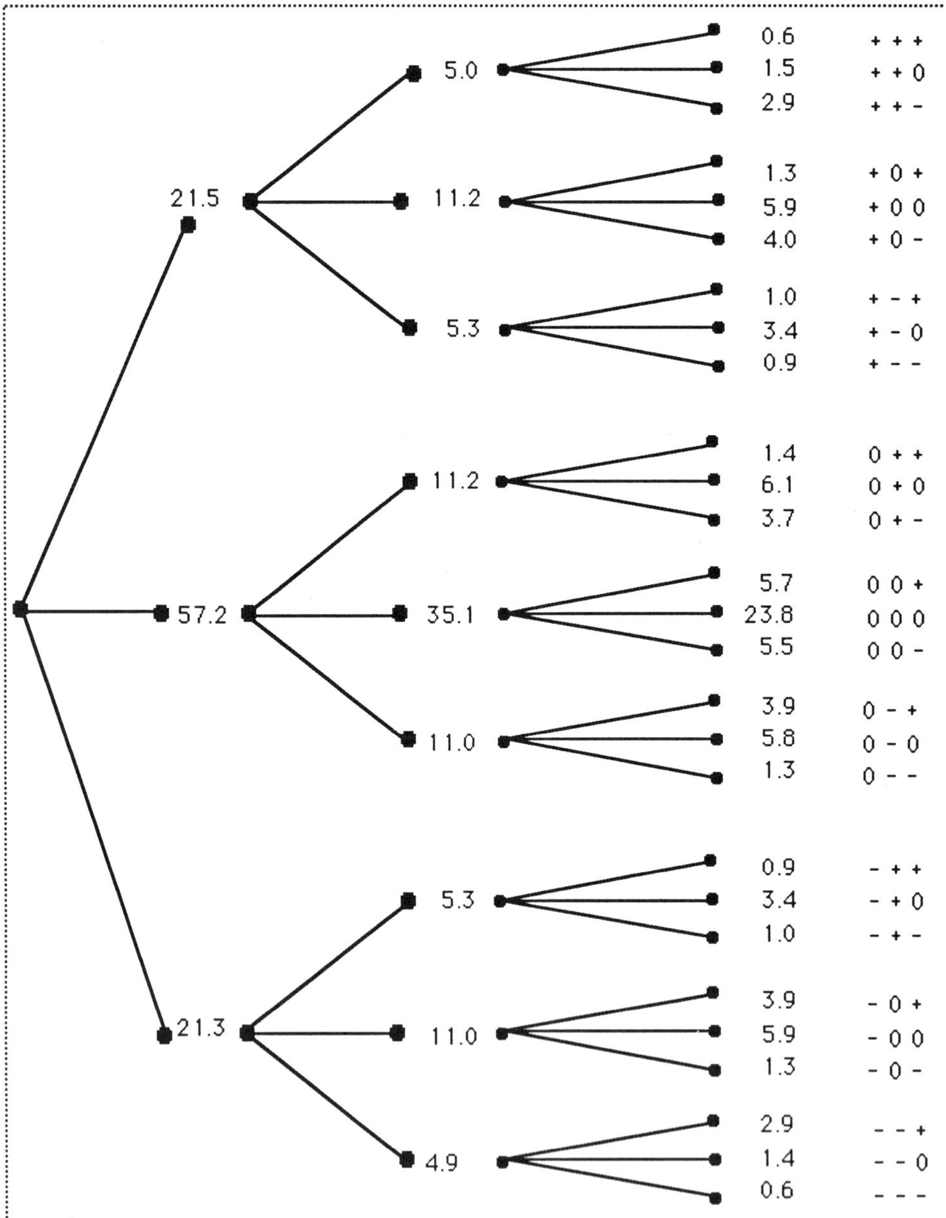

EXHIBIT 4-3
CALENDAR TIME ANALYSIS, MEAN SECURITY RETURNS: DISTRIBUTION STATISTICS OF AUTOCORRELATION COEFFICIENTS FOR DIFFERENT HOLDING PERIODS

.1 DECILE	1 MIN	5 MIN	10 MIN	15 MIN	60 MIN	120 MIN	240 MIN	361 MIN
r_1	–.07	–.15	–.16	–.16	–.15	–.13	–.08	–.09
r_2	–.05	–.06	–.05	–.05	–.04	–.02	–.06	–.08
r_3	–.04	–.03	–.03	–.03	–.02	–.03	–.07	–.08
r_4	–.03	–.02	–.02	–.03	–.02	–.05	–.06	–.09
.25 QUARTILE								
r_1	–.03	–.09	–.10	–.10	–.10	–.06	–.03	–.03
r_2	–.03	–.03	–.04	–.03	–.02	.00	–.03	–.04
r_3	–.03	–.02	–.02	–.02	.00	–.01	–.03	–.05
r_4	–.02	–.02	–.02	–.02	–.01	–.03	–.03	–.05
.5 DECILE								
r_1	–.01	–.04	–.05	–.05	–.05	–.01	.02	.01
r_2	–.01	–.02	–.02	–.02	.00	.02	–.00	–.01
r_3	–.01	–.01	–.01	–.01	.02	.02	.00	–.01
r_4	–.01	–.01	–.01	–.01	.01	–.01	–.00	–.02
.75 QUARTILE								
r_1	.00	–.02	–.02	–.02	–.01	.03	.07	.07
r_2	.00	.00	.00	.00	.03	.05	.03	.03
r_3	.00	.00	.00	.00	.04	.04	.03	.02
r_4	.00	.00	.00	.00	.03	.02	.02	.01
.9 DECILE								
r_1	.00	.00	.00	.01	.02	.07	.11	.11
r_2	.00	.01	.01	.01	.05	.07	.06	.07
r_3	.00	.01	.01	.01	.05	.07	.06	.06
r_4	.00	.01	.01	.01	.04	.03	.05	.05
MEAN								
r_1	–.03	–.06	–.07	–.07	–.06	–.02	.02	.01
r_2	–.02	–.02	–.02	–.02	.01	.02	.00	–.01
r_3	–.02	–.01	–.01	–.01	.02	.02	.00	–.01
r_4	–.01	–.01	–.01	–.01	.01	–.01	.00	–.02

FIGURE 4-1
TRANSACTION TIME: MEAN SECURITY RETURNS

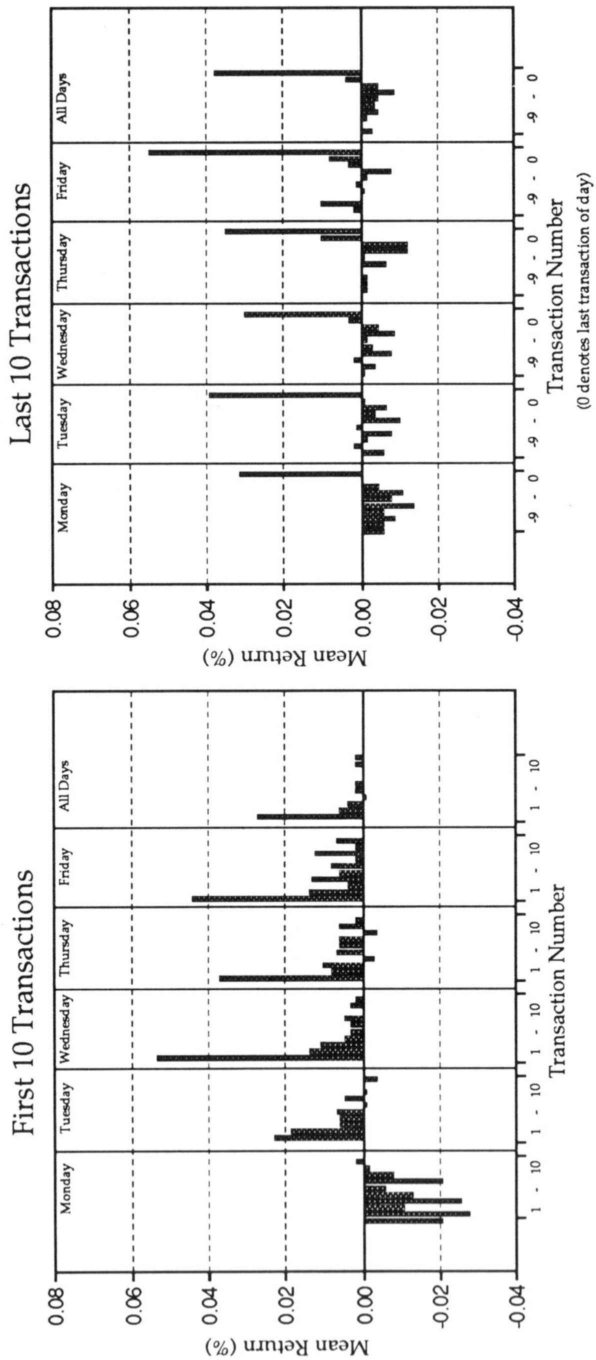

FIGURE 4-2
TRANSACTION TIME: VARIABILITY OF SECURITY RETURNS

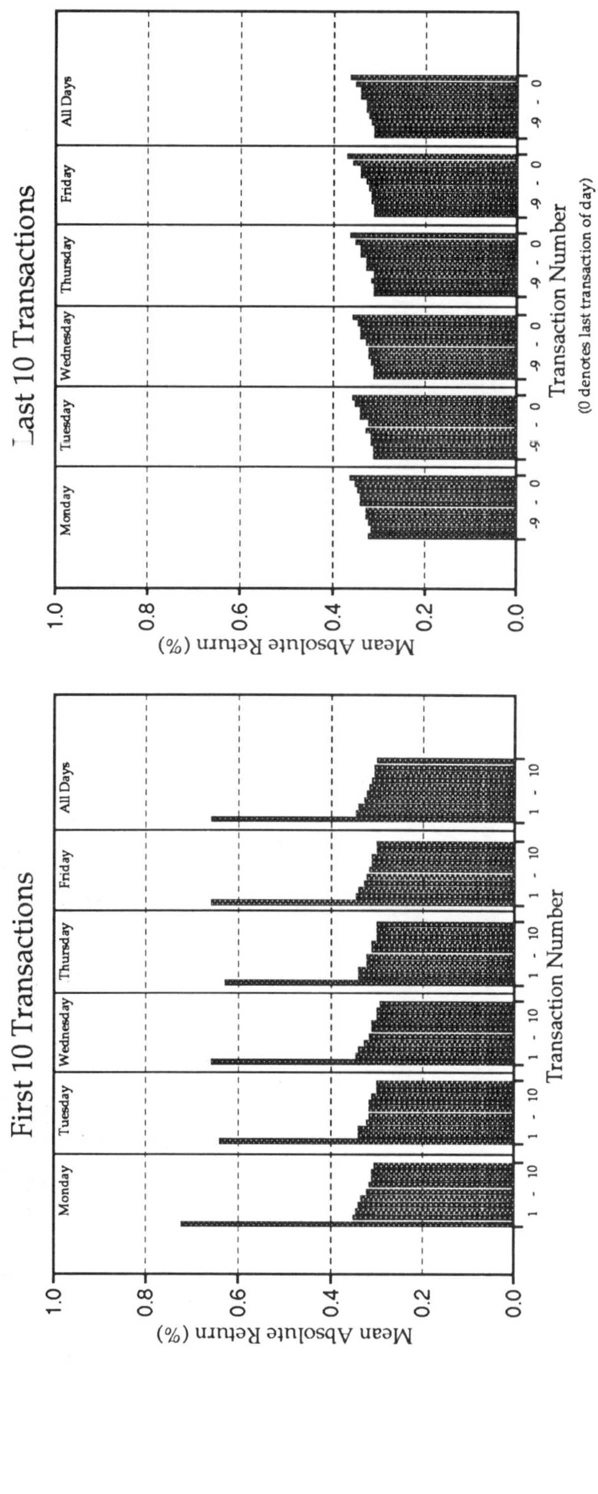

FIGURE 4-3
TRANSACTION TIME: TRADING FREQUENCY (TIME BETWEEN TRANSACTIONS)

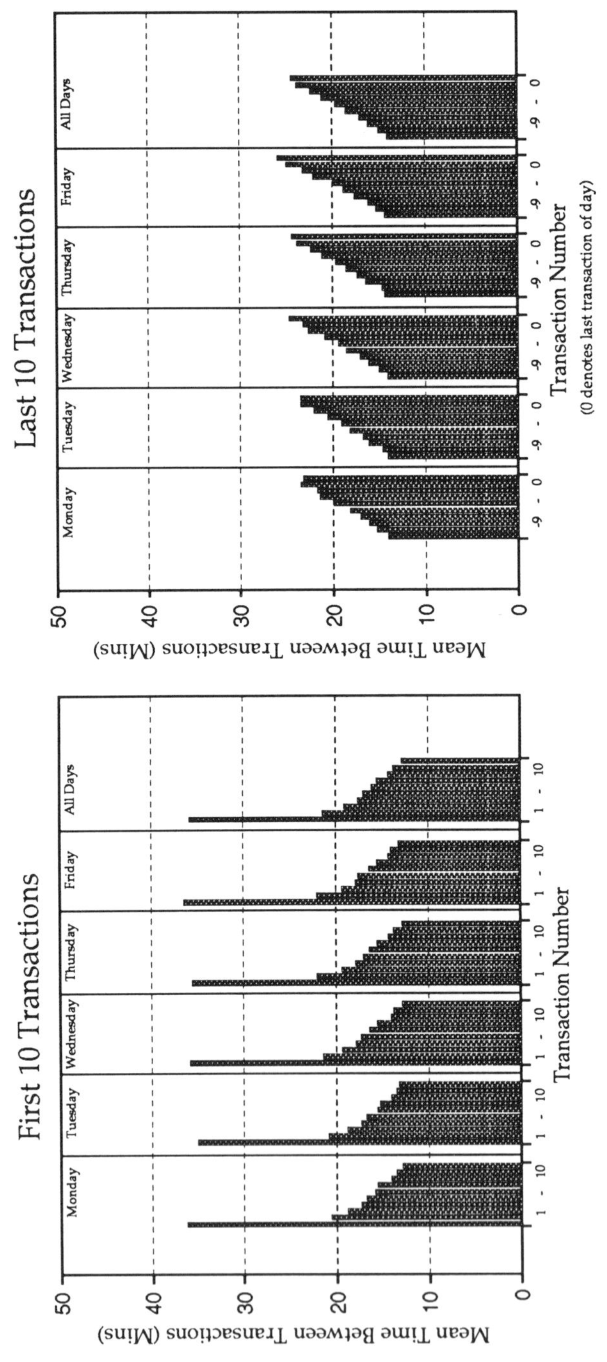

FIGURE 4-4
TRANSACTION TIME: MEAN NUMBER OF SHARES TRADED PER TRANSACTION

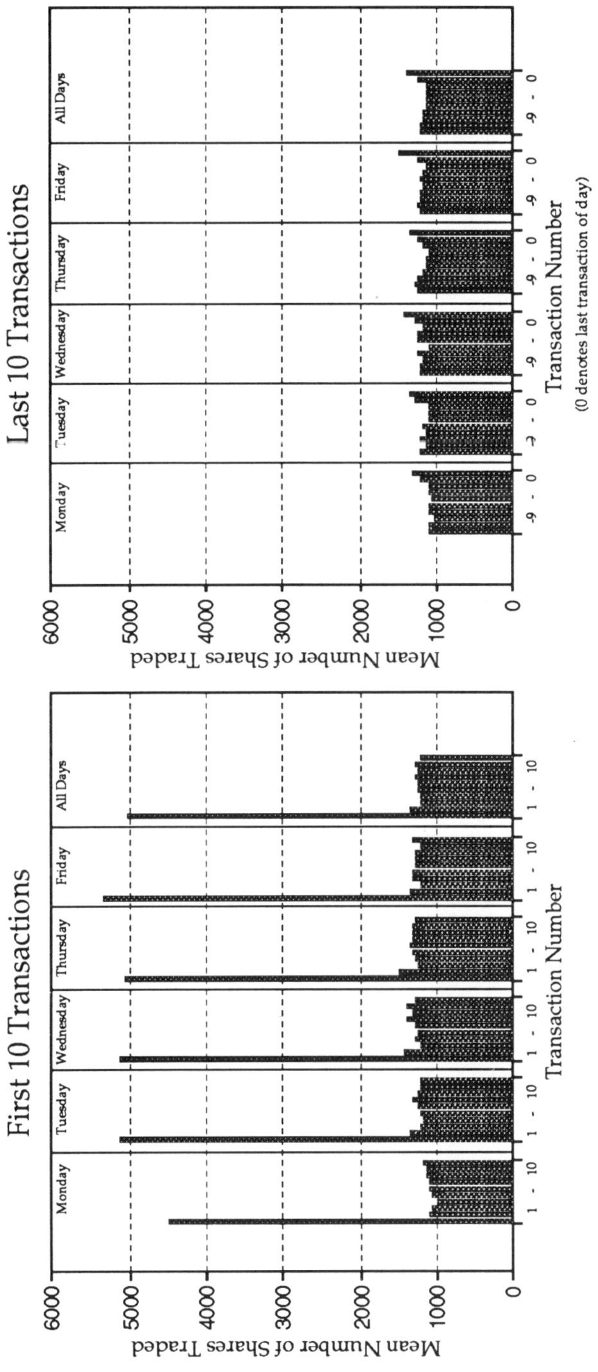

FIGURE 4-5
CALENDAR TIME: MEAN SECURITY RETURNS

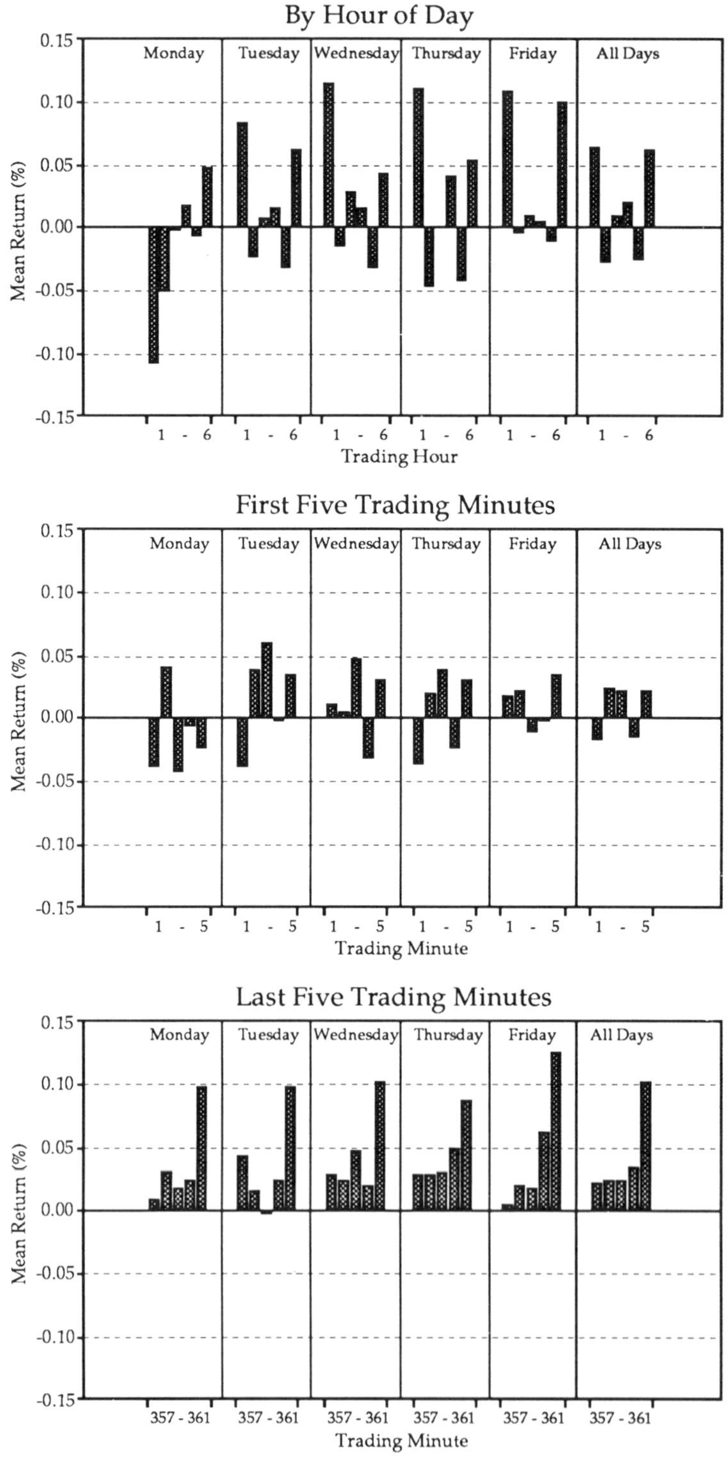

FIGURE 4-6
CALENDAR TIME: VARIABILITY OF SECURITY RETURNS*

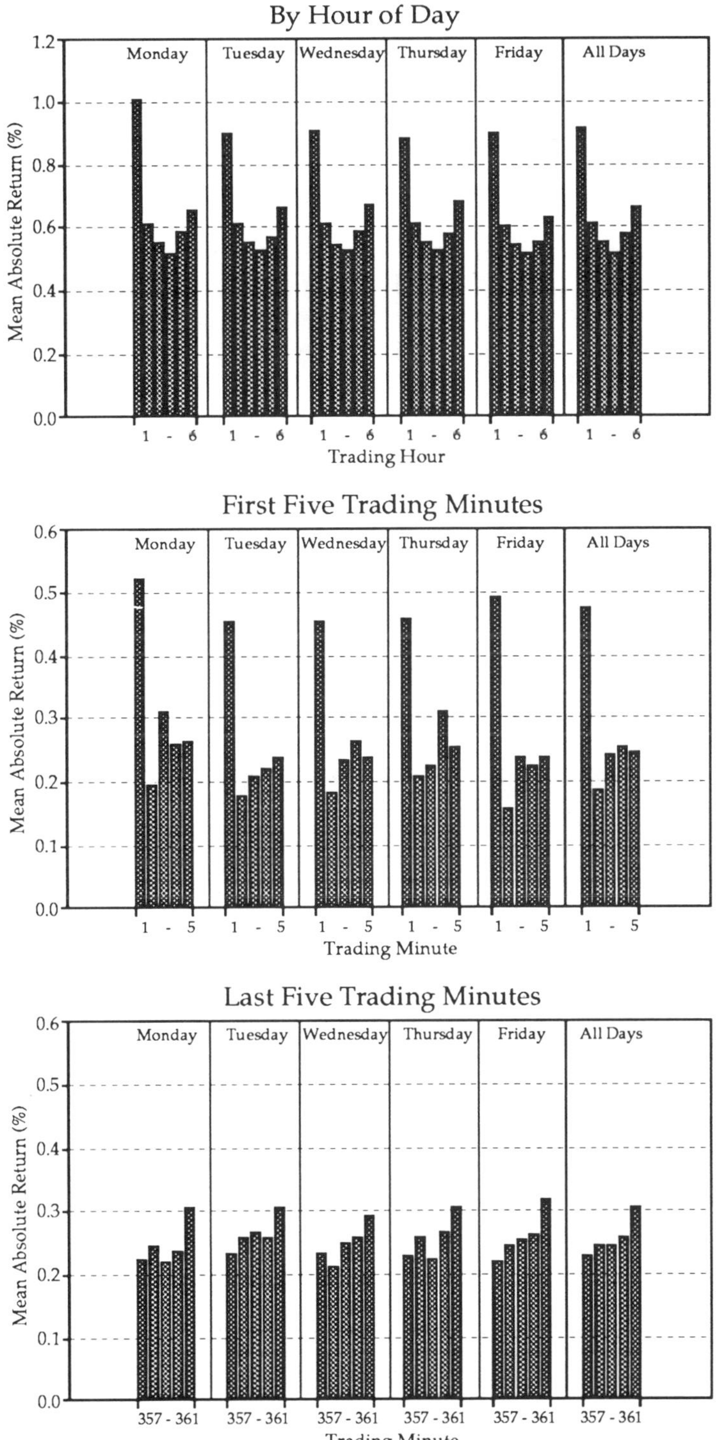

* Different scales are used in the hour-by-hour and the minute-by-minute plots

FIGURE 4-7
CALENDAR TIME: TRADING FREQUENCY
(MEAN NUMBER OF TRANSACTIONS PER CALENDAR TIME UNIT)*

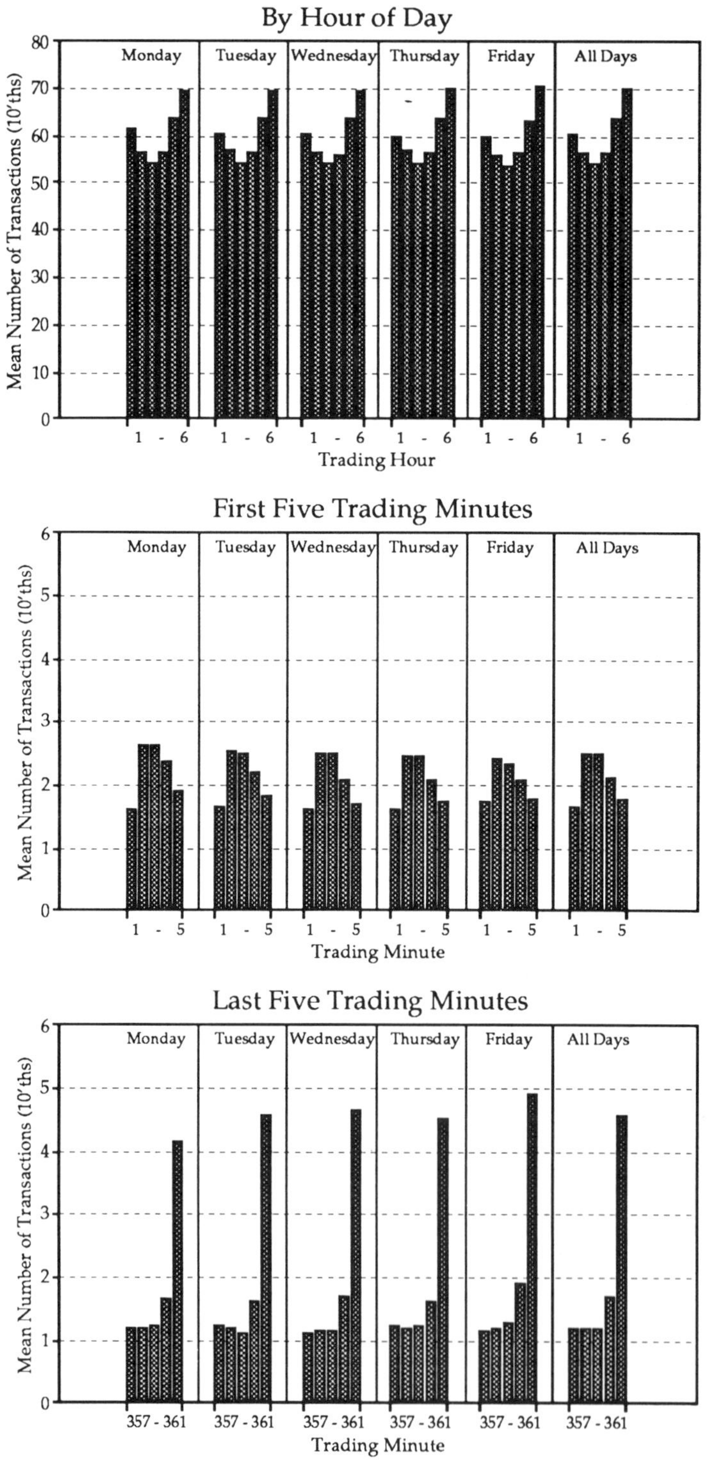

* Different scales are used in the hour-by-hour and the minute-by-minute plots

FIGURE 4-8
CALENDAR TIME: MEAN NUMBER OF SHARES TRADED PER TRANSACTION

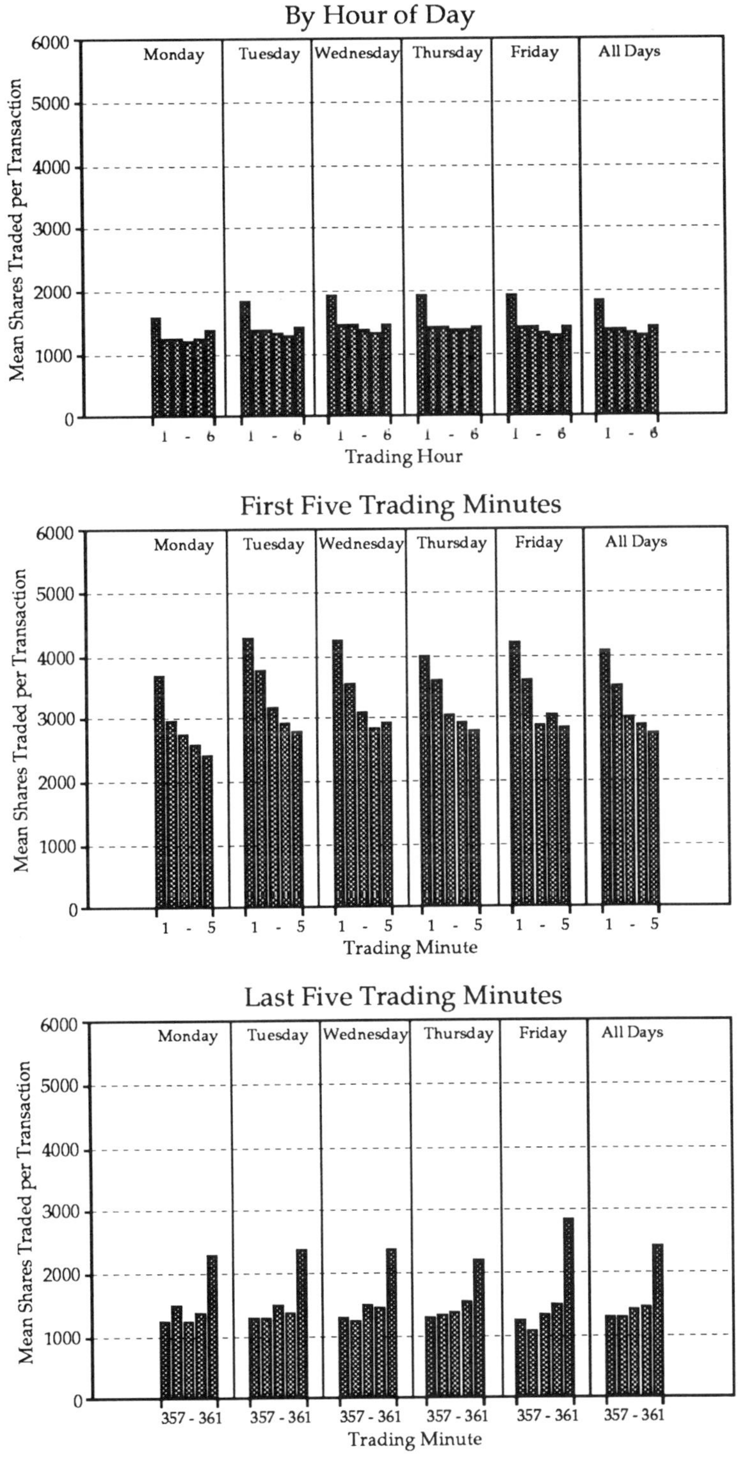

FIGURE 4-9
CALENDAR TIME: MEAN NUMBER OF SHARES TRADED PER CALENDAR TIME UNIT*

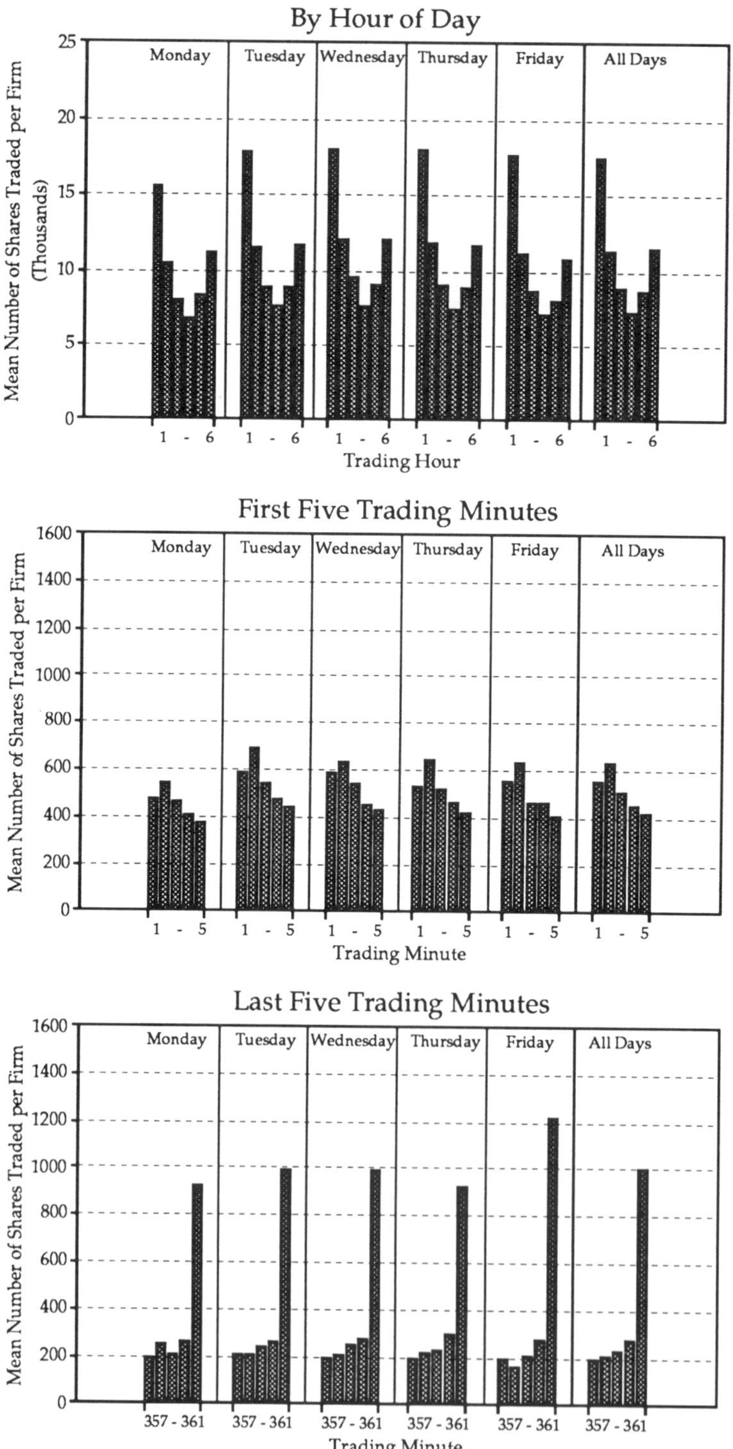

* Different scales are used in the hour-by-hour and the minute-by-minute plots

Chapter 5
Earnings Association Analysis: Transaction Time and Calendar Time

5.1: Introduction

This chapter analyzes the intraday behavior of four financial series at the time of earnings releases—security return variability, trading frequency, trading volume, and cumulative security returns. The major findings presented here include:

1. Earnings releases are associated with an immediate change in security returns, return variability and frequency of trading. For example, prior to the minute of the earnings release, there is a reduction in trading frequency. Immediately subsequent to the release, there is a significant increase in trading frequency. This significant increase in trading frequency extends over the first twenty-two transactions after the release for the total sample. This finding is consistent with comments made in interviews with security analysts, specialists and traders that (i) earnings releases are a major information cue, (ii) their release times are relatively predictable, and (iii) immediately prior to their release there is a reduction in trading activity.

The financial series examined in this monograph are not homogeneous in the way they behave at the time of earnings releases. Security return variability exhibits statistically significant abnormal behavior at only transaction 0 while trading frequency exhibits significant abnormal behavior for each of the twenty-two transactions subsequent to the release. Such differences highlight the importance of examining multiple series to gain insight into the adjustment process that occurs at the time of earnings releases.

2. The significant increase in trading volume observed in a calendar-time analysis immediately subsequent to an earnings release is primarily due to an increase in trading frequency rather than an increase in the number of shares traded per transaction. Security analysts, specialists and traders interviewed attributed the rapid increase in trading frequency (especially within the first 15 minutes subsequent to the release) mostly to floor traders rather than to increased trading by individual or institutional investors.

Only the subsample with earnings releases made outside trading hours shows a statistically significant increase in shares traded per transaction at transaction 0. However, due to market microstructure differences in intraday trading on the NYSE, it is not possible to distinguish between a trading frequency and a trading volume per order explanation for this finding. Transaction 0 is the first transaction of the day for earnings releases made outside trading hours. The first transaction is conducted with an auction trading regime in which many overnight orders may be batched into a single transaction. An increase in shares traded for the opening transaction subsequent to an overnight earnings release could be due to (a) an increase in the number of shares per overnight order, (b) an increase in the number of overnight orders batched into the opening transaction, or (c) a combination of (a) and (b).

The statistically significant increase in security return variability at transaction 0 for the full sample is observed for the subsample with earnings releases made outside trading hours and the subsample with earnings releases made between 10:30 A.M. and 3:30 P.M.

3. A transaction time analysis highlights the spiked increase in security return variability at the time of earnings releases. In contrast, the more traditionally used calendar time analysis results in these spiked increases appearing as a more smoothed path of adjustment when a very granular time-unit (such as a trading minute) is used.

4. Systematic intraday patterns of the kind documented in Chapter 4 can result in marked empirical regularities appearing in both the transaction time and calendar time financial series that are unrelated to the earnings releases of interest. These systematic patterns, most marked for the subsample with earnings releases made outside trading hours, vary with the financial series examined and whether a transaction time or calendar time mode of analysis is used. For example, transaction 0 for the trading volume series in transaction time (number of shares traded per transaction) for this subsample captures the high opening trading volume for the first transaction of each trading day. In contrast, trading minute -1 in calendar time for the trading frequency series captures the high trading frequency in the last minute of each trading day for this same subsample.

5.2: Analysis Based on Timing of Earnings Releases

This section reports both transaction time and calendar time results for three financial variables—security return variability, trading frequency, and trading volume. The analysis here uses only the timing of each quarterly earnings release when examining each variable. Section 5.3 presents an analysis using both the timing of the release and the magnitude of the unexpected earnings content of that release.

Significance testing is based on the empirical distribution of each series—see Appendix 5.A. Three series (the earnings announcement series, the control series, and the abnormal series) are reported for each variable in this and subsequent sections of this chapter. Because each transaction and each trading minute is tested separately, our procedure may understate the significance of observations taken over longer holding periods.

EARNINGS ANNOUNCEMENT SERIES. In transaction time, the event window is the eighty-one transaction period which starts with the twentieth transaction prior to transaction 0 and ends with the sixtieth transaction subsequent to it—designated [-20T,+60T]. Transaction 0 is the first transaction in the same minute as, or after, the Broadtape announcement time. For earnings releases made outside trading hours, transaction 0 is the first transaction after the

Broadtape announcement time (which also is the first transaction of the subsequent trading day). For earnings releases made during trading hours, transaction 0 is the first transaction after the earnings release for observations when no transaction occurs in the Broadtape earnings release minute. When transactions occur in the same minute as the Broadtape release minute, it is not possible to unambiguously classify each transaction as occurring either before or after that earnings release.[1]

Chapter 3 (see Exhibit 3-2) reported the following distribution data on the average number of transactions per day for the companies in our sample:

	1980	1985
Minimum	3	3
.1 Decile	8	9
.5 Decile	29	25
.9 Decile	90	65
Maximum	281	266

The [-20T, +60T] transaction interval will incorporate a wide range of calendar time intervals. For example, for the .1 decile firm in 1985 it will cover approximately 15 trading hours prior to the release and 40 trading hours subsequent to the release while for the .9 decile firm it will cover approximately 1 hour prior to and 6 hours subsequent to the release.

In calendar time, the event window is from the 421st trading minute prior to the earnings release to the 421st trading minute subsequent to the earnings release—designated [–421M, +421M]. This event window highlights the effect of the start of day/end of day patterns documented in Chapter 4. The [–421M, +421M] window will include start of day/end of day patterns for at least three trading days: the trading day prior to, the trading day of, and the trading day subsequent to the earnings release.

CONTROL SERIES. This series is centered on the actual quarterly earnings announcement minute and is averaged over 400 control portfolios—see Appendix 5.A.

ABNORMAL SERIES. This series is the difference between the earnings announcement series and the control series. The abnormal series examines the incremental change in the earnings announcement series relative to the control series. Thus, for instance, the abnormal series will have extracted from it any start of day or end of day empirical regularities captured by the control series.

Samples Examined

Results for three subsamples, as well as for the total sample, are presented in this chapter to incorporate into the research design the systematic patterns documented in Chapter 4:

---

[1] Approximately 84.0% of the earnings observations have no transaction occurring in the Broadtape earnings release minute. A breakdown of the remaining observations is: 11.8% with one transaction in the Broadtape earnings release minute, 3.0% with two and 0.5% with four to seven transactions.

SUBSAMPLE (a): Earnings releases made outside trading hours—comprises 28.9 percent of the total sample. In transaction time, event time 0 will be the first transaction of the following trading period for all observations in this subsample. In calendar time, event time 0 will be the first trading minute of the day (10:00:00 A.M. to 10:00:59 A.M.).

SUBSAMPLE (b): Earning releases made in the first half hour of trading (between 10:00 A.M. and 10:29 A.M.) or the last half hour of trading (between 3:31 P.M. and 4:00 P.M.)—comprises 12.9 percent of the total sample. In transaction time, event time 0 will be the first transaction in the same minute as, or after, the Broadtape announcement time. In calendar time, event time 0 will be the trading minute in which the earnings report appears on the Broadtape.

SUBSAMPLE (c): Earnings releases made between 10:30 A.M. and 3:30 P.M.—comprises 58.2 percent of the sample. The definitions of event time 0 in transaction time and calendar time are the same as for subsample (b). Subsample (c) reduces, but does not eliminate, the confounding effects problem associated with start of day/end of day empirical regularities. For infrequently traded firms, the first or last transaction could occur in the 10:30 A.M. to 3:30 P.M. period.

Two factors will influence the subsample into which each earnings release will fall—(a) the release time chosen by the firm, and (b) the speed with which Dow Jones reports details of the release on the Broadtape. In periods of high news traffic at Dow Jones, there may be time delays between the release time chosen by the firm and the time the earnings information appears on the Broadtape. Dow Jones officials indicated that releases by firms to Dow Jones just prior to the start of trading (near the end of trading) may not always be placed on the Broadtape before the start of trading (before the end of trading). They indicated, however, that releases by firms to Dow Jones after trading but before the end of the calendar day are placed (almost without exception) on the Broadtape before the start of trading on the next trading day.

The body of this chapter presents most results via figures. Appendix 5.B reports selected observations underlying the figures in Chapter 5. Exhibits 5-1 to 5-4 report statistical significance results for the three financial series examined in this section. Exhibit 5-1 reports results for the total sample while 5-2 to 5-4 report results for the three subsamples described above.

A. Security Return Variability

Security return variability is measured by the absolute value of the security return. In transaction time, this return is from transaction to transaction. In calendar time, it is from trading minute to trading minute.

TRANSACTION TIME: Figure 5-1 presents the variability of security returns for the total sample. Panel A reports the earnings announcement series, Panel B the control series and Panel C the abnormal series (the difference between the earnings announcement series and the control series).

The most dramatic pattern in Panel A of Figure 5-1 is the spiked increase in security return variability at transaction 0. Panel B indicates that a sizable increase at transaction 0 also occurs in non-earnings announcement periods. However, even after the increase in the control series is extracted from the earnings announcement series, there remains a marked increase in variability at transaction 0—see Panel C of Figure 5-1. (Note that Panel C in Figure 5-1, as well as other figures in Chapter 5 where indicated, uses a different scale than in Panels A and B to highlight time-series patterns in the abnormal series.) This increase at transaction 0 is consistent with little prior anticipation of the content of the earnings release by the capital market. Significance tests are reported in Exhibit 5-1. The earnings announcement security return variability series for the total sample exhibits significantly higher variability than the control series only for transaction 0.

Figure 5-2 presents subperiod results for the security return variability series. The spiked increase in the aggregate control series in Figure 5-1 is most marked in the outside trading hours subsample—see Panel B of Figure 5-2. This pattern reflects the increase in variability of the first transaction of the day documented in Chapter 4. The smaller increases in variability for the control group in the first/last half hour and 10:30 to 3:30 subsamples are also consistent with the Chapter 4 first transaction of the day pattern; both subsamples will include the first transaction for a subset of their observations.

The abnormal subseries pattern in Figure 5-2 shows that the increase in security return variability at the time of the earnings release is most marked in the outside trading hours release and in the 10:30 to 3:30 release subsamples. The first/last half hour subsample, which has the smallest number of observations, shows little evidence of increased variability at transaction 0 in the abnormal series. The significance levels reported in Exhibits 5-2 to 5-4 are consistent with the visual patterns in Figure 5-2. The 10:30 to 3:30 subsample shows significantly higher security return variability (at the .05 level) for transactions 0, 1 and 2 compared to only transaction 0 for the outside trading hours subsample. No transaction in the [-20T, +60T] period shows significantly higher return variability at the .05 period for the first/last half hour subsample.

The relative magnitude of the increase in security return variability at transaction 0 for the earnings announcement series can be illustrated in several ways:

(i) Relative to the control group transaction 0 observation. The ratio of security return variability at transaction 0 for the earnings announcement series, relative to transaction 0 for the control series, is:

	Earnings Announcement Series
• Full sample	1.21
• Subsamples	
a. Outside trading hours	1.25
b. First/last half hour	1.02
c. Between 10:30 and 3:30	1.21

The aggregate sample increase in variability of 21 percent at transaction 0, relative to the control group, is not uniform across the three subsamples examined. It ranges from a 25 percent increase for the outside trading hours subsample to a 2 percent increase for the first/last half hour subsample.

(ii) Relative to the [-20T,-1T] and [+1T,+60T] observations for the same series. The ratio of return variability at transaction 0, relative to the mean variability over the [-20T,+60T] period (excluding transaction 0) for the same series, is:

	Earnings Announcement Series	**Control Series**
• Full sample	1.68	1.42
• Subsamples		
a. Outside trading hours	2.50	2.00
b. First/last half hour	1.47	1.43
c. Between 10:30 and 3:30	1.28	1.09

The outside trading hours subsample has a ratio for the earnings announcement series that is 25 percent higher than the control series ratio; the comparable figures for the first/last half hour and the 10:30 to 3:30 subsamples are 2.8 percent and 17.4 percent respectively. This ranking of the three subsamples is the same as with the control group transaction 0 benchmark.

CALENDAR TIME: Security return variability per trading minute is presented in Figures 5-3 and 5-4. The total sample results in the [-421M, +421M] and in the [-60M, +60M] periods are in Figure 5-3.

One pattern highlighted in Figure 5-3 (Panel B) is the systematic spiked increase in security return variability for the control group every 361 minutes apart. Figure 5-4 (Panel B) shows this increase in variability to be concentrated in the outside trading hours subsample. Both the announcement effect series and the control series of this subsample have increases in variability at event time -1M; -1M corresponds to the final trading minute of the prior trading day. The abnormal security return variability series in Figure 5-3 shows above average variability in calendar time in the [0M, +60M] period. Statistically, the earnings announcement series differs from the control series at the .05 level in each minute of the [0M, +15M] period—see Exhibit 5-1.

Figure 5-3 shows three spiked increases in security return variability for the calendar-time based control group. In transaction time, the same underlying observations occur for the control group. However, only one spiked increase is apparent in Figure 5-1. One explanation is that transaction time diversifies the spiked increases at -361M and +361M across different transactions in event time. A second explanation is that Figure 5-1 reports only 81 transactions (from -20T to +60T), which for a subset of the firms (approximately 20 percent) likely would not extend to one trading day before or to one trading day subsequent to transaction 0.

The abnormal series in Figure 5-3 (calendar time) appears to exhibit a less rapid speed of adjustment than the comparable series in Figure 5-1 (transaction time). However, comparisons between the two series should be made with caution, due to the "smoothing phenomenon" that can arise with calendar time results—see Chapter 4 (pp. 45-6) for a discussion of this phenomenon. This smoothing phenomenon in calendar time vis-a-vis transaction time will be most marked when: (i) the adjustment in transaction time is very rapid (in the limit 1 transaction), and (ii) stocks differ sizably in the calendar time lag from the information release to the first transaction subsequent to that release.

The 10:30 to 3:30 subsample shows the strongest evidence of increased security return variability over an extended calendar time period. Panel A of Exhibit 5-5 reports the number of individual trading minutes in successive ten minute periods that are significant at the .05 level in the [0M, +119M] calendar period. In the first 60 trading minutes following an earnings release in the 10:30 to 3:30 period, 48 minutes are statistically significantly different from the control group at the .05 level. The 10:30 to 3:30 subsample has a longer run of observations in transaction time that are statistically significant (transactions 0, 1 and 2) than the other two subsamples. As a result, the smoothing phenomenon is likely to be most marked in the 10:30 to 3:30 subsample.

B. Trading Frequency

Trading frequency in transaction time is measured as the trading time between successive transactions.[2] In calendar time, trading frequency is measured as the number of transactions per trading minute (scaled up by 10).

TRANSACTION TIME. Figures 5-5 and 5-6 present the behavior of the mean trading time between successive transactions in the [-20T, +60T] event window. The arrival of the earnings release on the Broadtape is associated with a marked increase in trading frequency. The general pattern for the abnormal series in Figures 5-5 and 5-6 is above normal trading frequency in the [0T, +21T] period. Significance levels are reported in Exhibits 5-1 to 5-4. For the total sample, every one of the first 22 transactions subsequent to the earnings release ([0T, +21T]) has a statistically significant increase in trading frequency relative to a control period.

Dramatic evidence of the rapid increase in trading frequency at the time of earnings releases can be gained by focusing on the time from transaction -1 to transaction 0. Panel A of Figure 5-7 plots the average time from transaction -1 to transaction 0 for the earnings announcement series and the control series. Panels B and C of Figure 5-7 subdivide the average time in Panel A into:

- average time from transaction -1 to the earnings release minute.
- average time from the earnings release minute to transaction 0.

The arrival of an earnings release sizably reduces the average time until the next transaction. The following ratio quantifies this reduction:

---

[2] Calendar time outside trading hours is not counted in computing this trading frequency measure in transaction time.

$$\frac{\dfrac{\text{Average Time from Transaction -1 to Actual Release}}{\text{Average Time from Actual Release to Transaction 0}}}{\dfrac{\text{Average Time from Transaction -1 to "Pseudo" Release in Control Series}}{\text{Average Time from "Pseudo" Release in Control Series to Transaction 0}}}$$

A ratio greater than one signifies a reduction in the average time until the next transaction for the earnings announcement series vis-a-vis the control series. Values of this ratio are:

- Total Sample 1.70
- Subsamples
  - a. Outside trading hours 1.32
  - b. First/last half hour 1.81
  - c. Between 10:30 and 3:30 1.68

There is a reduction in the average time until the next transaction across all three subsamples. The decomposition of Panel A in Exhibit 5-7 into Panels B and C highlights the offsetting decrease in trading frequency immediately prior to the earnings release and the increase immediately subsequent to the release.

The control group in Exhibits 5-5 and 5-6 shows increased time between transaction -1 and transaction 0. The time between successive transactions in the [–2T, +2T] event window for the control group is:

Transaction	All Firms	Outside Trading Hours	First/Last Half Hour	Between 10:30 and 3:30
–2	18.60	18.89	17.78	20.23
–1	18.22	18.83	16.58	20.01
0	40.69	28.09	32.66	52.09
1	18.80	18.60	16.02	21.22
2	18.61	17.08	16.86	21.43

The 10:30 to 3:30 control group subsample has the longest time between transactions for transaction 0. One explanation for this pattern is that less frequently traded firms have a higher proportion of their earnings releases in the 10:30 to 3:30 time period. Less frequently traded firms have dramatically longer times between transactions than do more frequently traded firms and have a more delayed first trade at the start of the day. The average time between transactions for the first five transactions of the day, and for the last five transactions of the day, for five portfolios based on trading frequency are (from Section 4-3):

Transaction	(Least Frequently Traded) I	II	III	IV	(Most Frequently Traded) V
1 (First)	97.57	40.36	20.30	12.95	8.78
2	51.14	28.12	15.65	9.45	4.60
3	45.66	26.56	14.37	8.27	3.87
4	41.62	26.06	13.98	7.98	3.56
5	39.42	26.53	14.52	7.96	3.52
–4	43.91	29.18	17.62	9.95	4.33
–3	49.32	30.54	17.59	10.00	4.29
–2	53.26	31.02	17.25	9.80	4.11
–1	59.09	31.43	16.83	9.55	4.04
0 (Last)	63.49	29.99	15.96	9.06	3.70

The least frequently traded 20 percent of firms have time lags between successive transactions up to 11 times the lag for the most frequently traded 20 percent of firms. A second possible explanation arises from a higher percentage of earnings releases occurring in the earlier hours of trading than in the later hours of trading—see Exhibit 3-3. Transaction 0 for the control group for earnings releases made during the earlier hours of trading is more likely to be the first transaction of the day (with its longer time between transactions) than for the control group associated with earnings releases made during the later hours of trading.

The spiked increase in time between transaction -1 and transaction 0 in the 10:30 to 3:30 subsample is observed in both the earnings announcement series and the control series. The abnormal series will extract this commonality found in both series. The abnormal series for the 10:30 to 3:30 subsample shows the same marked increase in trading frequency in the [0T, +10T] as the other two subsamples examined in this chapter.

CALENDAR TIME: The behaviors of the transactions per trading minute variable in the [-421M, +421M] and [-60M, +60M] event periods are in Figures 5-8 and 5-9. The abnormal series in Figure 5-8 highlights for the total sample the above normal trading frequency over an extended calendar time period. Each of the first 80 trading minutes subsequent to an earnings release for the total sample has significantly higher trading frequency than a control group—see Exhibit 5-5.

Chapter 4 documented a dramatic increase in the number of transactions per minute in the last trading minute of the day (3:59 to 4:00)— See Figure 4-7. The control series in Figure 5-8 over the [-420M, +420M] event period highlights this systematic pattern; minutes -362, -1, and +360 each have a spiked increase in trading frequency. The control series for the outside trading hours subsample also highlights this end of trade empirical regularity. Indeed, the magnitude of this last minute of the day trading frequency pattern exceeds the magnitude of the abnormal series trading frequency patterns for any minute in the [-60M, +60M] period for all of the three subsamples examined in Figure 5-9.

The trading frequency variable shows a considerably longer period of adjustment than security return variability in both transaction time and calendar time. This finding underlies the importance of examining multiple series to gain insight into the adjustment process that occurs at the time of earnings releases.

C. Trading Volume

Trading volume in transaction time is measured by the number of shares traded per transaction. In calendar time, trading volume is measured by the number of shares traded per trading minute.

TRANSACTION TIME: The behavior of the shares traded per transaction variable in the [-20T, +60T] event period is in Figure 5-10 for the total sample and Figure 5-11 for the three subsamples. There is only limited evidence of abnormal behavior in the shares traded per transaction at the time of earnings releases. For the full sample in Figure 5-10, transaction 0 has significantly higher shares traded per transaction from the control group at the .10 level (but not the .05 level). None of the other transactions in the [-20T, +60T] event period has an average number of shares traded that is significantly different from the control series at either the .05 or .10 significance level. Figure 5-12 (and Exhibits 5-2 to 5-4) shows that only the outside trading hours earnings release subsample has an immediate, statistically significant increase in trading volume per transaction. However, for this subsample transaction 0 is the first transaction of the day which is conducted with an auction trading regime in which many overnight orders may be batched into a single transaction. This transaction 0 effect for the outside trading hours subsample could be due to (a) an increase in the number of shares per overnight order, or (b) an increase in the number of overnight orders batched into the opening transaction, or (c) a combination of (a) and (b).

Chapter 4 documented that the number of shares traded in the first transaction is over 375 percent above those in the second transaction of the day and over 360 percent above those in the last transaction of the prior trading day—see Figure 4-4. This empirical regularity is sizably larger than any incremental change in the number of shares traded per transaction at the time of an earnings release. Consider the ratio of (i) the number of shares traded at transaction 0 to (ii) the average number of shares traded per transaction in the [-20T, -1T] and [+1, +60T] period:

	Earnings Announcement Series	Control Series
• Total sample	2.68	2.37
• Subsamples		
a. Outside trading hours	6.00	5.08
b. First/last half hour	1.40	2.01
c. Between 10:30 and 3:30	1.29	1.04

For the outside trading hours control subsample, the first trade in the day has a 508 percent increase vis-a-vis the surrounding observations. When an earnings release occurs outside trading hours, the first trade has a 600 percent increase. Failure to recognize this first transaction effect in the control subsample would vastly overestimate the change in the number of shares traded per transaction at the time of an earnings release.

Interviews were conducted with specialists about the finding of no sizable increase in the number of shares traded per transaction at the time of an earnings release for the first/last half-hour of trading and the 10:30 A.M. to 3:30 P.M. subsamples. Several institutional factors were cited (anecdotally) as to possible reasons the Fitch data base may understate any increase in the number of shares traded per transaction: (a) some large institutions do not make all their transactions through specialists and it may be these institutions that increase the size of their buy or sell trading orders at the time of a major information release, and (b) specialists may increase the percentage of orders that are debundled (broken into smaller trading units) when major information releases occur.

CALENDAR TIME: Figures 5-12 and 5-13 present the number of shares traded per minute in the [-420M, +420M] and [-60M, +60M] event periods. For the total sample, the number of shares traded per minute is significantly different from that observed in the control group (at the .05 level) in nine of the ten trading minutes in the [0M, +9M] period. Chapter 4 documented that (a) the last trading minute of the day has a dramatic increase in the number of shares traded per trading minute, and (b) the start of day (including at least the first five trading minutes) has an above average number of shares traded per trading minute—see Figure 4-9. The control group observations in Figures 5-12 and 5-13 evidence both these empirical regularities. For example, trading minute -1 for the outside trading hours subsample reflects this last trading minute regularity.

This variable is a composite of two variables previously examined in this chapter—the number of shares traded per transaction (a transaction time variable) and the number of transactions per minute (a calendar time variable). Figures 5-10 and 5-11 show little evidence of abnormal behavior in the number of shares traded per transaction at the time of earnings releases. In contrast, Figures 5-8 and 5-9 show a significant increase in the number of transactions per minute at the time of earnings releases. The calendar time patterns observed in Figures 5-12 and 5-13 are primarily driven by the increase in the number of transactions per minute at the time of earnings releases.

5.3: Analysis Based on Sign and Magnitude of Unexpected Earnings

A. Cumulative Security Returns

This section reports transaction time and calendar time results for the cumulative returns series of five portfolios formed using the sign and magnitude of unexpected earnings. Unexpected earnings is measured relative to the Value Line EPS quarterly forecast issued just prior to the start of the relevant quarter:

$$\frac{\text{Actual Quarterly EPS} - \text{Quarterly EPS Forecast by Value Line}}{\text{Security Price Immediately Prior to Forecast Date}}$$

Announcements with zero forecast error (totalling 74) are placed into Portfolio 6. The remaining announcements (1660) are ranked and placed into five equal-sized portfolios. Distribution statistics on the forecast error observations in each portfolio are in Exhibit 5-6. Panel A has statistics on the full sample while Panel B has a year-by-year breakdown. There is a wide range in the unexpected earnings across the five portfolios for the full sample; the median ranges from -0.017 for Portfolio 1 to 0.015 for Portfolio 5.

TRANSACTION TIME: Figures 5-14 and 5-15 present cumulative returns in transaction time over the [-20T, +60T] period. The control series for the aggregate sample in Figure 5-14 shows little difference across the five earnings change portfolios in the behavior of their cumulative returns. As a consequence the results for the earnings announcement series and the abnormal series are virtually identical.

For the aggregate series in Figure 5-14, there is little evidence of anticipation of the earnings release prior to transaction 0. The marked differences across portfolios 1 to 5 in their CAR behavior are concentrated in the [-1T, +60T] period. Portfolios with unexpected bad news have negative CARs in the [-1T, +60T] period while portfolios with unexpected good news have positive CARs in the same period. Some insight into the speed of adjustment can be gained by examining how much of the [-1T, +60T] CAR has occurred at designated points in this event window. This measure is analogous to the "path to full adjustment" method described in Appendix B:

Ratio of $\frac{[-1T, XT]}{[-1T, +60T]}$

	Portfolio I (Extreme Bad News)	Portfolio V (Extreme Good News)
[-1T, 0T]	18.6%	23.7%
[-1T, +5T]	41.4	61.1
[-1T, +10T]	60.0	65.6
[-1T, +20T]	77.9	70.2
[-1T, +30T]	85.0	76.3
[-1T, +40T]	103.6	84.7
[-1T, +50T]	101.4	87.0
[-1T, +60T]	100.0	100.0

By transaction +10, 60 percent of the movement in the [-1T, +60T] period has occurred for Portfolio I and 65.6 percent for Portfolio V. Chapter 6 examines speed of adjustment issues in more detail. The focus of the current chapter is the impact of intraday regularities on the observed behavior of financial series at the time of earnings releases.

Further insight into speed of adjustment is provided by the magnitude of the security return adjustment at each transaction in the [-1T, +60T] event period. Transaction 0 for both Portfolio I and Portfolio V has the largest security return in the direction of the unexpected earnings change of all transactions in the [-1T, +60T] period. The mean returns at transaction 0 for the five unexpected earnings change portfolios are:

	(Most Negative) I	II	III	IV	(Most Positive) V
Announcement Effect Series	−0.26	−0.15	0.12	0.13	0.31
Control Series	0.00	0.01	0.00	0.01	0.01

These results are consistent with the capital market reacting in a very rapid manner.[3]

[3] These results for transaction 0 may understate the magnitude of the security return adjustment at the time of an earnings release. Some transactions may occur in minute 0 before the earnings release occurs. In addition, we may potentially misclassify the magnitude of unexpected earnings due to the use of Value Line earnings expectations formed some time prior to the earnings release.

Figure 5-15 shows the CAR patterns for the three subsamples examined in Section 5-2—(a) earnings releases made outside trading hours, (b) earnings releases made in the first/last half hour of trading and (c) earnings releases made between 10:30 A.M. and 3:30 P.M. Across all three subsamples, the general patterns observed for the full sample in Figure 5-14 hold. However, because of their smaller sizes, there is more variability in the series for each of the subsamples. For example, in the first/last half hour subsample the relationship between the sign and magnitude of the portfolio unexpected earnings and the sign and magnitude of the portfolio CAR is not monotonic (unlike the monotonic relationship observed in Figure 5-14 over the [0T, +60T] period).

The control group for the outside trading hours (see Figure 5-15, Panel B) subsample reflects the systematic end of trading effect. Chapter 4 (Figure 4-1) documents that both the last transaction and the first transaction, on average, have positive mean returns. For the outside trading hours earnings release subsample, the last and first transactions are transactions -1 and 0 respectively in transaction time. This pattern is reflected in the mean returns of the control series for this subsample for each portfolio in Exhibit 5-15:

	Portfolio I	Portfolio II	Portfolio III	Portfolio IV	Portfolio V
Transaction -1	.08	.04	.03	.03	.05
Transaction 0	.04	.05	.02	.02	.03

The magnitude of this intraday empirical regularity, however, is still small relative to the CAR patterns observed for this subsample in the earnings announcement series for the five portfolios:

	Portfolio I	Portfolio II	Portfolio III	Portfolio IV	Portfolio V
CAR [-1T, 0T]	-0.35	-0.23	0.15	0.12	0.60
CAR [-1T, +60T]	-1.17	-0.59	-0.37	0.44	1.64

For both the other two subsamples in Exhibit 5-15, the intraday mean return regularities are not centered on the same control series transactions and are also small relative to the CAR patterns in those subsamples.

CALENDAR TIME: Cumulative returns for calendar time over the [-421M, +421M] event period are presented in Figure 5-16. One marked pattern in Figure 5-16 is the limited evidence of prior anticipation of the content of the earnings release in the [-421M, -1M] time period. All five unexpected earnings change portfolios behave in a similar way in the [-421M, -1M] period. Over the [-1M, +421M] period, there is strong positive association between the sign and magnitude of the portfolio unexpected earnings change and the portfolio CAR. This strong positive association is evident soon after the earnings release. By the +30M event minute, 51.3 percent of the CAR adjustment in the [-1M, +421M] period has occurred for Portfolio I and 57.1 percent for Portfolio V:

Ratio of $\frac{[-1M, XT]}{[-1M, +421M]}$

	Portfolio I	Portfolio V
[-1M, 0M]	0.9%	0.9%
[-1M, +10M]	21.7	41.1
[-1M, +20M]	39.1	51.8
[-1M, +30M]	51.3	57.1
[-1M, +60M]	70.4	58.9
[-1M, +120M]	83.5	68.7
[-1M, +240M]	88.7	72.3
[-1M, +421M]	100.0	100.0

These figures relate to the percentage of the total CAR adjustment in the [-1M, +421M] period. There is no implication that by +421M the capital market has fully adjusted to the "information content" of the earnings release being examined.

Subsample results are reported in Figure 5-17. Across all three subsamples the general patterns apparent in Figure 5-16 exist. However, there is more variability in the subsample patterns than in the aggregate sample (see especially the first /last half hour subsample).

5.4: Summary

The analysis in this chapter is at a relatively macro level. The earnings/capital market variable associations are examined using a pooled set of earnings releases of 100 firms (or subsets thereof) over 18 interim earnings periods for each firm. The noise level inherent in estimating earnings/capital market variable associations is diversified across firms and over time in this macro approach. Chapter 6 adopts a more micro approach than Chapter 5. In Chapter 6 we estimate a separate speed of adjustment (SOA) measure for each individual earnings release. The pro of this more micro approach is an ability to empirically examine determinants of SOA at the individual earnings release level. The con is a higher level of noise in the experiment vis-a-vis the results presented in Chapter 5.

Appendix 5.A
Significance Testing

Significance testing is done by comparing a metric (e.g., trading frequency) for the experimental portfolio with the corresponding metrics for 400 randomly selected, control portfolios. We used the following procedure, which is illustrated by reference to Ford Motor Company's quarterly EPS announcement made at 11:02 A.M. on Monday February 13, 1984.

1. Define the experimental calendar time window as corresponding to the calendar time interval beginning 421 trading minutes before the event and ending 421 trading minutes after it. Thus the calendar time window for Ford's announcement opens at 10:02 A.M. on Friday February 10 and closes at 12:02 P.M. on Tuesday February 14. According to our database there were 556 transactions in Ford stock while the calendar time window was open, 276 of them being before 11:02 A.M. on February 13.
2. Define transaction 0 as the first transaction that occurs either in the same minute as the announcement, or if there was no trading that minute, then the first transaction thereafter. The transaction time window opens 20 transactions before transaction 0 and closes 60 transactions after transaction 0. For the Ford announcement, transaction 0 occurred at 11:02 A.M. on February 13. The transaction time window opened at 10:35 A.M. on February 13 and closed at 1:00 P.M. the same day. Because Ford stock was actively traded—in 1984 there were 64,983 transactions in Ford stock in our database—the transaction time window was open for less than 2.5 hours.
3. Identify the set {S} of "complete windows" that occurred in the same calendar year as the announcement. Each window extends for 843 minutes [-421M, +421M] in calendar time and 81 transactions [-20T, +60T] in transaction time, and is centered on the same hour and minute as the event (11:02 A.M. in the case of Ford's announcement). A "complete window" can be centered on any trading day of the year, including the "experimental day". Each element of {S} has the following properties:
   - at least one trade occurred before *both* calendar and transaction time windows were opened;
   - at least 60 transactions occurred after transaction 0;
   - there was no change in the stock's basis of quotation within either the calendar or transaction time window (a change occurs when, e.g., a stock is quoted ex dividend).

   For Ford's February 13 announcement, there were 235 elements in {S}.
4. Randomly sample, with replacement, from the set {S}, and place the randomly selected window into the first control portfolio.
5. Step 4 is repeated 399 times, each time placing the randomly selected window into the next control portfolio in the sequence of 400 portfolios.

6. When Steps 1 to 5 have been completed for all announcements, then for each calendar and transaction time metric, calculate:
   - the metric for the experimental portfolio and for each of the 400 control portfolios;
   - the average of the 400 control portfolios' metrics—this average is labelled the "control series" in the tables and figures; and
   - the relative frequency with which the experimental portfolio's metric exceeded those of the 400 control portfolios.

Available computer memory set the upper limit of 400 control portfolios. We compromised in our decision to confine the set {S} to windows centered on trading days in the same calendar year as the event itself. The compromise was necessitated by (a) available computer memory, which restricted the number of control portfolios and the number of transactions that could be stored simultaneously, (b) the need to have sufficiently homogeneous market conditions across the control windows, and (c) a desire to limit the expected number of control portfolios that would include any given window. The last issue arises because there were at most 251 "complete windows" from which each of the 400 samples was drawn.

Our statistical tests use each firm as its own control group. The sample includes firms that differ sizably in such dimensions as stock market variability, trading frequency and trading volume. To reduce problems arising from time-series heterogeneity at the individual firm level, only the year of the earnings release being examined is used to develop the control portfolio of each firm.

Each transaction and each trading minute is tested separately. Consequently, our procedure may understate the significance of observations taken over longer holding periods.

Appendix 5.B
Tables of Data Underlying Chapter 5 Figures

Exhibits 5-7 to 5-10 present selected data points underlying the figures in Chapter 5 for the following variables:

Transaction Time Series

• Exhibit 5-7	– Security return variability
	– Trading frequency
	– Trading volume
• Exhibit 5-8	– Cumulative security returns

Calendar Time Series

• Exhibit 5-9	– Security return variability
	– Trading frequency
	– Trading volume
• Exhibit 5-10	– Cumulative security returns

EXHIBIT 5-1
STATISTICAL SIGNIFICANCE LEVELS OF FINANCIAL SERIES: ALL EARNINGS RELEASES

Transaction Time				Calendar Time			
Transaction	Security Return Variability	Trading Frequency	# Shares Per Transaction	Trading Minute	Security Return Variability	Trading Frequency	# Shares Per Firm
–20	0.88	0.73	0.05	–421	0.20	0.05	0.10
–10	0.51	0.30	0.19	–361	0.34	0.77	0.09
–9	0.82	0.80	0.19	–240	0.04*	0.50	0.52
–8	0.08	0.89	0.78	–120	0.47	0.91	0.34
–7	0.59	0.28	0.58	–60	0.53	0.68	0.66
–6	0.07	0.93	0.13	–10	0.78	0.86	0.33
–5	0.27	0.40	0.58	–5	0.21	0.17	0.17
–4	0.23	0.57	0.04*	–4	0.96*	0.91	0.97*
–3	0.10	0.91	0.19	–3	0.94	0.93	0.91
–2	0.39	0.05	0.37	–2	0.97*	1.00**	0.86
–1	0.35	1.00**	0.19	–1	0.96*	1.00**	0.90
0	1.00**	0.00**	0.97*	0	1.00**	1.00**	0.88
1	0.89	0.00**	0.86	1	1.00**	1.00**	1.00**
2	0.90	0.00**	0.91	2	1.00**	1.00**	1.00**
3	0.88	0.00**	0.84	3	1.00**	1.00**	1.00**
4	0.95*	0.00**	0.65	4	1.00**	1.00**	1.00**
5	0.49	0.00**	0.81	5	1.00**	1.00**	1.00**

EXHIBIT 5-1 CONTINUED

Transaction Time				Calendar Time			
Transaction	Security Return Variability	Trading Frequency	# Shares Per Transaction	Trading Minute	Security Return Variability	Trading Frequency	# Shares Per Firm
6	0.34	0.00**	0.93	6	1.00**	1.00**	0.99**
7	0.34	0.00**	0.82	7	1.00**	1.00**	0.99**
8	0.05*	0.00**	0.58	8	1.00**	1.00**	1.00**
9	0.57	0.00**	0.62	9	1.00**	1.00**	0.95*
10	0.10	0.00**	0.89	10	1.00**	1.00**	0.99**
11	0.25	0.00**	0.07	11	1.00**	1.00**	0.98**
12	0.22	0.00**	0.75	12	1.00**	1.00**	0.95*
13	0.55	0.00**	0.85	13	1.00**	1.00**	0.98**
14	0.64	0.00**	0.80	14	1.00**	1.00**	0.98**
15	0.26	0.00**	0.13	15	1.00**	1.00**	0.98**
20	0.05*	0.01**	0.29	60	0.58	1.00**	0.96*
30	0.09	0.01**	0.85	120	0.97*	1.00**	0.36
40	0.38	0.04**	0.86	240	0.38	0.94	0.91
50	0.69	0.05*	0.99**	361	0.88	0.97*	0.76
60	0.03*	0.06	0.89	421	0.78	0.91	0.65

Key: **Significant at .05 level (2 tailed test)
*Significant at .10 level (2 tailed test)

EXHIBIT 5-2
STATISTICAL SIGNIFICANCE LEVELS OF FINANCIAL SERIES: EARNINGS RELEASES OUTSIDE TRADING HOURS

Transaction Time				Calendar Time			
Transaction	Security Return Variability	Trading Frequency	# Shares Per Transaction	Trading Minute	Security Return Variability	Trading Frequency	# Shares Per Firm
–20	0.97*	0.54	0.58	–421	0.32	0.13	0.25
–10	0.40	0.41	0.11	–361	0.17	0.32	0.25
–9	0.40	0.41	0.69	–240	0.09	0.36	0.66
–8	0.28	0.61	0.73	–120	0.53	0.56	0.42
–7	0.64	0.51	0.88	–60	0.54	0.45	0.71
–6	0.13	0.14	0.18	–10	0.85	0.76	0.32
–5	0.33	0.02**	0.67	–5	0.58	0.17	0.32
–4	0.52	0.32	0.53	–4	0.90	0.93	0.62
–3	0.06	0.73	0.09	–3	0.18	0.37	0.96*
–2	0.85	0.19	0.17	–2	0.61	0.57	0.63
–1	0.38	0.57	0.06	–1	0.33	0.75	0.33
0	0.99**	0.25	0.98**	0	0.68	0.25	0.40
1	0.07	0.00**	0.92	1	0.44	0.73	0.51
2	0.16	0.00**	0.73	2	0.18	0.50	0.55
3	0.38	0.00**	0.98**	3	0.49	0.87	0.44
4	0.34	0.00**	0.14	4	0.48	0.35	0.39
5	0.07	0.00**	0.78	5	0.76	0.77	0.95*

EXHIBIT 5-2 CONTINUED

Transaction Time				Calendar Time			
Transaction	Security Return Variability	Trading Frequency	# Shares Per Transaction	Trading Minute	Security Return Variability	Trading Frequency	# Shares Per Firm
6	0.77	0.00**	0.83	6	0.61	0.92	0.96*
7	0.02**	0.17	0.35	7	0.50	0.49	0.56
8	0.10	0.00**	0.46	8	1.00**	1.00**	0.96*
9	0.31	0.04*	0.54	9	0.95*	0.82	0.58
10	0.00**	0.00**	0.96*	10	0.80	0.99**	0.82
11	0.16	0.00**	0.29	11	0.63	0.87	0.95*
12	0.20	0.01**	0.48	12	0.77	0.72	0.99**
13	0.02**	0.19	0.79	13	0.92	0.76	0.96
14	0.02**	0.01**	0.52	14	0.98**	1.00**	0.95*
15	0.19	0.01**	0.49	15	0.93	0.96*	0.91
20	0.06	0.04**	0.09	60	0.09	0.98**	0.95*
30	0.28	0.01**	0.36	120	0.92	0.94	0.62
40	0.88	0.01**	0.78	240	0.29	0.86	0.89
50	0.89	0.08	0.86	361	0.82	0.46	0.91
60	0.17	0.23	0.30	421	0.92	0.82	0.59

Key: **Significant at .05 level (2 tailed test)
* Significant at .10 level (2 tailed test)

EXHIBIT 5-3
STATISTICAL SIGNIFICANCE LEVELS OF FINANCIAL SERIES:
EARNINGS RELEASES IN FIRST AND LAST HALF HOURS OF TRADING

Transaction Time				Calendar Time			
Transaction	Security Return Variability	Trading Frequency	# Shares Per Transaction	Trading Minute	Security Return Variability	Trading Frequency	# Shares Per Firm
–20	0.94	0.50	0.03*	–421	0.35	0.09	0.17
–10	0.78	0.53	0.64	–361	0.57	0.59	0.22
–9	0.54	0.94	0.17	–240	0.34	0.93	0.64
–8	0.33	0.86	0.32	–120	0.79	0.94	0.54
–7	0.81	0.04	0.46	–60	0.88	0.99**	0.95*
–6	0.79	0.61	0.91	–10	0.88	0.38	0.47
–5	0.61	0.68	0.74	–5	0.22	0.62	0.37
–4	0.34	0.63	0.04*	–4	0.95	0.83	0.99**
–3	0.35	0.06	0.17	–3	0.61	0.92	0.10
–2	0.39	0.30	0.73	–2	0.77	0.95*	0.83
–1	0.54	0.74	0.15	–1	0.86	0.99**	0.73
0	0.51	0.00*	0.13	0	1.00**	1.00**	0.79
1	0.79	0.00*	0.02**	1	0.99**	1.00**	0.81
2	0.67	0.00*	0.21	2	1.00**	1.00**	0.96*
3	0.91	0.05*	0.22	3	1.00**	1.00**	0.95*
4	0.51	0.05*	0.38	4	0.96*	1.00**	0.70
5	0.49	0.00**	0.84	5	1.00**	1.00**	0.86

EXHIBIT 5-3 CONTINUED

Transaction Time				Calendar Time			
Transaction	Security Return Variability	Trading Frequency	# Shares Per Transaction	Trading Minute	Security Return Variability	Trading Frequency	# Shares Per Firm
6	0.95*	0.05*	0.77	6	1.00**	1.00**	0.40
7	0.73	0.00**	0.94	7	0.99**	0.99**	0.89
8	0.17	0.01**	0.48	8	0.94	1.00**	0.64
9	0.54	0.01**	0.86	9	0.91	1.00**	0.67
10	0.15	0.13	0.57	10	0.92	1.00**	0.88
11	0.07	0.14	0.50	11	0.83	1.00**	0.97*
12	0.78	0.71	0.73	12	0.75	1.00**	0.76
13	0.93	0.17	0.96	13	1.00**	1.00**	0.78
14	0.70	0.00**	0.82	14	0.69	1.00**	0.78
15	0.36	0.02**	0.32	15	0.84	0.96*	0.51
20	0.08	0.22**	0.91	60	0.96*	1.00**	0.94
30	0.69	0.13	0.86	120	0.69	0.70	0.22
40	0.03*	0.17	0.62	240	0.52	0.90	0.82
50	0.07	0.67	0.47	361	0.91	0.98**	0.87
60	0.06	0.09	0.94	421	0.13	0.68	0.53

Key: **Significant at .05 level (2 tailed test)
* Significant at .10 level (2 tailed test)

EXHIBIT 5-4
STATISTICAL SIGNIFICANCE LEVELS OF FINANCIAL SERIES: EARNINGS RELEASES BETWEEN 10:30 A.M. AND 3:30 P.M.

Transaction Time				Calendar Time			
Transaction	Security Return Variability	Trading Frequency	# Shares Per Transaction	Trading Minute	Security Return Variability	Trading Frequency	# Shares Per Firm
–20	0.32	0.75	0.09	–421	0.29	0.13	0.31
–10	0.42	0.29	0.43	–361	0.57	0.86	0.13
–9	0.92	0.75	0.16	–240	0.20	0.35	0.49
–8	0.13	0.86	0.89	–120	0.35	0.84	0.45
–7	0.52	0.41	0.24	–60	0.33	0.29	0.16
–6	0.07	0.98*	0.03*	–10	0.29	0.83	0.53
–5	0.21	0.77	0.45	–5	0.18	0.21	0.31
–4	0.16	0.65	0.09	–4	0.62	0.39	0.68
–3	0.35	0.99**	0.56	–3	1.00**	0.98**	0.77
–2	0.17	0.12	0.49	–2	0.98**	1.00**	0.90
–1	0.37	0.99**	0.69	–1	1.00**	1.00**	0.99**
0	0.99**	0.00**	0.91	0	0.99**	1.00**	0.97*
1	0.99**	0.00**	0.89	1	1.00**	1.00**	1.00**
2	0.98**	0.00**	0.96*	2	1.00**	1.00**	1.00**
3	0.86	0.00**	0.45	3	1.00**	1.00**	0.99**
4	0.97*	0.00**	0.93	4	1.00**	1.00**	1.00**
5	0.85	0.00**	0.64	5	1.00**	1.00**	1.00**

EXHIBIT 5-4 CONTINUED

Transaction Time				Calendar Time			
Transaction	Security Return Variability	Trading Frequency	# Shares Per Transaction	Trading Minute	Security Return Variability	Trading Frequency	# Shares Per Firm
6	0.05*	0.00**	0.92	6	1.00**	1.00**	0.99**
7	0.76	0.00**	0.63	7	1.00**	1.00**	0.99**
8	0.22	0.00**	0.72	8	1.00**	1.00**	1.00**
9	0.77	0.00**	0.48	9	1.00**	1.00**	0.99**
10	0.63	0.01**	0.75	10	1.00**	1.00**	1.00**
11	0.66	0.02**	0.09	11	1.00**	1.00**	0.95*
12	0.15	0.02**	0.70	12	1.00**	1.00**	0.99**
13	0.85	0.01**	0.46	13	1.00**	1.00**	1.00**
14	0.96*	0.01**	0.80	14	1.00**	1.00**	0.94
15	0.44	0.00**	0.12	15	1.00**	1.00**	0.99**
20	0.31	0.03*	0.36	60	0.71	0.90	0.80
30	0.04*	0.11	0.67	120	0.89	0.99**	0.49
40	0.35	0.27	0.88	240	0.54	0.78	0.92
50	0.61	0.12	0.99**	361	0.56	0.86	0.08
60	0.05*	0.18	0.88	421	0.66	0.87	0.83

Key: **Significant at .05 level (2 tailed test)
*Significant at .10 level (2 tailed test)

EXHIBIT 5-5
NUMBER OF INDIVIDUAL MINUTES IN SUCCESSIVE TEN MINUTE PERIODS STATISTICALLY SIGNIFICANT AT .05 LEVEL

	TOTAL SAMPLE	SUBSAMPLES: OUTSIDE TRADING HOURS	SUBSAMPLES: FIRST/LAST HALF HOURS	SUBSAMPLES: 10:30 TO 3:30
PANEL A: SECURITY RETURN VARIABILITY				
0-9 Trading Minutes	10	1	7	10
10-19	9	2	2	10
20-29	10	1	2	10
30-39	7	0	2	7
40-49	7	4	2	6
50-59	5	2	0	5
60-69	5	1	1	3
70-79	5	1	1	4
80-89	4	3	0	3
90-99	5	0	1	4
100-109	2	1	2	1
110-119	1	0	0	1
PANEL B: TRADING FREQUENCY				
0-9 Trading Minutes	10	1	10	10
10-19	10	5	10	8
20-29	10	7	10	5
30-39	10	6	10	6
40-49	10	6	10	7
50-59	10	3	9	7
60-69	10	1	9	7
70-79	10	3	6	4
80-89	9	2	8	3
90-99	8	5	6	1
100-109	8	0	4	2
110-119	6	0	5	4
PANEL C: # OF SHARES PER FIRM				
0-9 Trading Minutes	8	0	0	9
10-19	6	0	0	6
20-29	2	1	1	1
30-39	1	1	2	1
40-49	2	1	2	1
50-59	2	2	1	2
60-69	1	1	2	1
70-79	1	2	1	1
80-89	1	1	0	1
90-99	3	2	0	1
100-109	0	0	0	0
110-119	2	0	0	3

EXHIBIT 5-6
EARNINGS FORECAST ERROR DISTRIBUTION STATISTICS*

	PORT.1	PORT.2	PORT.3	PORT.4	PORT.5	PORT.6	ALL
PANEL A							
MIN	−0.892	−0.009	−0.002	0.001	0.004	0.000	−0.892
.1	−0.072	−0.008	−0.002	0.001	0.005	0.000	−0.016
.3	−0.031	−0.006	−0.001	0.001	0.006	0.000	−0.004
.5	−0.017	−0.004	−0.001	0.002	0.009	0.000	−0.000
.7	−0.013	−0.003	−0.000	0.003	0.015	0.000	0.002
.9	−0.010	−0.003	0.000	0.003	0.032	0.000	0.009
MAX	−0.009	−0.002	0.001	0.004	0.352	0.000	0.352
AVERAGE	−0.040	−0.005	−0.001	0.002	0.017	0.000	−0.005
NOB	332	332	332	332	332	74	1734
PANEL B							
MEDIANS							
1980	−0.022	−0.004	−0.001	0.002	0.012	0.000	0.001
1981	−0.018	−0.005	−0.001	0.002	0.010	0.000	0.000
1982	−0.016	−0.005	−0.001	0.002	0.010	0.000	−0.000
1983	−0.023	−0.005	−0.001	0.002	0.007	0.000	−0.000
1984	−0.015	−0.004	−0.001	0.002	0.008	0.000	−0.001
1985	−0.021	−0.004	−0.001	0.002	0.007	0.000	−0.002

* Earnings forecast error is defined by:

$$\frac{\text{Actual Quarterly EPS - Quarterly EPS Forecast by Value Line}}{\text{Security Price Immediately Prior to Forecast Date}}$$

Quarterly observations are ranked and placed into five equally-sized portfolios (after observations with zero earnings forecast error placed in Portfolio 6). Portfolio 1 is the portfolio with 20% lowest errors, 5 is the portfolio with 20% highest forecast errors.

EXHIBIT 5-7
TRANSACTION TIME. SECURITY RETURN VARIABILITY, TRADING FREQUENCY AND TRADING VOLUME

	ANNOUNCEMENT EFFECT SERIES			CONTROL SERIES		
SAMPLE/ TRANSACTION	SEC. RET. VARIAB.	TRADING FREQ.	TRADING VOLUME	SEC. RET. VARIAB.	TRADING FREQ.	TRADING VOLUME
A. TOTAL SAMPLE						
–20T	0.36	21.6	10.2	0.33	17.8	12.1
–2T	0.35	20.2	12.0	0.34	18.6	12.8
–1T	0.34	24.1	12.0	0.33	18.2	13.4
0T	0.57	38.8	34.6	0.47	40.7	29.4
+1T	0.35	14.5	14.6	0.32	18.8	13.0
+2T	0.36	14.2	14.0	0.33	18.6	12.2
+3T	0.36	15.5	13.5	0.33	18.3	12.3
+4T	0.36	15.9	12.5	0.33	18.4	12.2
+5T	0.34	14.6	13.3	0.33	18.2	12.4
+20T	0.33	18.2	11.7	0.33	17.8	12.8
+60T	0.32	18.6	14.3	0.33	17.5	12.6
B. OUTSIDE TRADING HOURS						
–2T	0.38	18.8	10.5	0.35	18.9	13.0
–1T	0.35	21.0	11.3	0.36	18.8	14.7
0T	0.85	29.0	79.3	0.68	28.1	62.8
+1T	0.31	14.9	18.9	0.33	18.6	14.4
+2T	0.32	13.6	13.6	0.34	17.1	12.2
+60T	0.32	16.5	11.0	0.34	16.6	12.2
C. FIRST/LAST HALF HOURS						
–2T	0.33	17.2	17.1	0.34	17.8	15.9
–1T	0.35	19.1	13.4	0.35	16.6	16.6
0T	0.44	21.7	19.6	0.43	32.7	25.9
+1T	0.34	11.0	9.7	0.31	16.0	15.1
+2T	0.33	13.2	12.9	0.31	16.9	13.9
+60T	0.26	14.5	19.8	0.30	16.8	12.9
D. 10:30 - 3:30						
–2T	0.34	21.5	11.4	0.35	20.2	11.9
–1T	0.33	26.9	12.0	0.33	20.0	11.8
0T	0.46	47.5	16.2	0.38	52.1	12.9
+1T	0.38	15.1	13.7	0.33	21.2	11.7
+2T	0.39	14.8	14.8	0.34	21.4	11.8
+60T	0.33	20.5	14.6	0.35	19.4	12.7

EXHIBIT 5-8
TRANSACTION TIME. CUMULATIVE SECURITY RETURNS ([-20T, +60T]) FOR FIVE UNEXPECTED EARNINGS CHANGE PORTFOLIOS

SAMPLE/ TRANSACTION	ANNOUNCEMENT EFFECT SERIES					CONTROL SERIES				
	PORT. I	PORT. II	PORT. III	PORT. IV	PORT. V	PORT. I	PORT. II	PORT. III	PORT. IV	PORT. V
A.TOTAL SAMPLE										
–20T	–0.04	–0.06	0.04	0.05	0.03	–0.01	–0.00	–0.00	–0.00	0.00
–2T	–0.16	–0.10	–0.07	–0.11	0.18	–0.12	–0.05	–0.04	–0.02	–0.06
–1T	–0.20	–0.09	–0.14	–0.14	0.19	–0.10	–0.05	–0.03	–0.02	–0.05
0T	0.46	–0.24	–0.02	–0.01	0.50	–0.10	–0.04	–0.03	–0.01	–0.04
+1T	–0.55	–0.33	–0.02	0.09	0.58	–0.10	–0.05	–0.03	–0.01	–0.04
+2T	–0.64	–0.43	–0.01	0.13	0.68	–0.10	–0.05	–0.03	–0.01	–0.04
+3T	–0.75	–0.42	–0.05	0.19	0.85	–0.10	–0.05	–0.03	–0.01	–0.03
+4T	–0.78	–0.54	–0.04	0.22	0.94	–0.11	–0.05	–0.03	–0.01	–0.03
+5T	–0.78	–0.63	–0.06	0.24	0.99	–0.12	–0.05	–0.03	–0.01	–0.04
+20T	–1.29	–0.96	–0.23	0.44	1.11	–0.12	–0.03	–0.01	0.03	–0.02
+60T	–1.60	–0.80	–0.42	0.61	1.50	–0.04	0.07	0.06	0.15	0.11
B. OUTSIDE TRADING HOURS										
–2T	–0.35	–0.16	0.27	–0.16	0.03	–0.16	–0.08	–0.04	–0.03	–0.09
–1T	–0.26	–0.11	0.15	–0.16	0.08	–0.08	–0.04	–0.01	–0.00	–0.04
0T	–0.61	–0.34	0.30	–0.04	0.68	–0.04	0.01	0.01	0.02	–0.01
+1T	–0.67	–0.36	0.26	0.03	0.67	–0.04	0.01	0.01	0.03	–0.00
+2T	–0.66	–0.43	0.29	–0.02	0.78	–0.04	0.01	0.01	0.03	–0.00
+60T	–1.43	–0.70	–0.22	0.28	1.72	–0.24	0.04	0.12	0.18	0.11

(Continued on next page)

EXHIBIT 5-8 CONTINUED

SAMPLE/ TRANSACTION	ANNOUNCEMENT EFFECT SERIES					CONTROL SERIES				
	PORT. I	PORT. II	PORT. III	PORT. IV	PORT. V	PORT. I	PORT. II	PORT. III	PORT. IV	PORT. V
C. FIRST/LAST HALF HOURS										
–2T	–0.38	0.21	–0.17	0.41	–0.12	–0.11	–0.04	–0.03	–0.01	–0.03
–1T	–0.40	0.27	–0.19	0.47	–0.16	–0.09	–0.04	–0.03	–0.01	–0.02
0T	–0.69	0.29	–0.16	0.56	0.04	–0.09	–0.03	–0.03	0.02	–0.03
+1T	–0.88	0.21	–0.13	0.70	0.14	–0.09	–0.03	–0.03	0.03	–0.01
+2T	–0.92	0.25	–0.24	0.74	0.36	–0.10	–0.03	–0.02	0.03	–0.01
+60T	–1.41	–0.39	–0.58	1.00	1.24	–0.15	–0.03	0.02	0.19	0.26
D. 10:30 – 3:30										
–2T	–0.01	–0.12	–0.21	–0.20	0.35	–0.11	–0.05	–0.04	–0.02	–0.05
–1T	–0.10	–0.14	–0.27	–0.27	0.34	–0.13	–0.06	–0.04	–0.03	–0.06
0T	–0.33	–0.29	–0.13	–0.11	0.53	–0.15	–0.07	–0.05	–0.03	–0.07
+1T	–0.41	–0.41	–0.13	–0.01	0.66	–0.15	–0.08	–0.05	–0.03	–0.07
+2T	–0.55	–0.55	–0.10	0.07	0.73	–0.16	–0.08	–0.06	–0.04	–0.08
+60T	–1.68	–0.90	–0.46	0.68	1.53	–0.03	0.08	0.04	0.13	0.08

PORTFOLIOS
I=20% most negative unexpected earnings
V=20% most positve unexpected earnings

EXHIBIT 5-9
CALENDAR TIME. SECURITY RETURN VARIABILITY, TRADING FREQUENCY AND TRADING VOLUME

SAMPLE/ TRANSACTION	ANNOUNCEMENT EFFECT SERIES SEC. RET. VARIAB.	ANNOUNCEMENT EFFECT SERIES TRADING FREQ.	ANNOUNCEMENT EFFECT SERIES TRADING VOLUME	CONTROL SERIES SEC. RET. VARIAB.	CONTROL SERIES TRADING FREQ.	CONTROL SERIES TRADING VOLUME
A. TOTAL SAMPLE						
–30M	0.033	1.38	1.63	0.032	1.38	2.14
–2M	0.045	1.89	2.96	0.038	1.59	2.39
–1M	0.069	2.93	5.98	0.061	2.33	4.91
0M	0.073	2.24	4.26	0.044	1.37	3.52
+1M	0.085	3.22	6.24	0.046	1.47	3.68
+2M	0.086	3.17	7.34	0.043	1.43	3.28
+3M	0.080	3.05	5.29	0.042	1.42	3.02
+4M	0.078	2.77	5.07	0.039	1.40	2.92
+5M	0.076	2.66	5.87	0.038	1.40	2.76
+30M	0.040	1.74	2.87	0.034	1.48	2.25
+60M	0.031	1.72	3.28	0.032	1.41	2.11
B. OUTSIDE TRADING HOURS						
–2M	0.055	2.22	3.19	0.055	2.27	3.15
–1M	0.124	4.93	9.73	0.135	4.82	11.76
0M	0.081	1.40	6.16	0.076	1.55	6.85
+1M	0.081	2.06	7.43	0.085	1.94	7.55
+2M	0.064	1.80	6.14	0.078	1.83	6.65
+60M	0.028	2.20	4.83	0.041	1.82	2.77
C. FIRST/LAST HALF HOURS						
–2M	0.053	2.32	5.43	0.045	1.76	3.68
–1M	0.059	2.49	4.55	0.043	1.68	3.65
0M	0.106	3.39	6.04	0.042	1.67	3.80
+1M	0.072	3.69	5.58	0.041	1.66	3.71
+2M	0.103	4.68	9.23	0.040	1.59	2.97
+60M	0.049	2.92	5.50	0.033	1.60	2.25
D. 10:30 - 3:30						
–2M	0.038	1.63	2.27	0.027	1.19	1.66
–1M	0.044	2.05	4.50	0.027	1.18	1.63
0M	0.061	2.44	3.16	0.028	1.18	1.69
+1M	0.090	3.69	5.96	0.027	1.18	1.67
+2M	0.096	3.61	8.00	0.027	1.18	1.60
+60M	0.027	1.22	2.01	0.026	1.13	1.70

EXHIBIT 5-10
CALENDAR TIME. CUMULATIVE SECURITY RETURNS
([-421M , +421M]) FOR FIVE UNEXPECTED EARNINGS CHANGE PORTFOLIOS

	ANNOUNCEMENT EFFECT SERIES					CONTROL SERIES				
SAMPLE/ TRANSACTION	PORT. I	PORT. II	PORT. III	PORT. IV	PORT. V	PORT. I	PORT. II	PORT. III	PORT. IV	PORT. V
A. TOTAL SAMPLE										
–30M	0.06	0.12	0.09	0.06	0.21	0.04	0.08	0.08	0.10	0.11
–2M	0.03	0.10	0.06	0.12	0.29	0.05	0.10	0.09	0.12	0.13
–1M	0.02	0.12	0.04	0.12	0.31	0.08	0.11	0.10	0.13	0.15
0M	0.01	0.11	0.03	0.15	0.32	0.08	0.11	0.10	0.13	0.15
+1M	–0.03	0.11	0.05	0.18	0.37	0.08	0.11	0.10	0.13	0.15
+2M	–0.03	0.09	0.07	0.21	0.49	0.08	0.11	0.10	0.13	0.15
+3M	–0.07	0.10	0.08	0.24	0.52	0.08	0.11	0.10	0.13	0.15
+4M	–0.04	0.09	0.08	0.26	0.60	0.08	0.11	0.10	0.13	0.15
+5M	–0.08	0.07	0.08	0.30	0.66	0.08	0.11	0.10	0.13	0.15
+30M	–0.57	–0.21	0.07	0.49	0.95	0.09	0.12	0.12	0.15	0.16
+60M	–0.79	–0.35	0.06	0.46	0.97	0.09	0.12	0.12	0.15	0.16
B. OUTSIDE TRADING HOURS										
–2M	–0.07	–0.11	0.10	0.21	–0.03	0.03	0.10	0.11	0.12	0.11
–1M	–0.08	–0.02	0.03	0.21	0.03	0.11	0.14	0.13	0.14	0.16
0M	–0.06	–0.03	–0.00	0.22	0.04	0.12	0.14	0.14	0.15	0.17
+1M	–0.07	–0.03	0.02	0.21	0.09	0.13	0.14	0.14	0.15	0.17
+2M	–0.05	–0.05	0.05	0.19	0.15	0.13	0.14	0.14	0.15	0.17
+60M	–1.00	–0.51	0.05	0.41	0.66	0.16	0.18	0.20	0.20	0.22

EXHIBIT 5-10 CONTINUED

SAMPLE/ TRANSACTION	ANNOUNCEMENT EFFECT SERIES					CONTROL SERIES				
	PORT. I	PORT. II	PORT. III	PORT. IV	PORT. V	PORT. I	PORT. II	PORT. III	PORT. IV	PORT. V
C. FIRST/LAST HALF HOURS										
–2M	0.23	0.62	0.05	0.84	0.50	0.11	0.12	0.10	0.18	0.20
–1M	0.16	0.65	0.06	0.84	0.49	0.11	0.12	0.10	0.18	0.20
0M	0.03	0.74	0.06	0.86	0.48	0.10	0.12	0.10	0.19	0.20
+1M	–0.01	0.77	0.05	0.91	0.53	0.11	0.13	0.11	0.19	0.20
+2M	–0.00	0.74	0.07	1.00	0.65	0.11	0.13	0.11	0.19	0.20
+60M	–0.61	0.37	–0.19	1.29	1.42	0.14	0.13	0.13	0.24	0.22
D. 10:30 - 3:30										
–2M	0.11	0.10	0.03	–0.07	0.40	0.04	0.09	0.09	0.10	0.12
–1M	0.11	0.09	0.02	–0.08	0.42	0.04	0.09	0.09	0.10	0.12
0M	0.11	0.07	0.03	–0.04	0.43	0.04	0.09	0.09	0.10	0.12
+1M	0.05	0.05	0.05	0.00	0.48	0.04	0.09	0.09	0.10	0.12
+2M	0.04	0.03	0.08	0.05	0.65	0.04	0.09	0.09	0.10	0.12
+60M	–0.67	–0.40	0.12	0.31	1.09	0.02	0.08	0.08	0.11	0.11

PORTFOLIOS
I=20% most negative unexpected earnings
V=20% most positive unexpected earnings

FIGURE 5-1
SECURITY RETURN VARIABILITY (MEAN ABSOLUTE RETURN): TRANSACTION TIME FOR FULL SAMPLE*

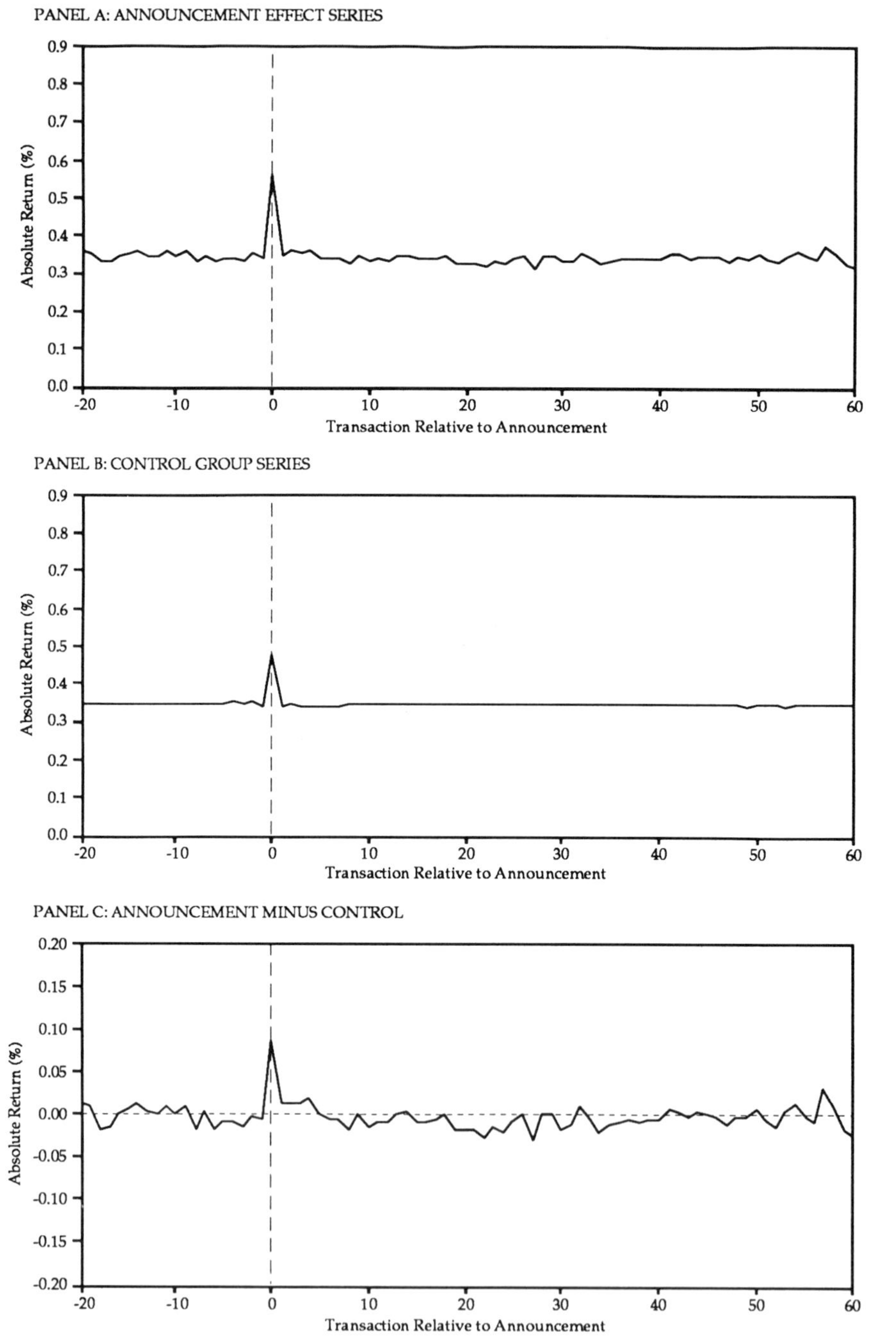

* Panel C uses a different scale than Panels A & B

FIGURE 5-2
SECURITY RETURN VARIABILITY (MEAN ABSOLUTE RETURN): TRANSACTION TIME FOR OUTSIDE TRADING HOURS SUBSAMPLE*

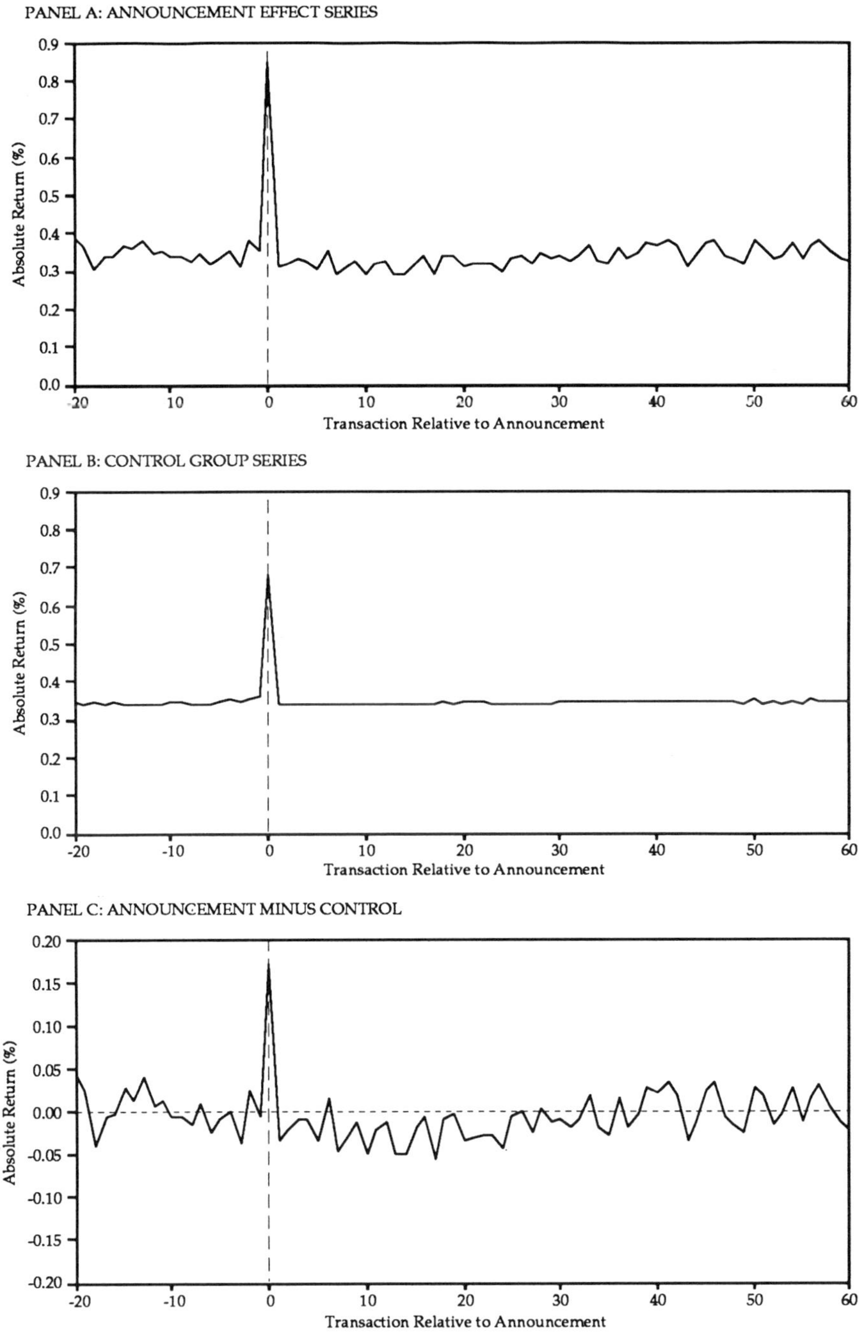

* Panel C uses a different scale than Panels A & B

FIGURE 5-2 (CONTINUED)
SECURITY RETURN VARIABILITY (MEAN ABSOLUTE RETURN): TRANSACTION TIME FOR FIRST/LAST HALF HOURS SUBSAMPLE*

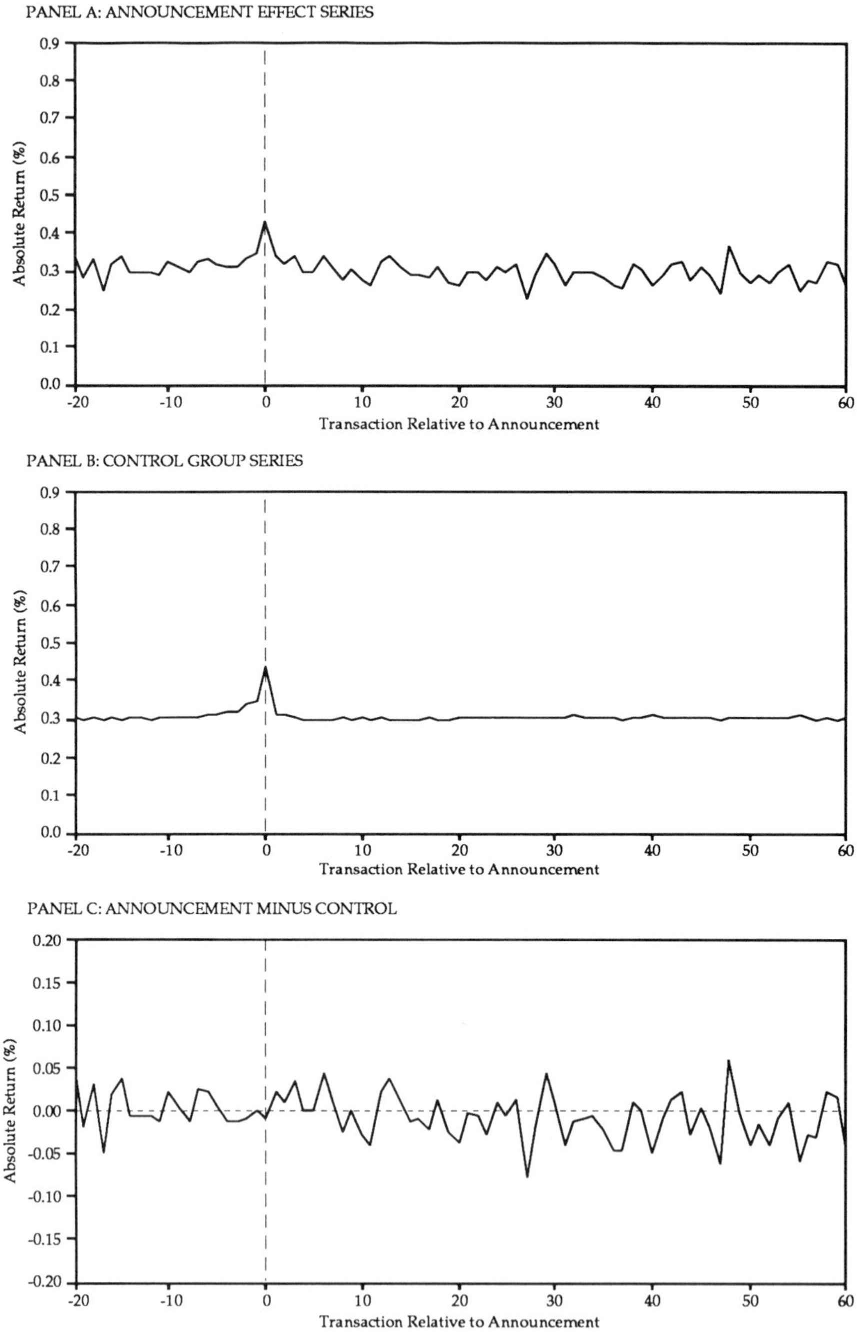

* Panel C uses a different scale than Panels A & B

FIGURE 5-2 (CONTINUED)
SECURITY RETURN VARIABILITY (MEAN ABSOLUTE RETURN): TRANSACTION TIME FOR 10:30 TO 3:30 SUBSAMPLE*

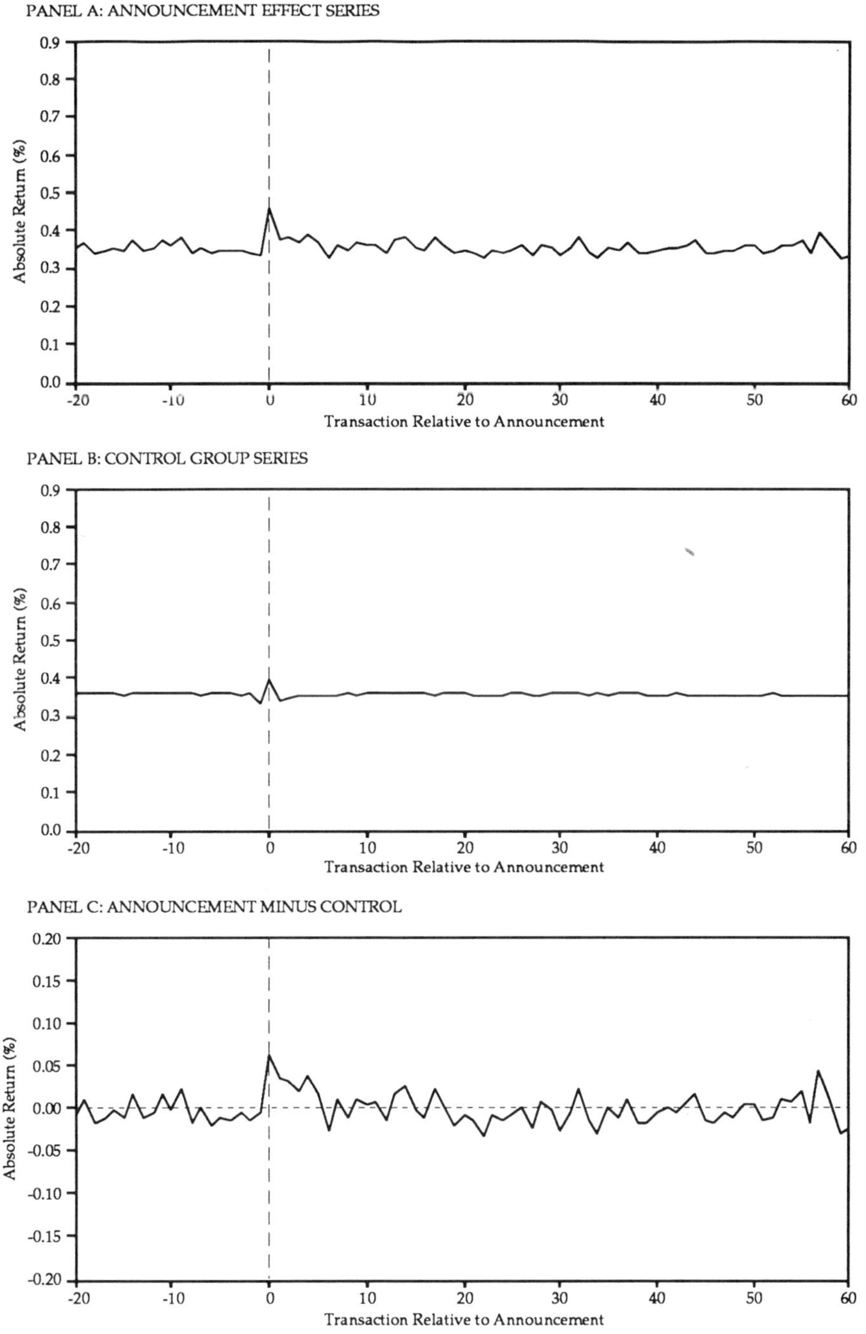

* Panel C uses a different scale than Panels A & B

FIGURE 5-3
SECURITY RETURN VARIABILITY (MEAN ABSOLUTE RETURN): CALENDAR TIME FOR FULL SAMPLE*

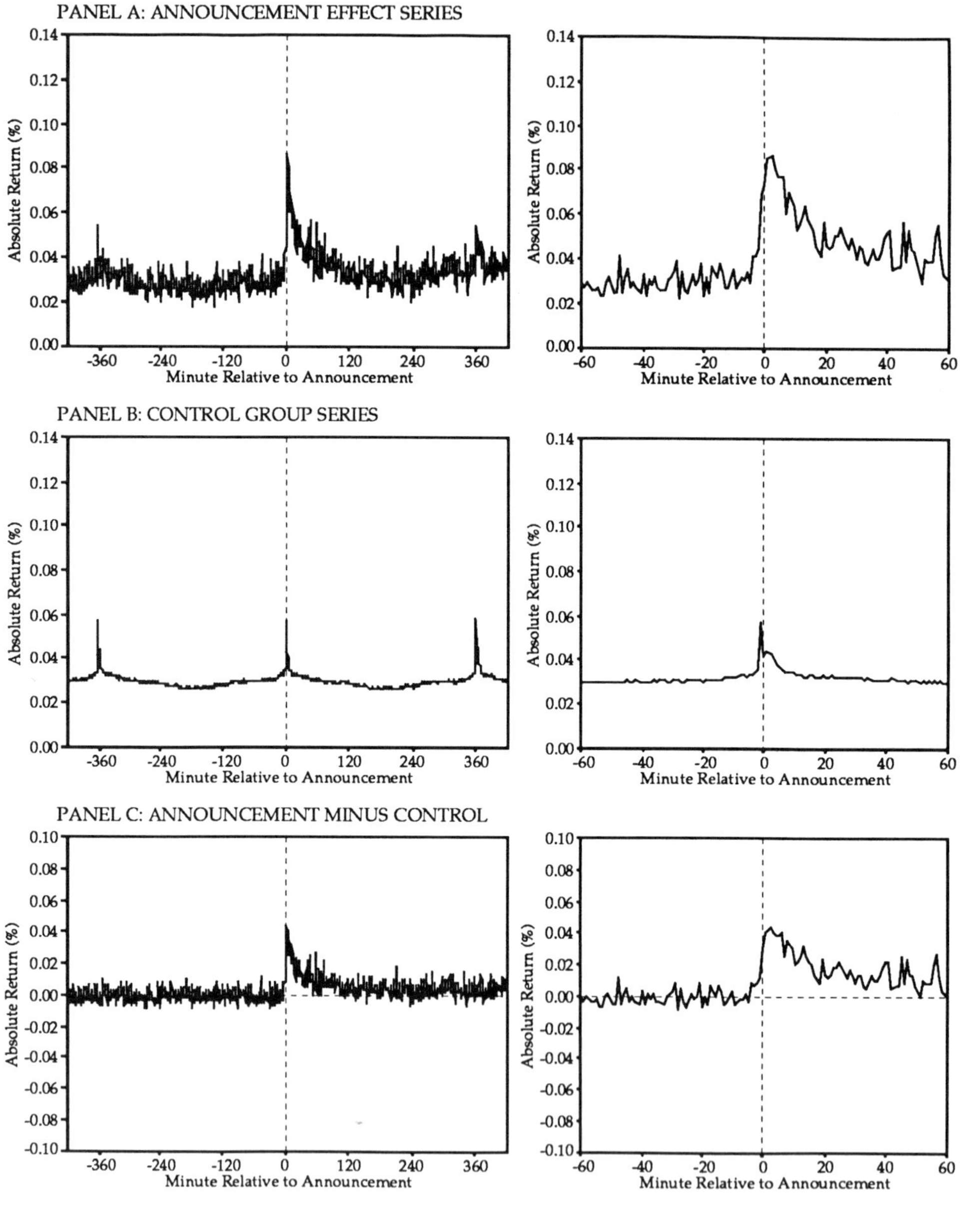

* Panel C uses a different scale than Panels A & B

FIGURE 5-4
SECURITY RETURN VARIABILITY (MEAN ABSOLUTE RETURN): CALENDAR TIME FOR OUTSIDE TRADING HOURS SUBSAMPLE*

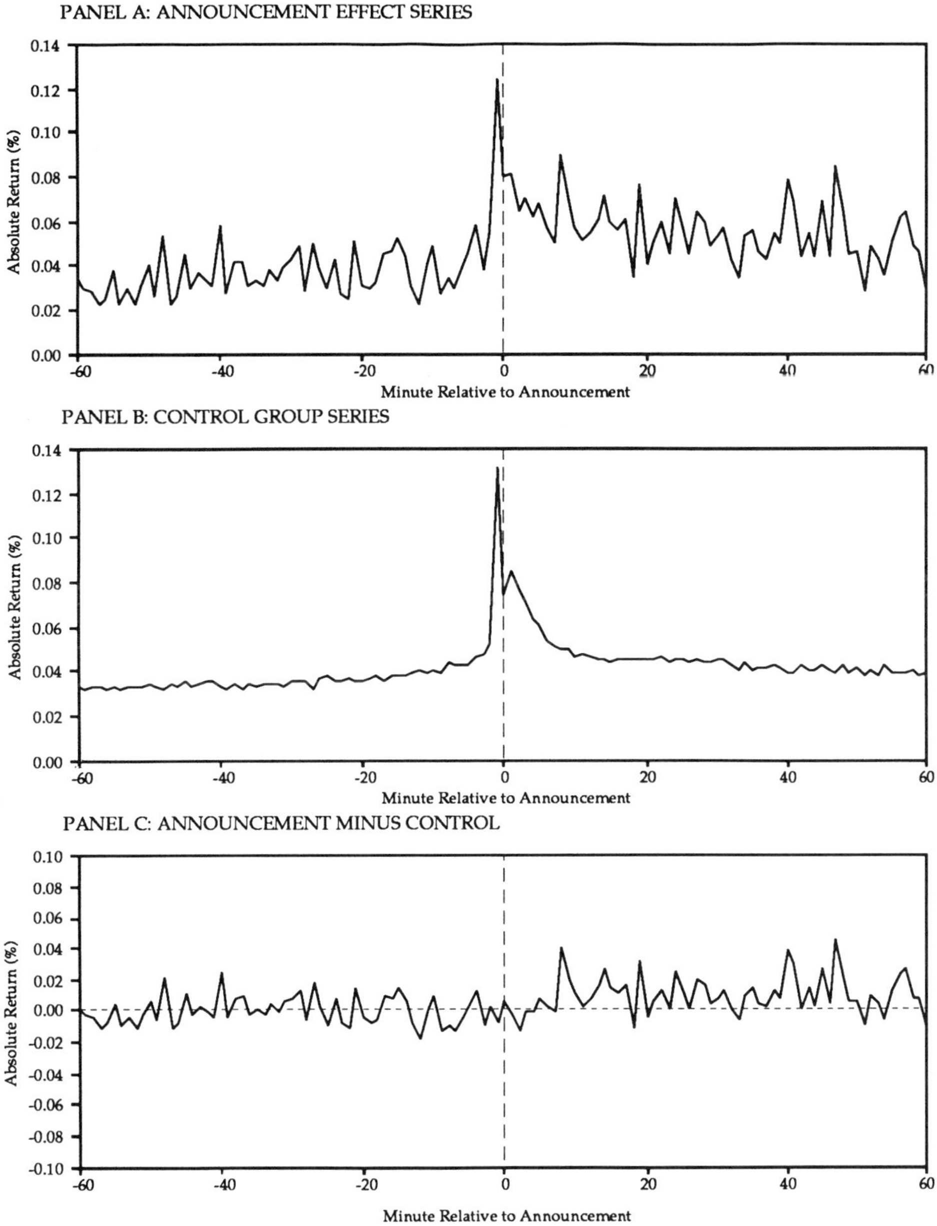

* Panel C uses a different scale than Panels A & B

FIGURE 5-4 (CONTINUED)
SECURITY RETURN VARIABILITY (MEAN ABSOLUTE RETURN):
CALENDAR TIME FOR FIRST/LAST HALF HOURS SUBSAMPLE*

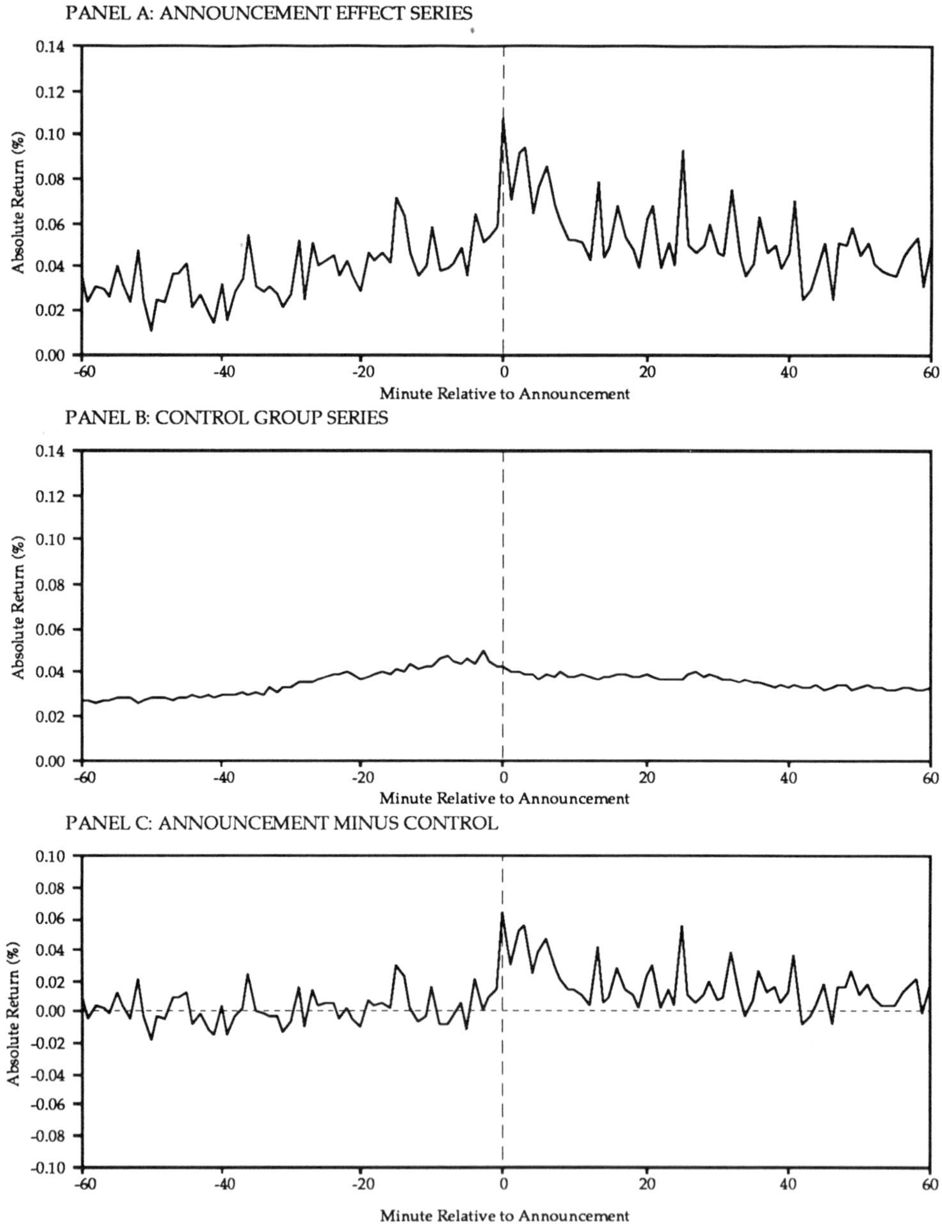

* Panel C uses a different scale than Panels A & B

FIGURE 5-4 (CONTINUED)
SECURITY RETURN VARIABILITY (MEAN ABSOLUTE RETURN):
CALENDAR TIME FOR 10:30 TO3:30 SUBSAMPLE*

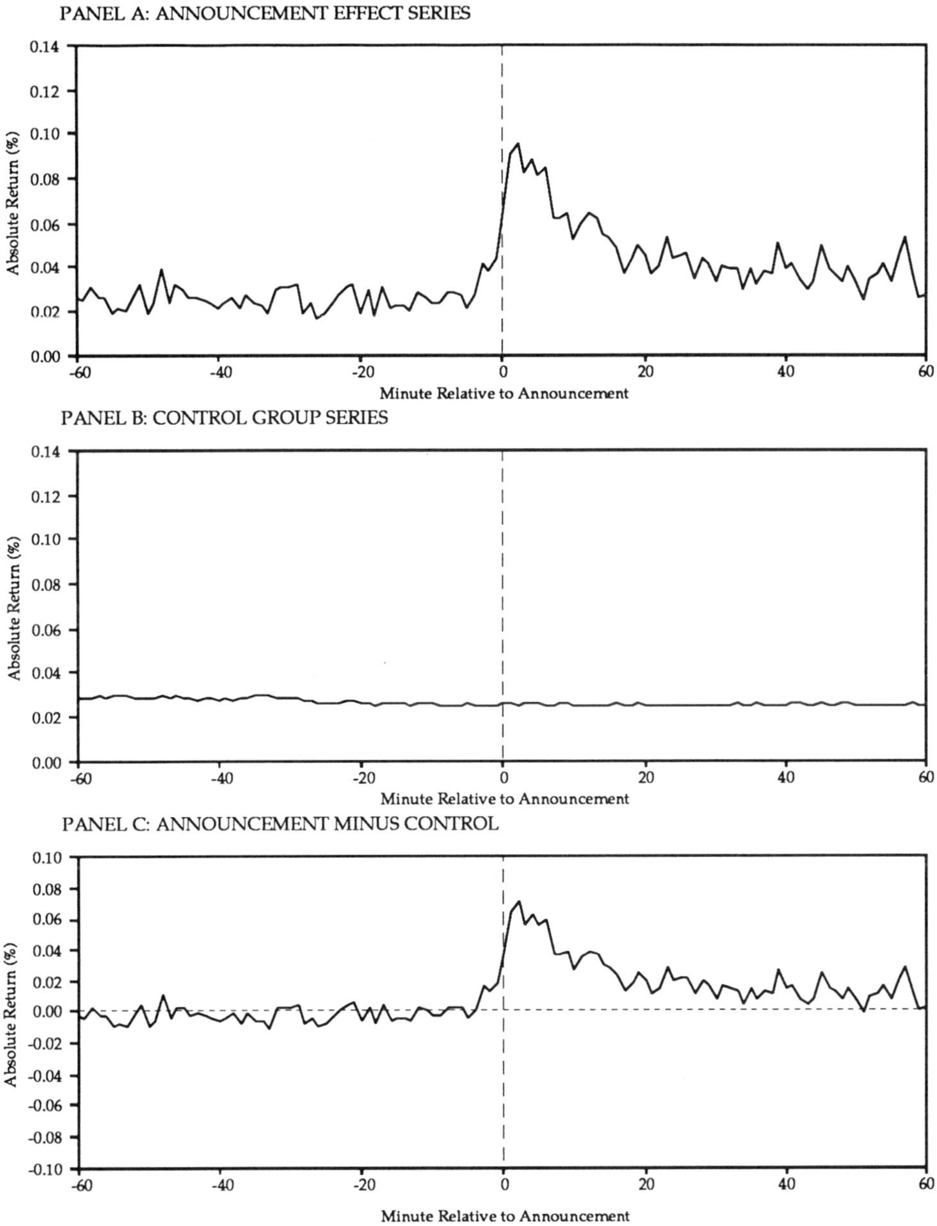

* Panel C uses a different scale than Panels A & B

FIGURE 5-5
TRADING FREQUENCY (TIME BETWEEN SUCCESSIVE TRANSACTIONS): TRANSACTION TIME FOR FULL SAMPLE*

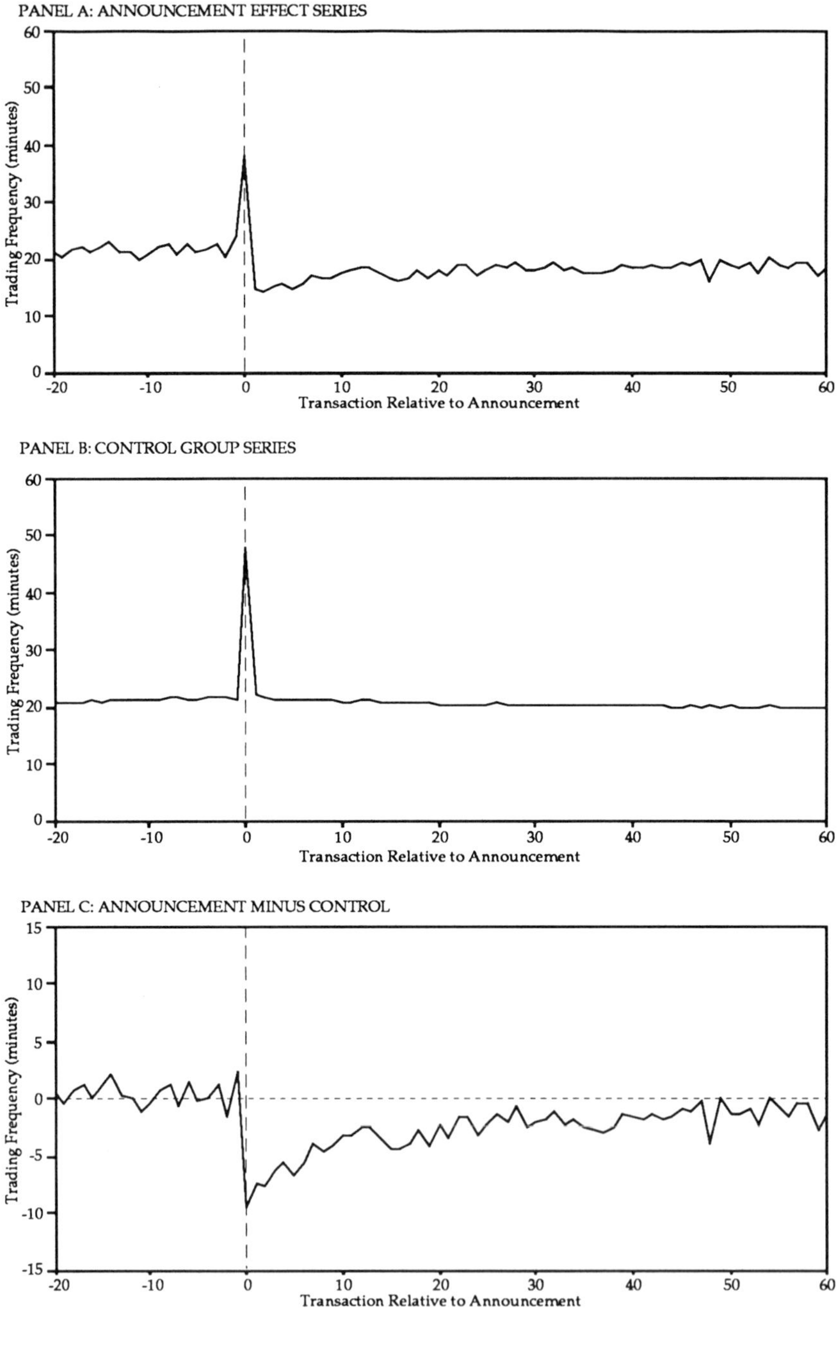

*** Panel C uses a different scale than Panels A & B**

FIGURE 5-6
TRADING FREQUENCY (TIME BETWEEN SUCCESSIVE TRANSACTIONS): TRANSACTION TIME FOR OUTSIDE TRADING HOURS SUBSAMPLE*

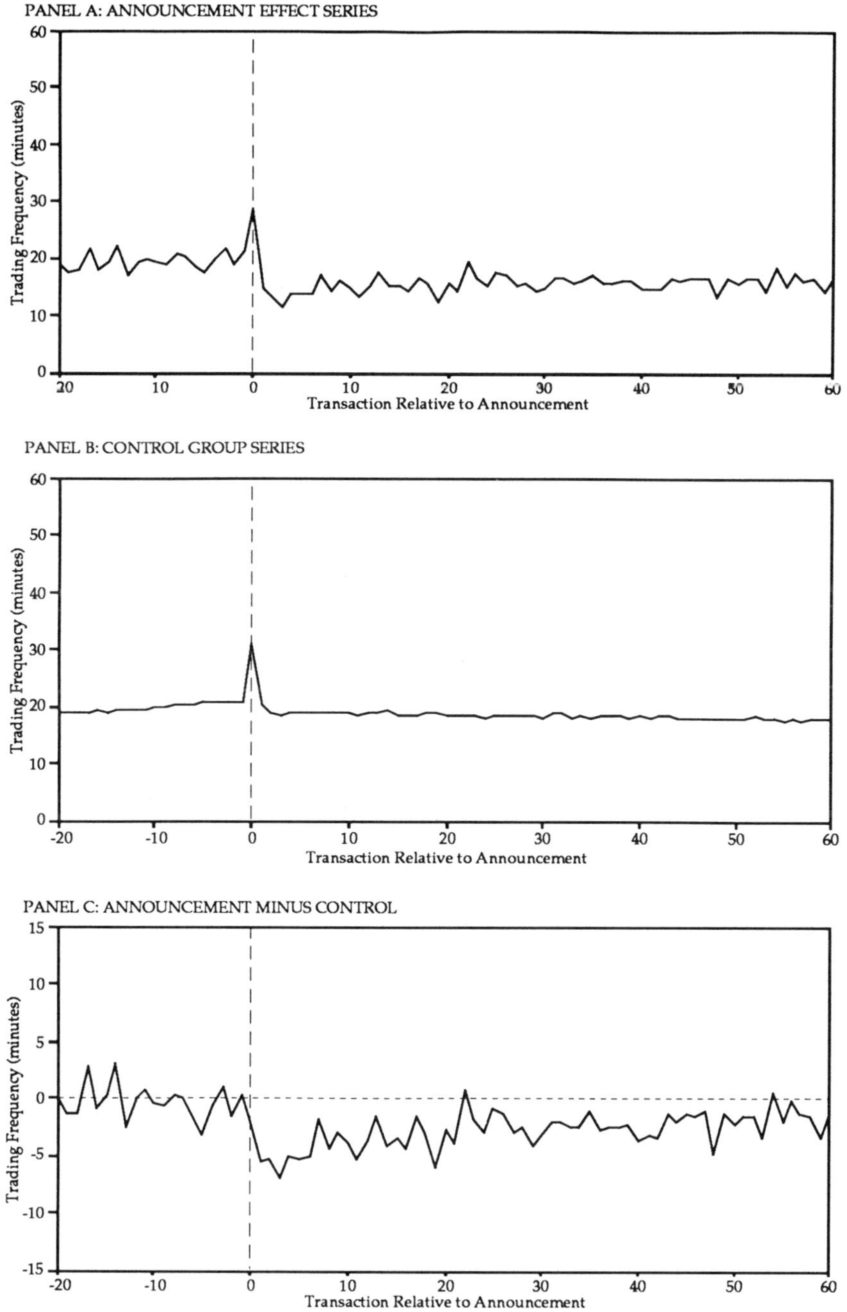

* Panel C uses a different scale than Panels A & B

FIGURE 5-6 CONTINUED
TRADING FREQUENCY (TIME BETWEEN SUCCESSIVE TRANSACTIONS): TRANSACTION TIME FOR FIRST/LAST HALF HOURS SUBSAMPLE*

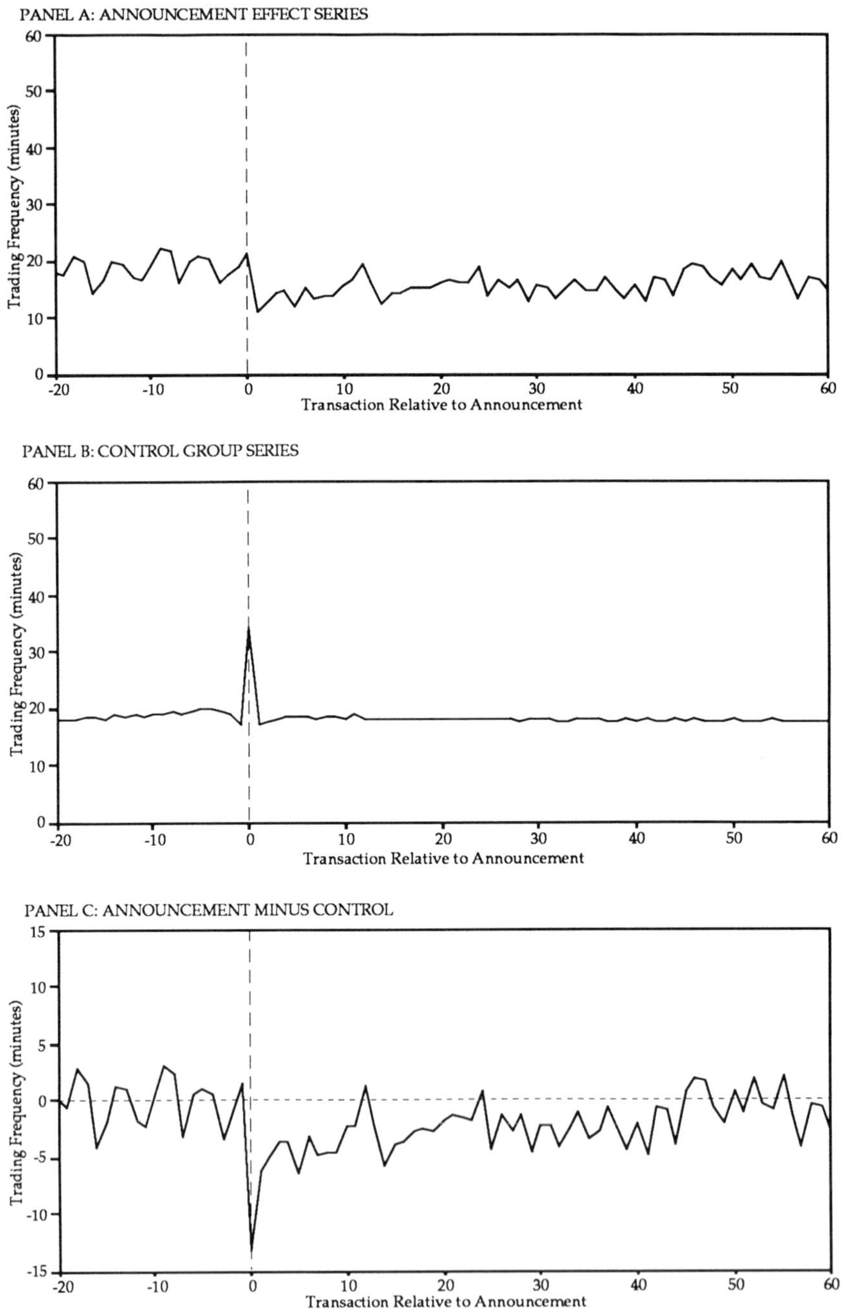

* Panel C uses a different scale than Panels A & B

FIGURE 5-6 CONTINUED
TRADING FREQUENCY (TIME BETWEEN SUCCESSIVE TRANSACTIONS): TRANSACTION TIME FOR 10:30 TO 3:30 SUBSAMPLE*

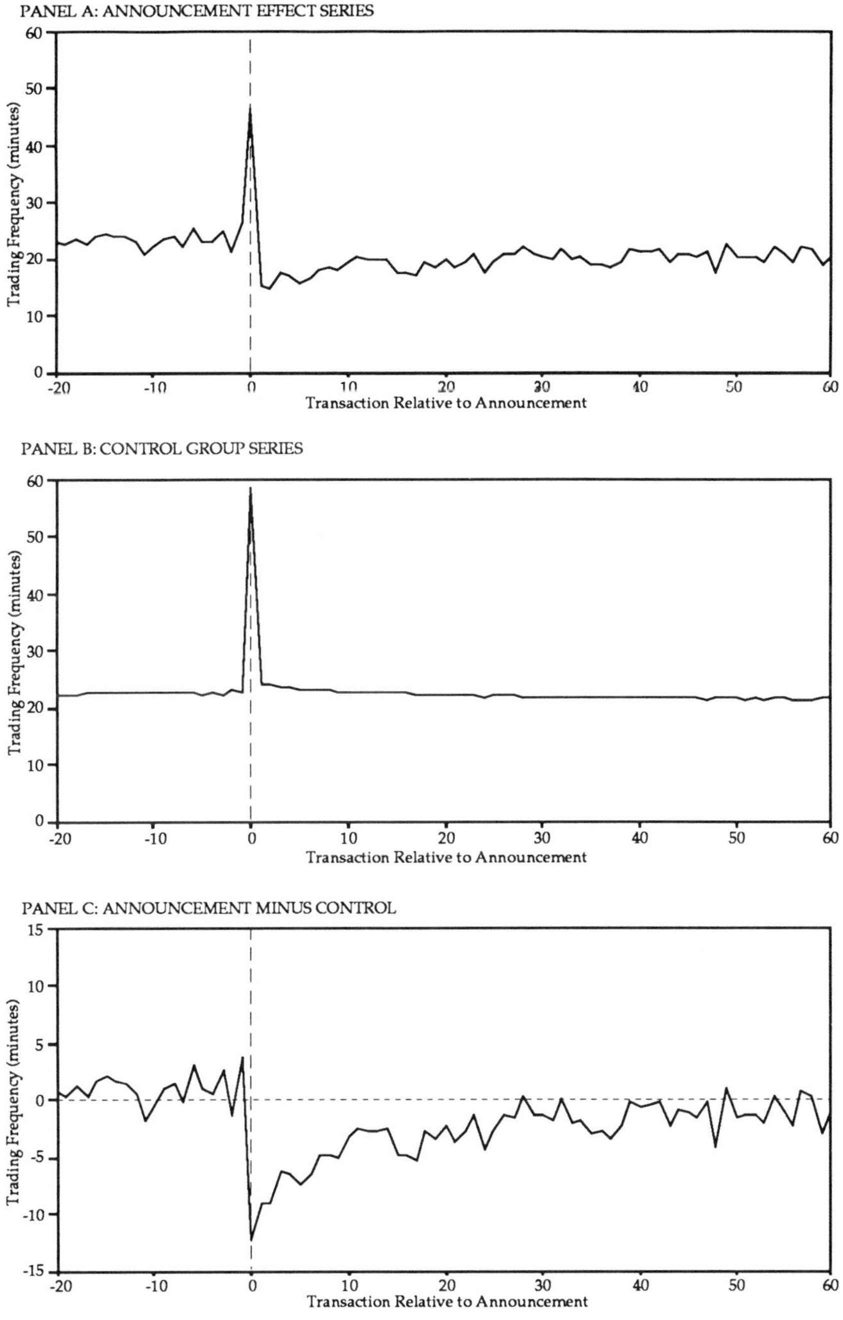

* Panel C uses a different scale than Panels A & B

FIGURE 5-7
BREAKDOWN OF TIME FROM TRANSACTION -1 TO TRANSACTION 0 RELATIVE TO EARNINGS RELEASE TIME (IN MINUTES)*

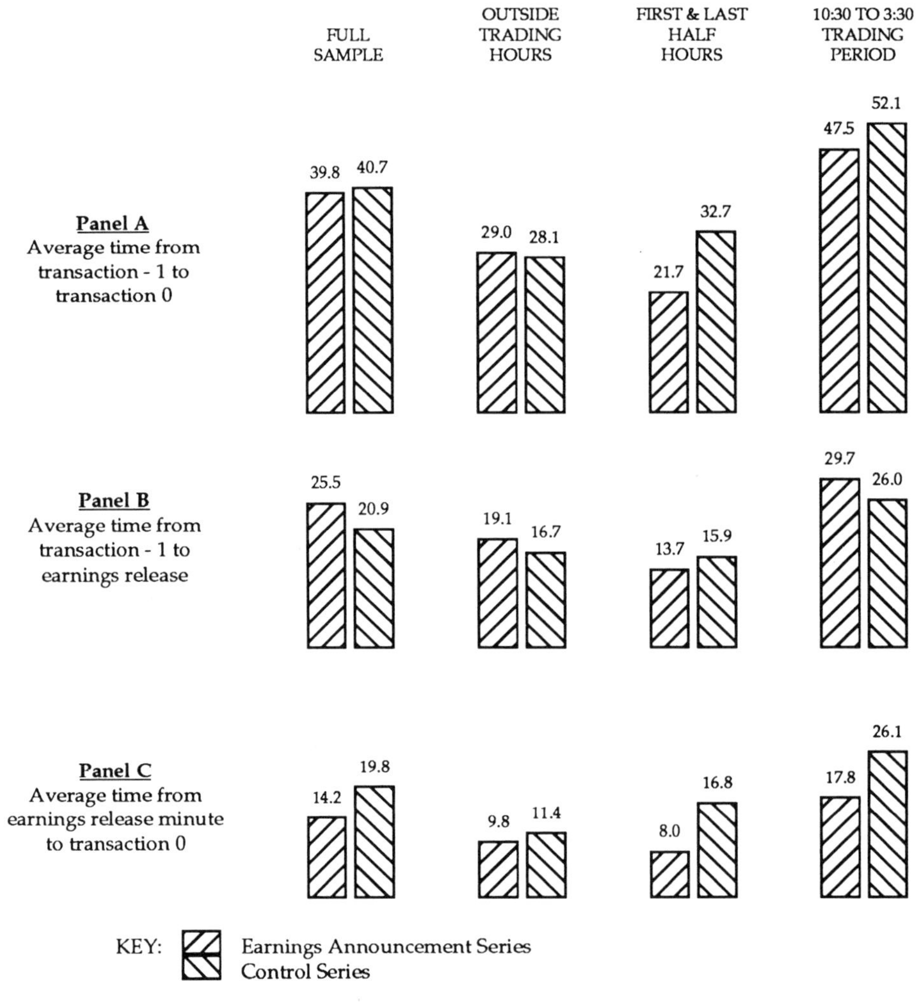

* Time (in minutes) between transactions is only counted while trading on NYSE is possible.

FIGURE 5-8
TRADING FREQUENCY (TRANSACTIONS PER MINUTE): CALENDAR TIME FOR FULL SAMPLE*

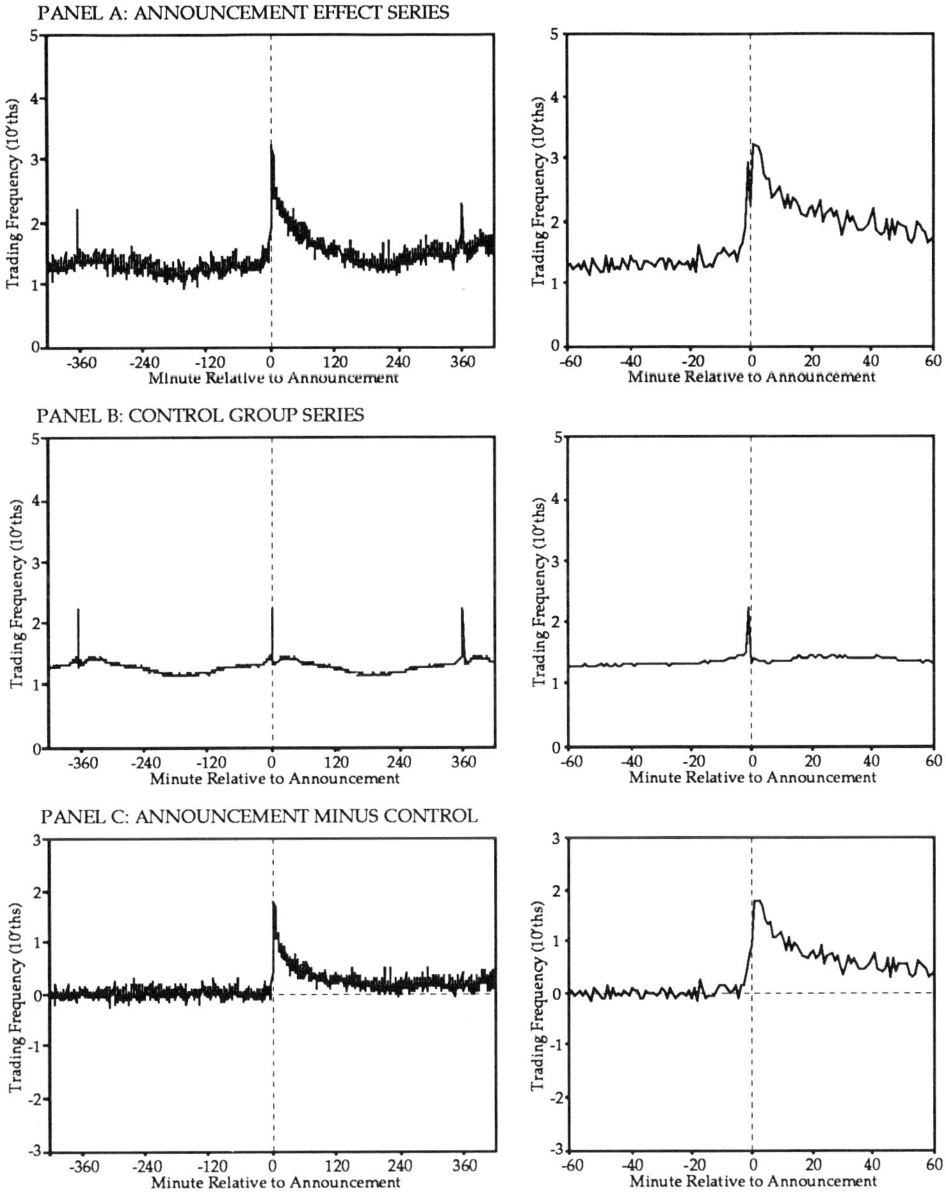

* Panel C uses a different scale than Panels A & B

FIGURE 5-9
TRADING FREQUENCY (TRANSACTIONS PER MINUTE):
CALENDAR TIME FOR OUTSIDE TRADING HOURS SUBSAMPLE*

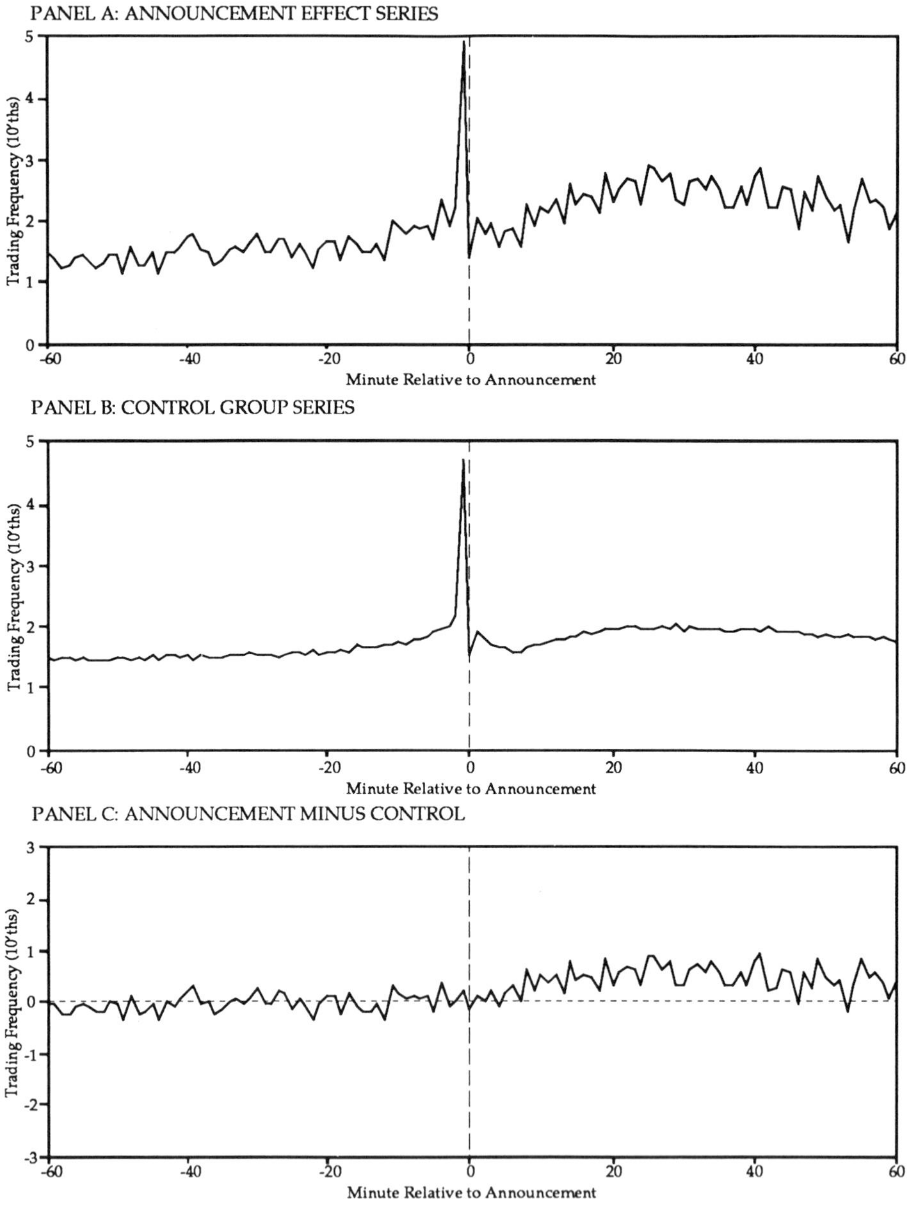

* Panel C uses a different scale than Panels A & B

FIGURE 5-9 CONTINUED
TRADING FREQUENCY (TRANSACTIONS PER MINUTE):
CALENDAR TIME FOR FIRST/LAST HALF HOURS SUBSAMPLE*

PANEL A: ANNOUNCEMENT EFFECT SERIES

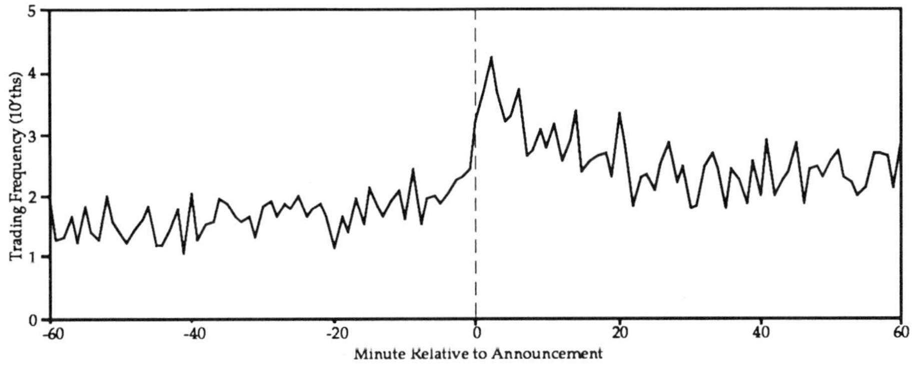

PANEL B: CONTROL GROUP SERIES

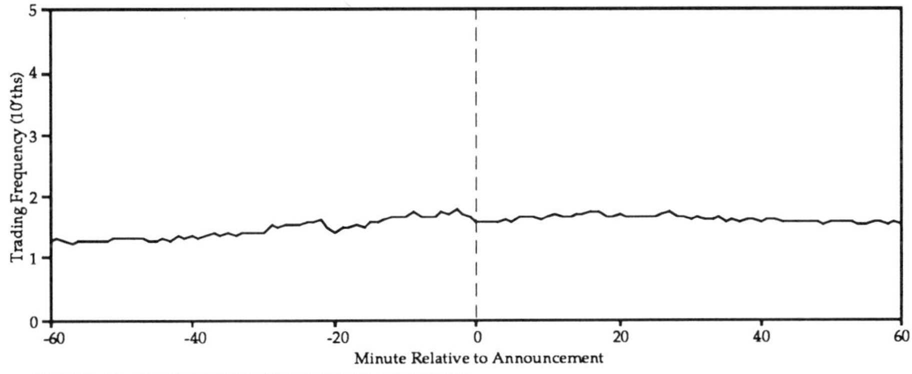

PANEL C: ANNOUNCEMENT MINUS CONTROL

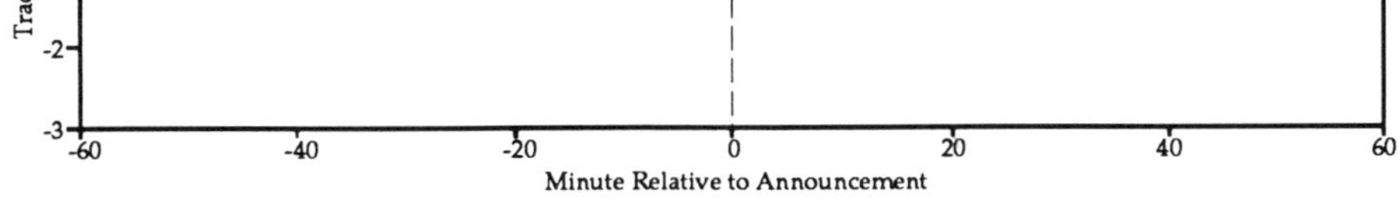

* Panel C uses a different scale than Panels A & B

FIGURE 5-9 CONTINUED
TRADING FREQUENCY (TRANSACTIONS PER MINUTE):
CALENDAR TIME FOR 10:30 TO 3:30 SUBSAMPLE*

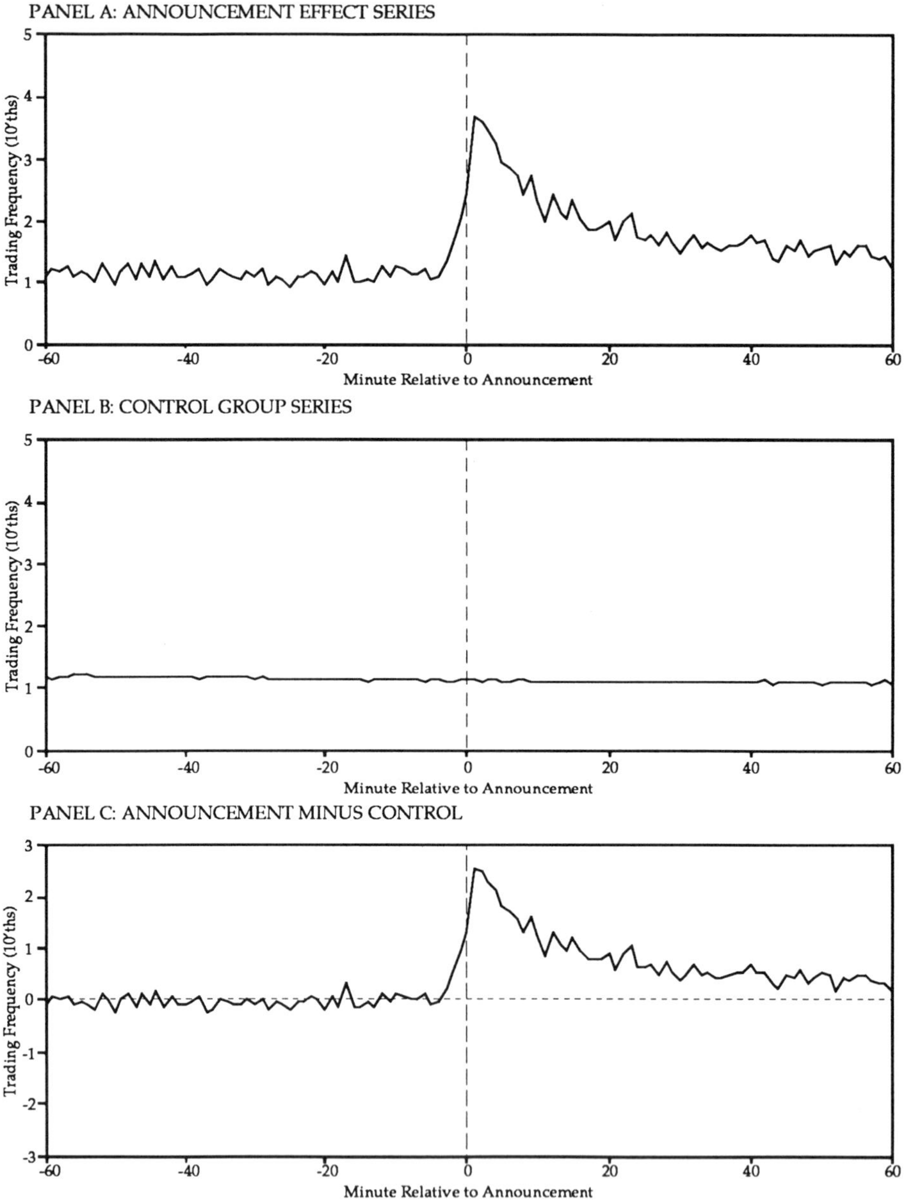

* Panel C uses a different scale than Panels A & B

FIGURE 5-10
TRADING VOLUME (SHARES TRADED PER TRANSACTION): TRANSACTION TIME FOR FULL SAMPLE*

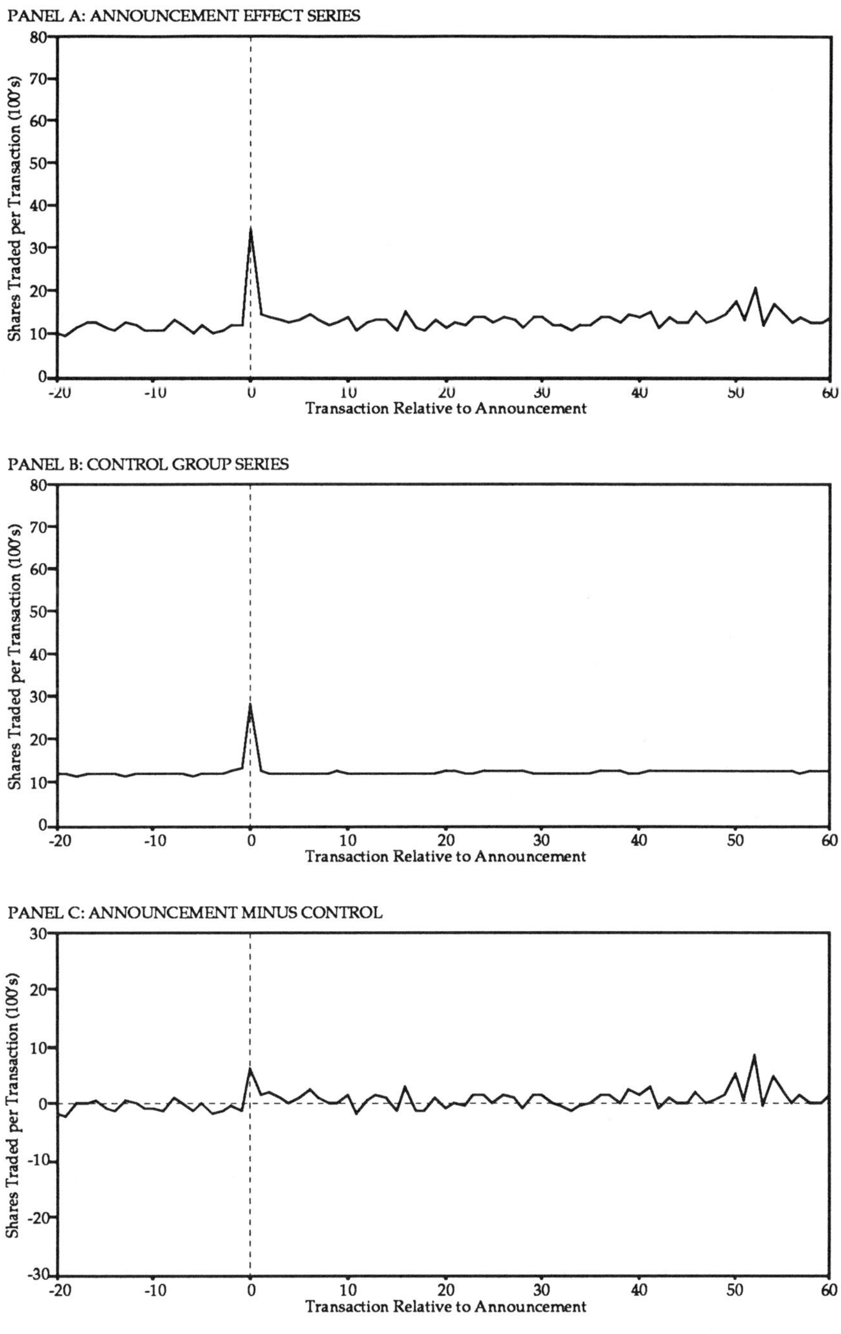

* Panel C uses a different scale than Panels A & B

FIGURE 5-11
TRADING VOLUME (SHARES TRADED PER TRANSACTION): TRANSACTION TIME FOR OUTSIDE TRADING HOURS SUBSAMPLE*

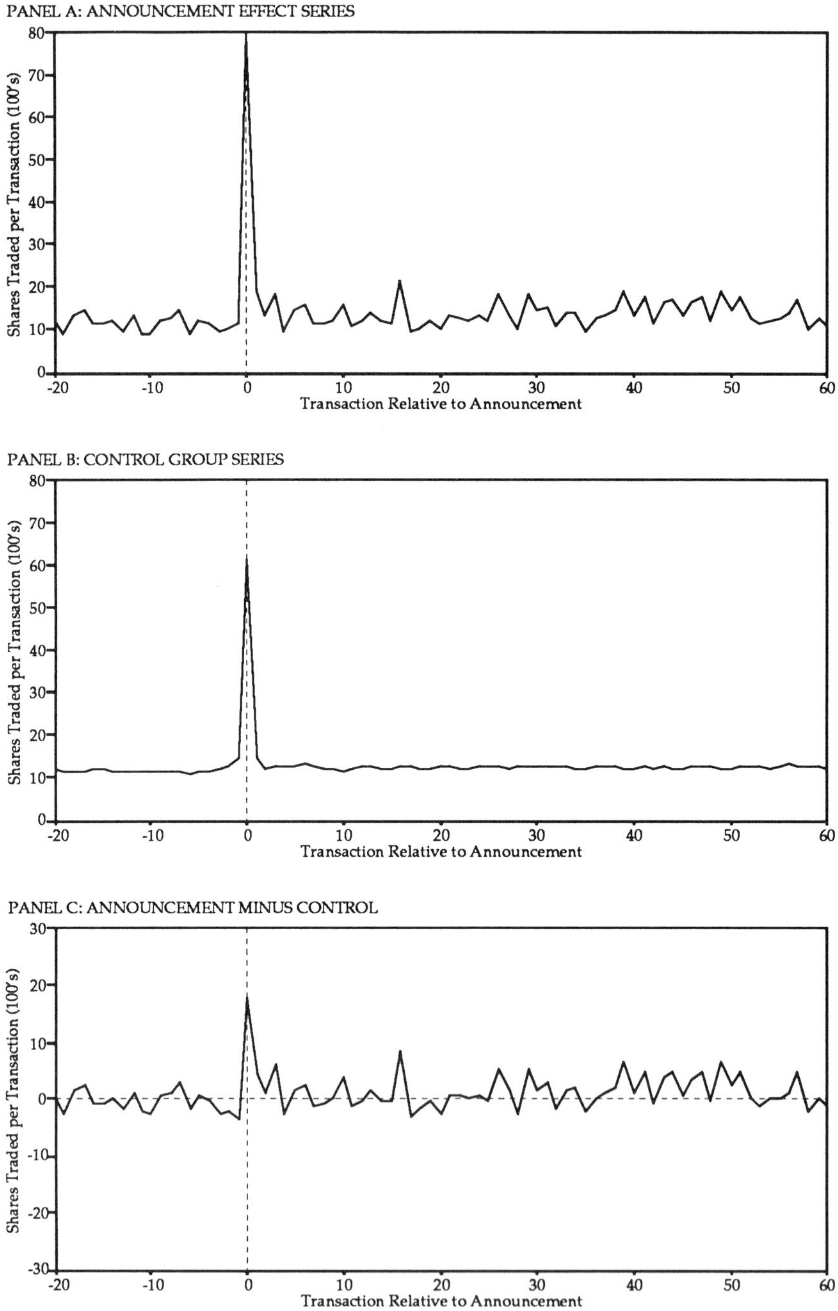

* Panel C uses a different scale than Panels A & B

FIGURE 5-11 CONTINUED
TRADING VOLUME (SHARES TRADED PER TRANSACTION):
TRANSACTION TIME FOR FIRST/LAST HALF HOURS SUBSAMPLE*

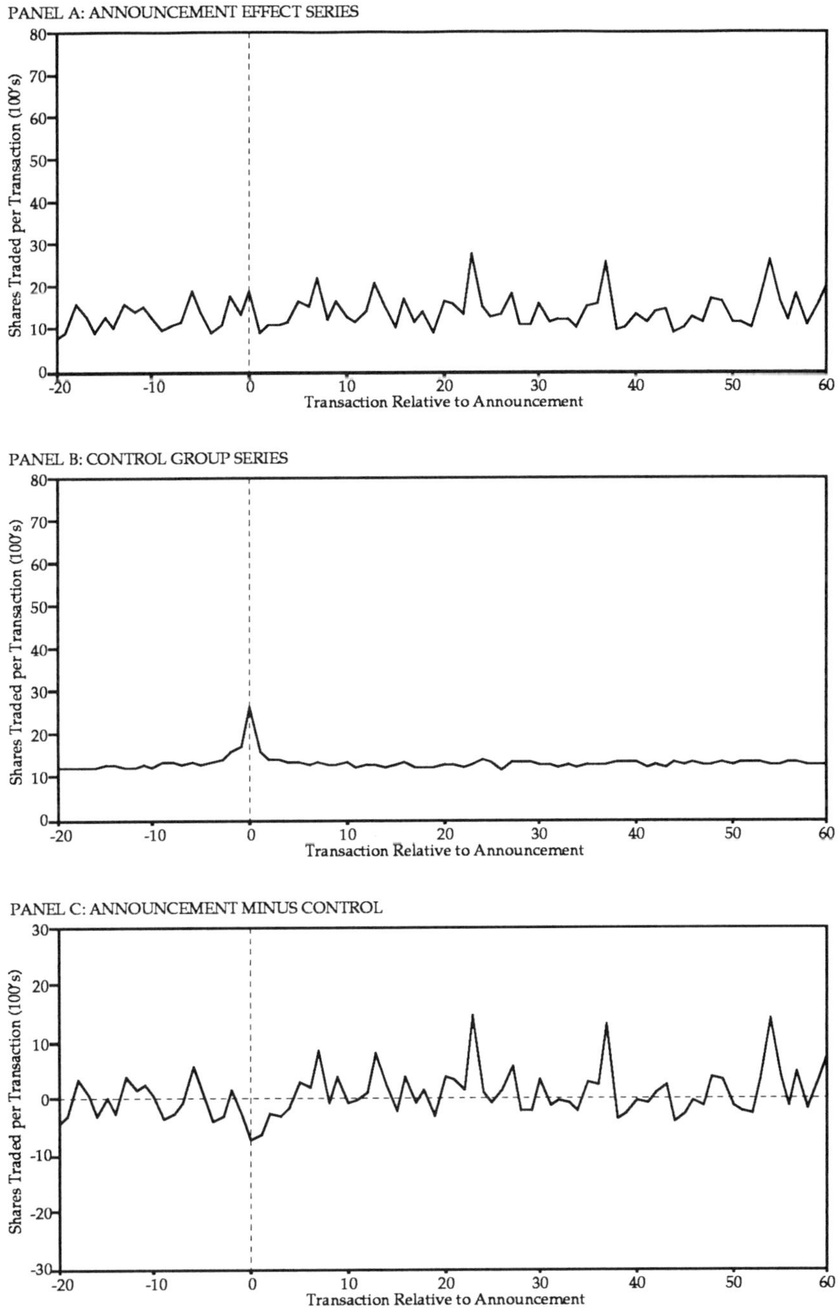

* Panel C uses a different scale than Panels A & B

FIGURE 5-11 CONTINUED
TRADING VOLUME (SHARES TRADED PER TRANSACTION): TRANSACTION TIME FOR 10:30 TO 3:30 SUBSAMPLE*

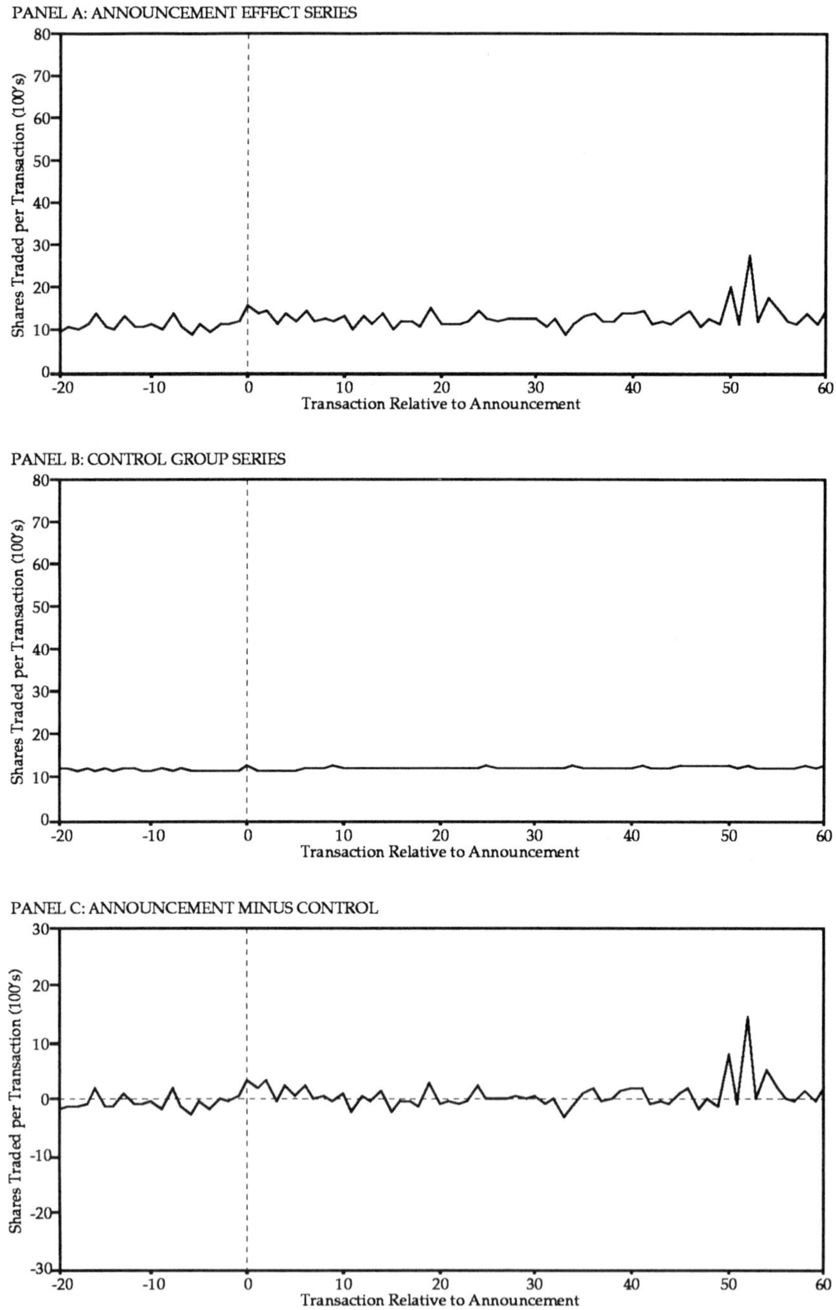

* Panel C uses a different scale than Panels A & B

FIGURE 5-12
TRADING VOLUME (SHARES TRADED PER MINUTE): CALENDAR TIME FOR FULL SAMPLE*

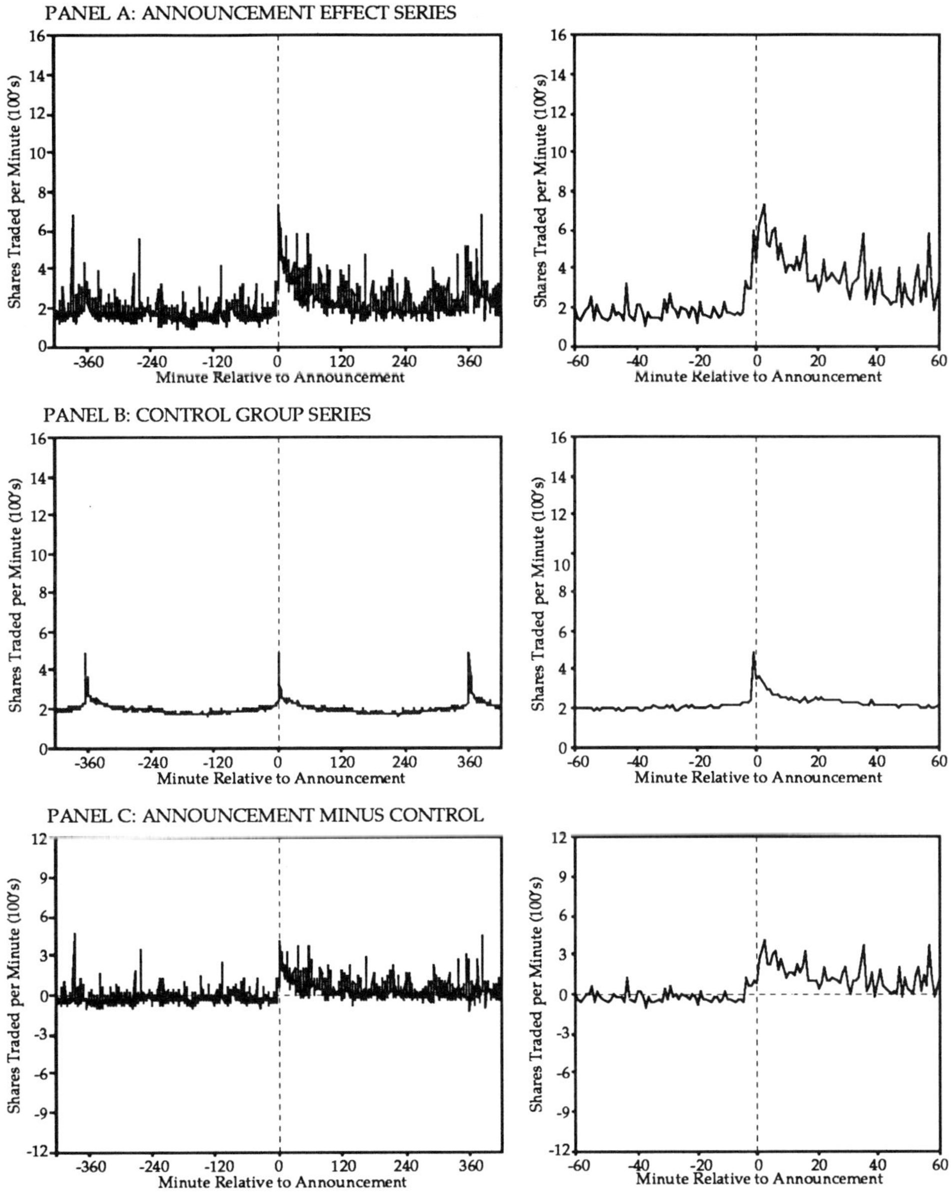

* Panel C uses a different scale than Panels A & B

FIGURE 5-13
TRADING VOLUME (SHARES TRADED PER MINUTE):
CALENDAR TIME FOR OUTSIDE TRADING HOURS SUBSAMPLE*

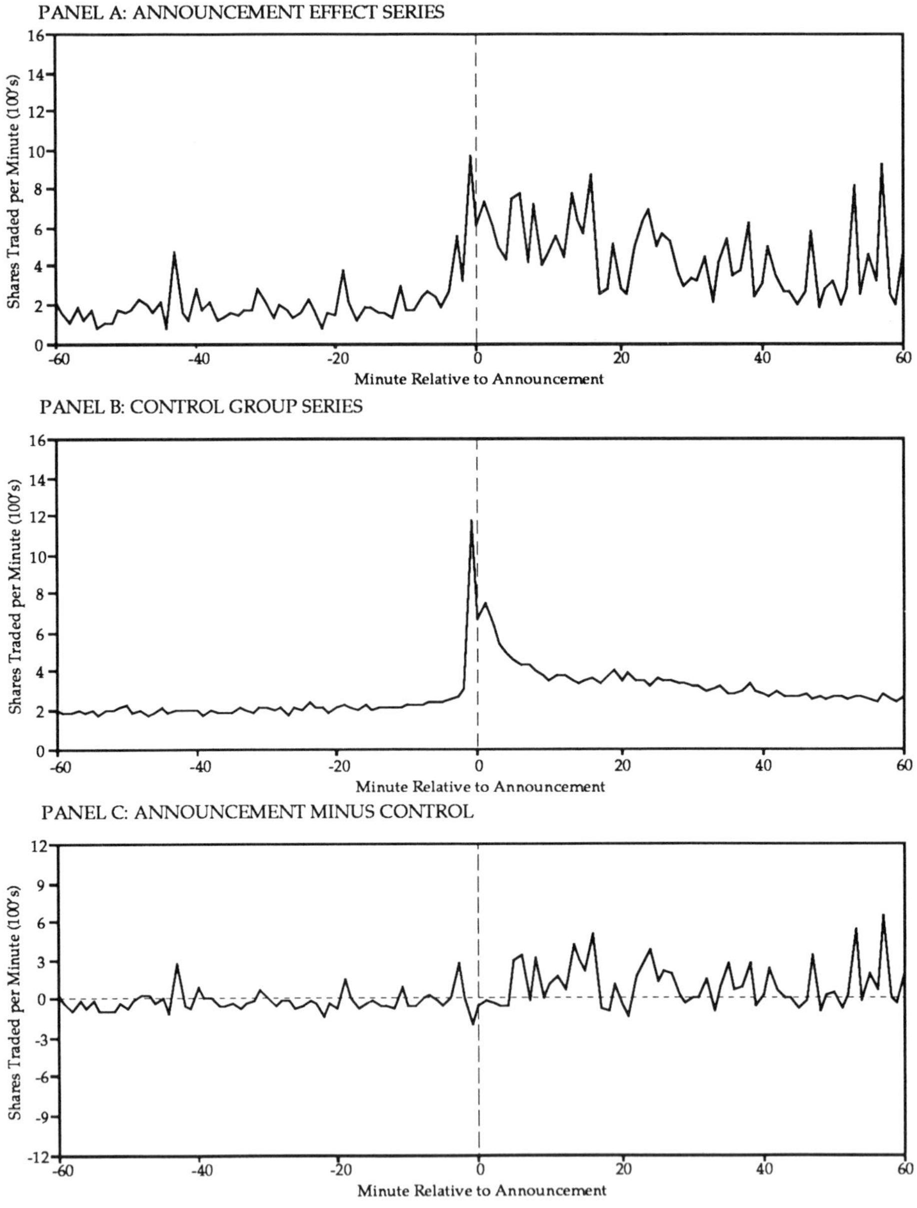

* Panel C uses a different scale than Panels A & B

FIGURE 5-13 CONTINUED
TRADING VOLUME (SHARES TRADED PER MINUTE):
CALENDAR TIME FOR FIRST/LAST HALF HOURS SUBSAMPLE*

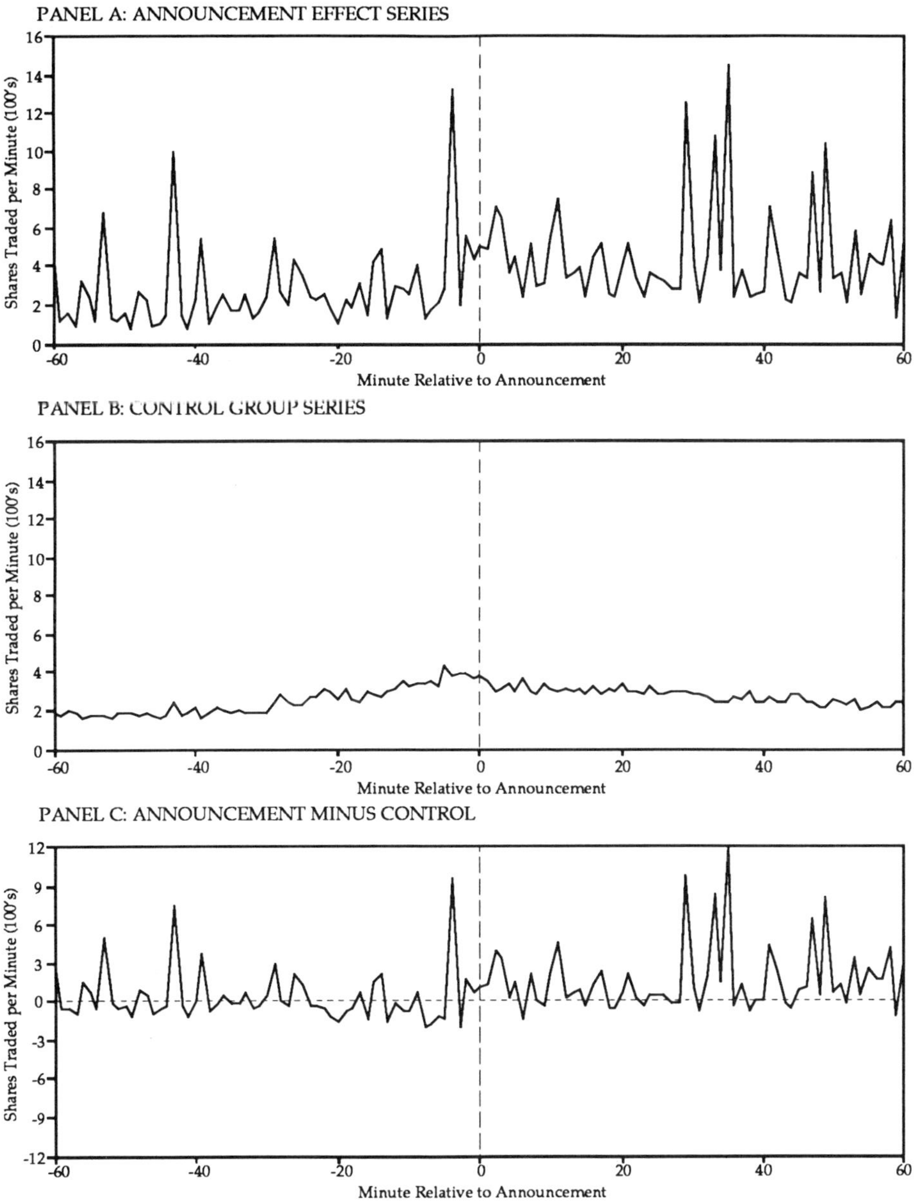

* Panel C uses a different scale than Panels A & B

FIGURE 5-13 CONTINUED
TRADING VOLUME (SHARES TRADED PER MINUTE): CALENDAR TIME FOR 10:30 TO 3:30 SUBSAMPLE*

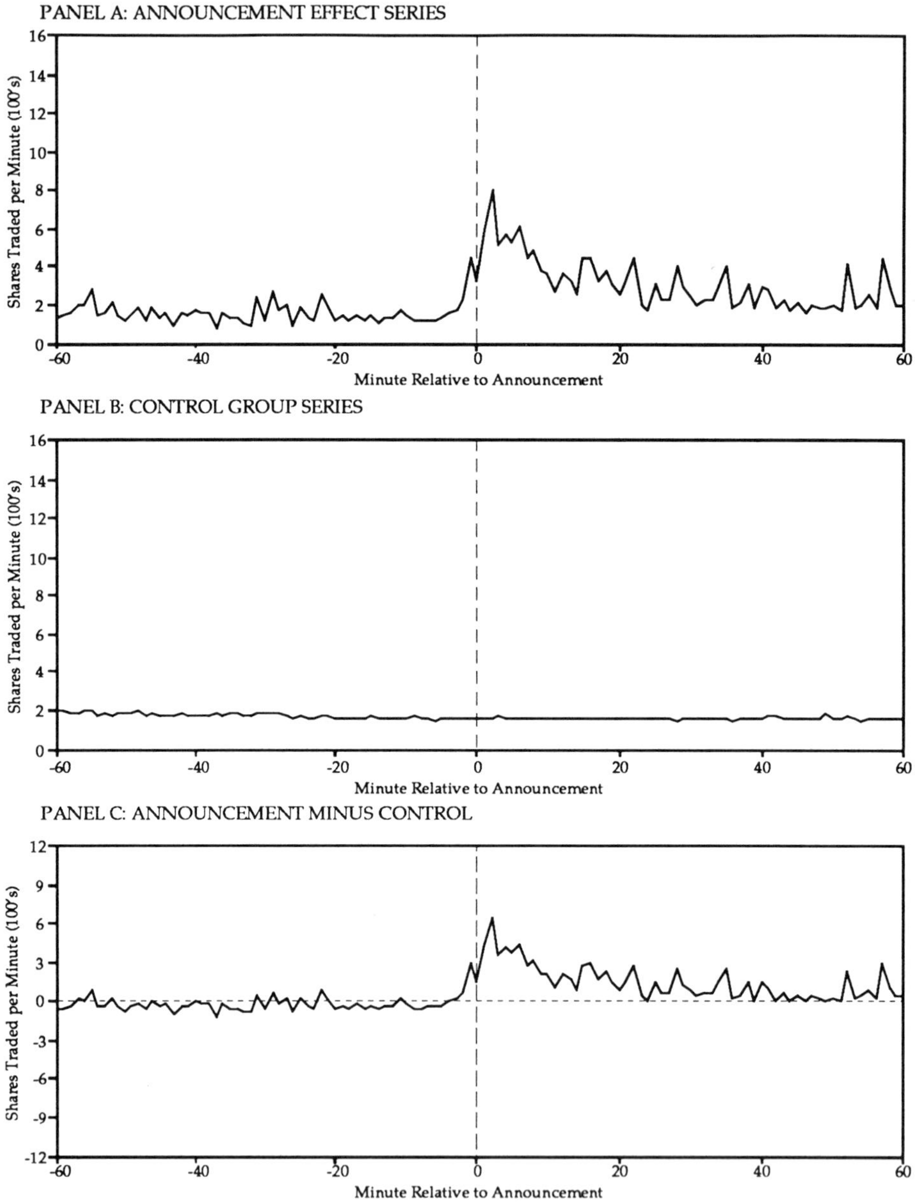

* Panel C uses a different scale than Panels A & B

FIGURE 5-14
CUMULATIVE RETURNS: TRANSACTION TIME FOR FULL SAMPLE

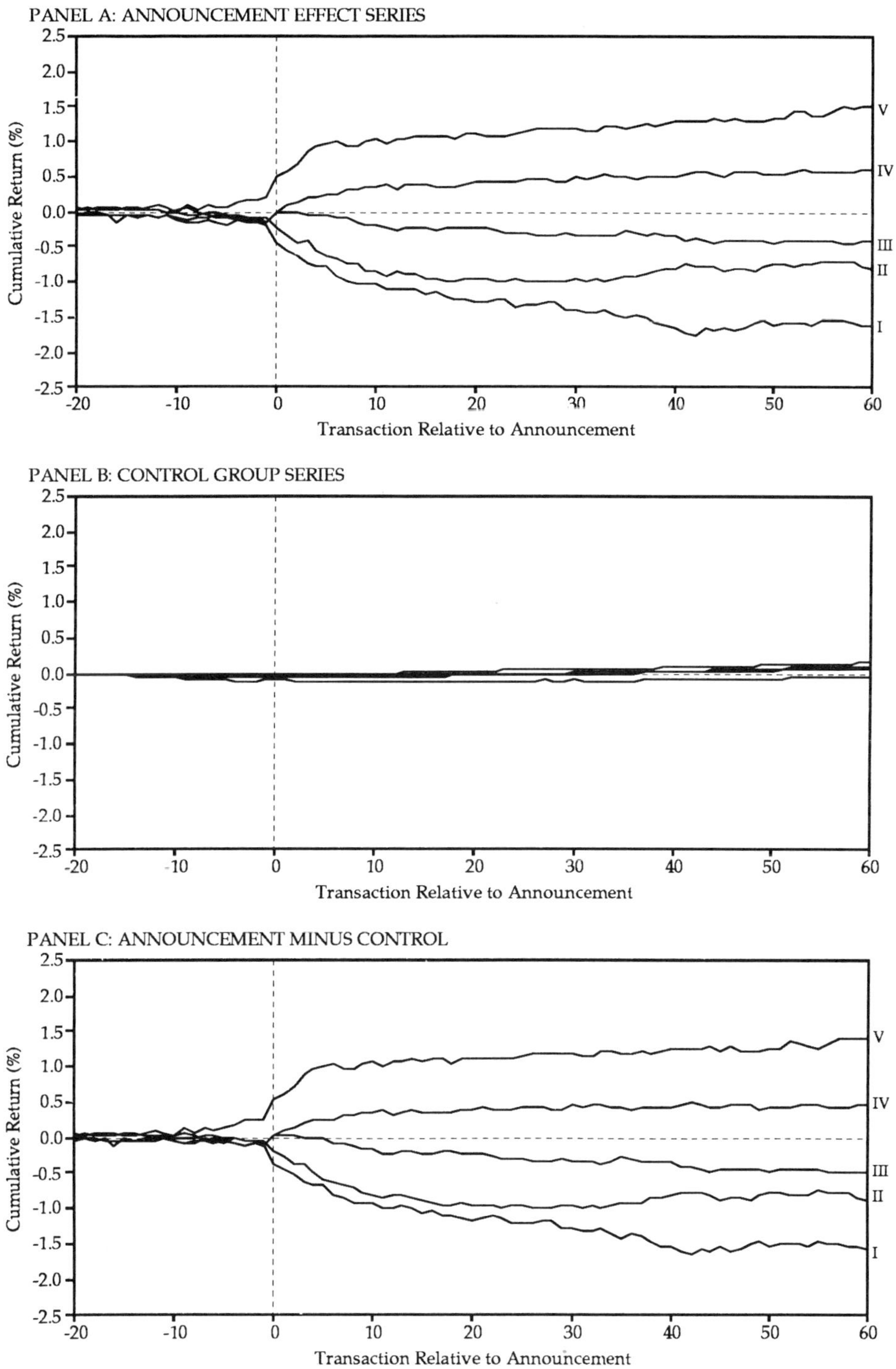

EXHIBIT 5-15
CUMULATIVE RETURNS: TRANSACTION TIME FOR OUTSIDE TRADING HOURS SUBSAMPLE

PANEL A: ANNOUNCEMENT EFFECT SERIES

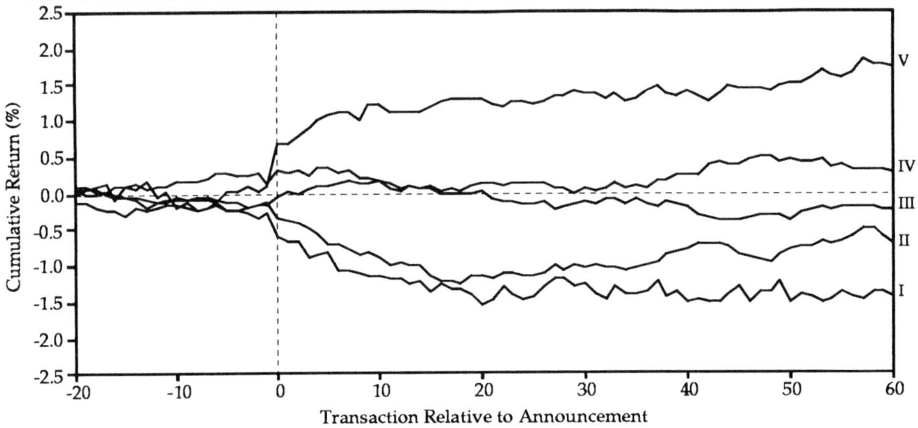

PANEL B: CONTROL GROUP SERIES

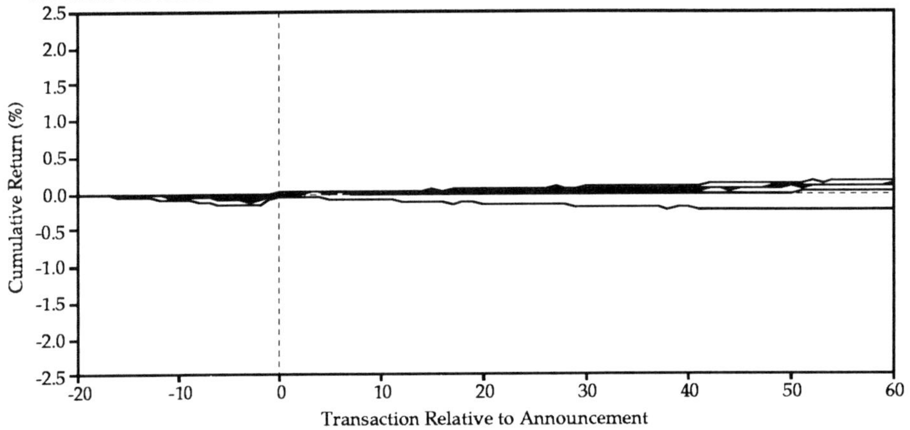

PANEL C: ANNOUNCEMENT MINUS CONTROL

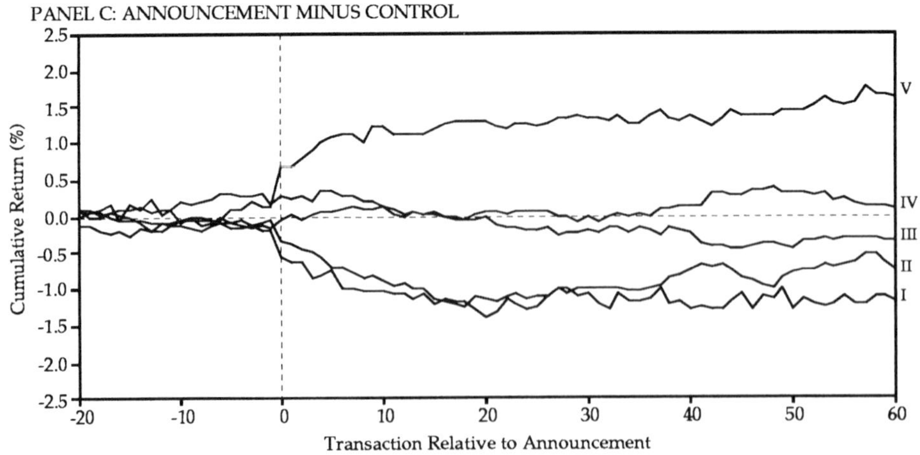

EXHIBIT 5-15 CONTINUED
CUMULATIVE RETURNS: TRANSACTION TIME FOR FIRST/LAST HALF HOURS SUBSAMPLE

PANEL A: ANNOUNCEMENT EFFECT SERIES

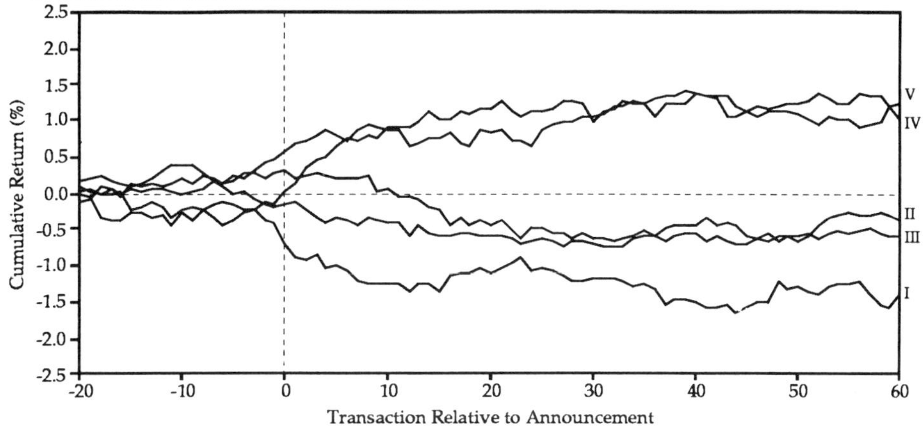

PANEL B: CONTROL GROUP SERIES

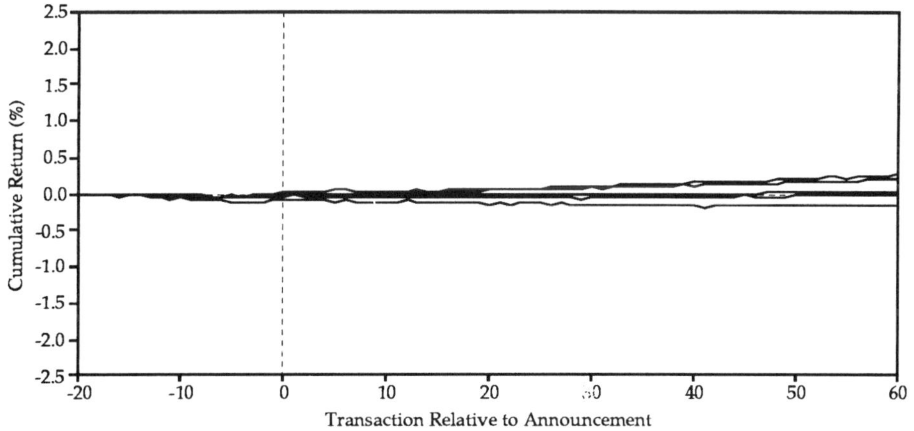

PANEL C: ANNOUNCEMENT MINUS CONTROL

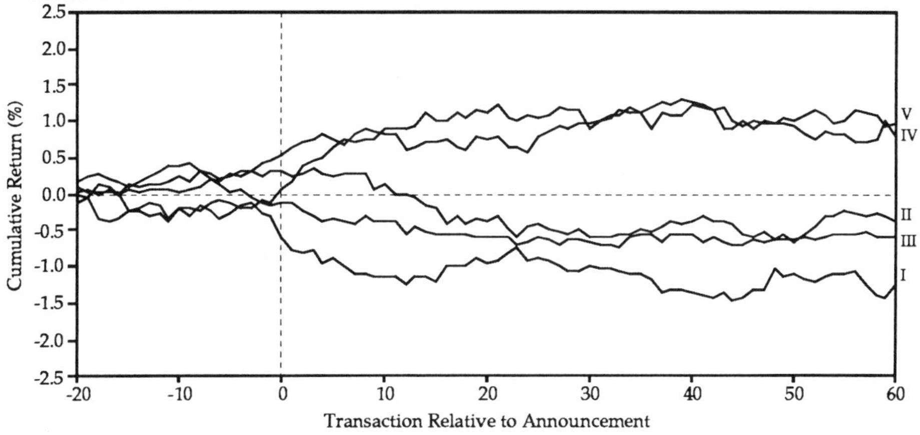

EXHIBIT 5-15 CONTINUED
CUMULATIVE RETURNS: TRANSACTION TIME FOR 10:30 TO 3:30 SUBSAMPLE

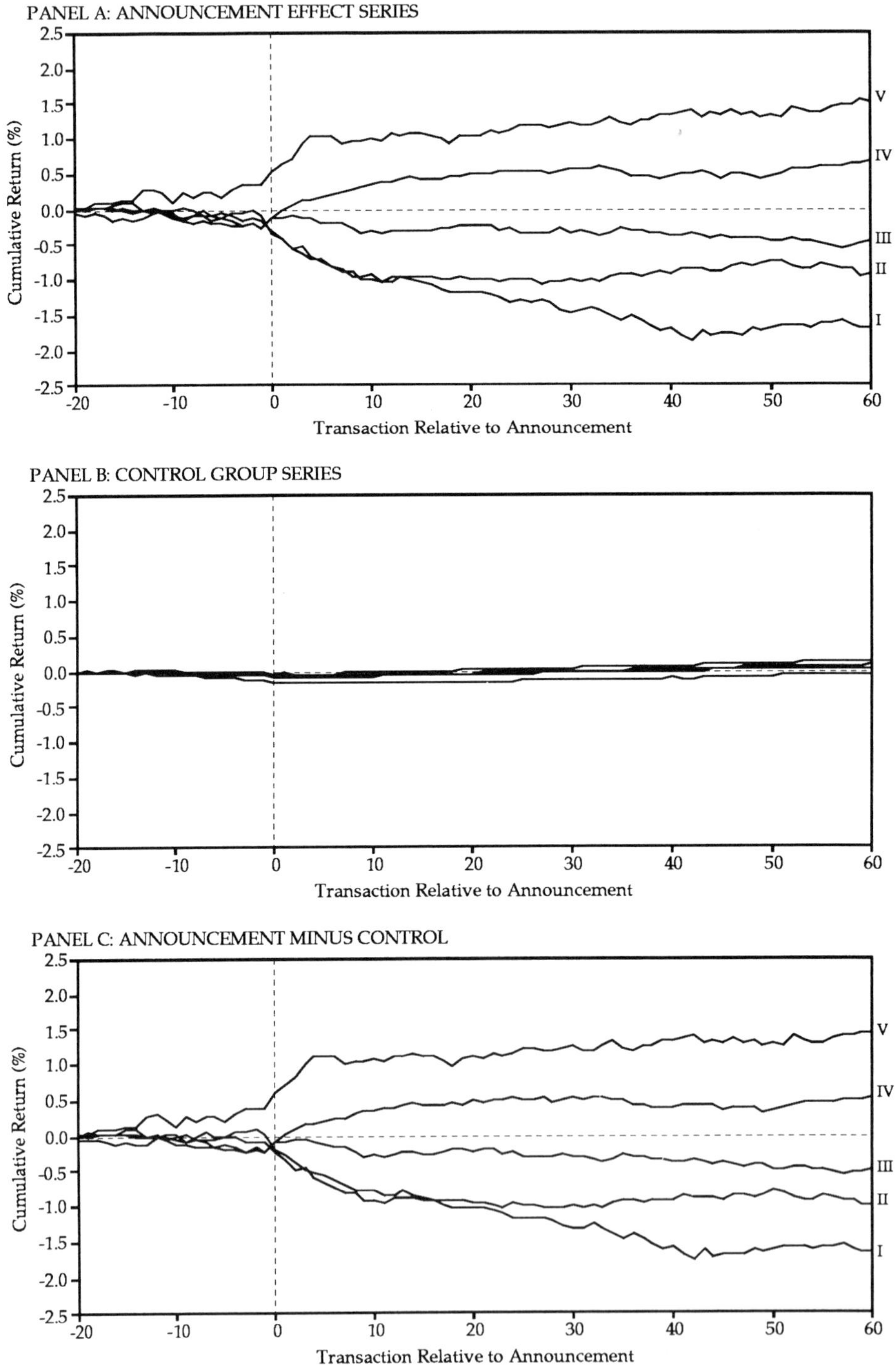

EXHIBIT 5-16
CALENDAR TIME: CUMULATIVE RETURNS FOR FULL-SAMPLE

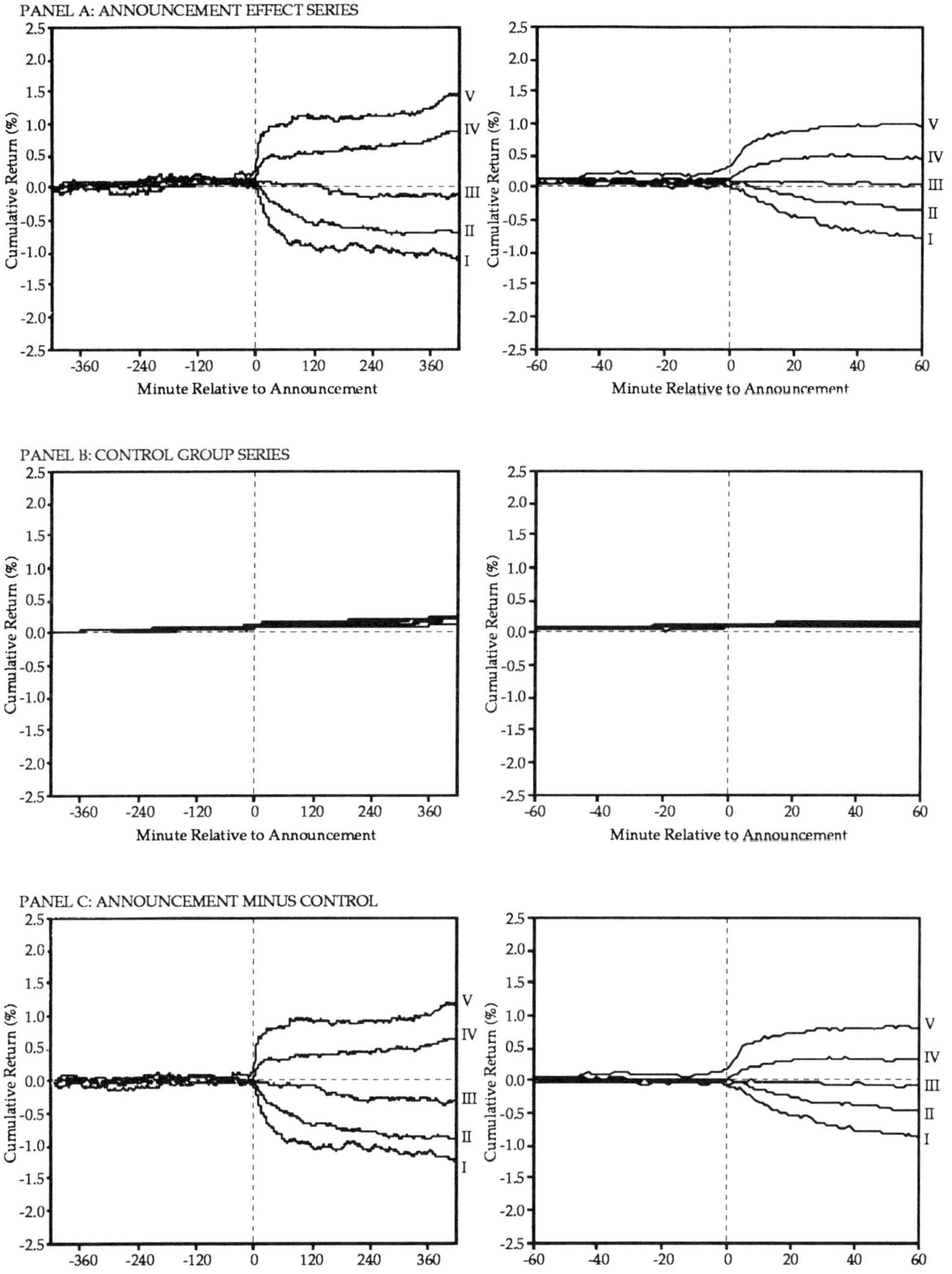

EXHIBIT 5-17
CUMULATIVE RETURNS:
CALENDAR TIME FOR OUTSIDE TRADING HOURS SUBSAMPLE

PANEL A: ANNOUNCEMENT EFFECT SERIES

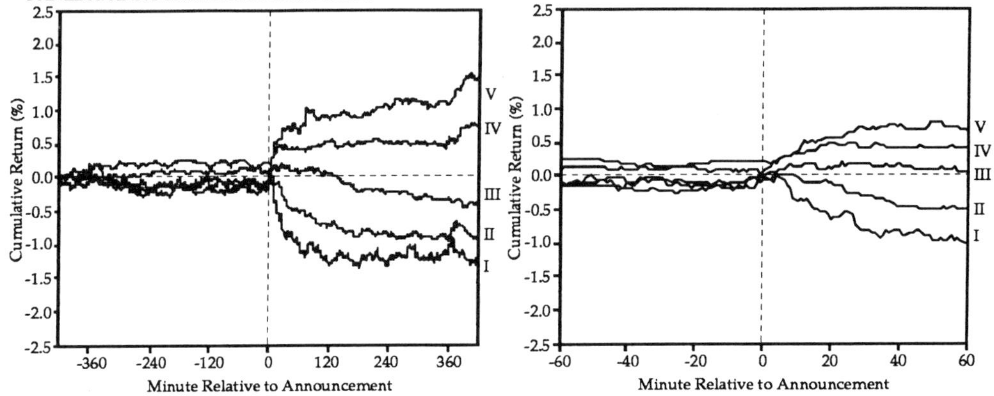

PANEL B: CONTROL GROUP SERIES

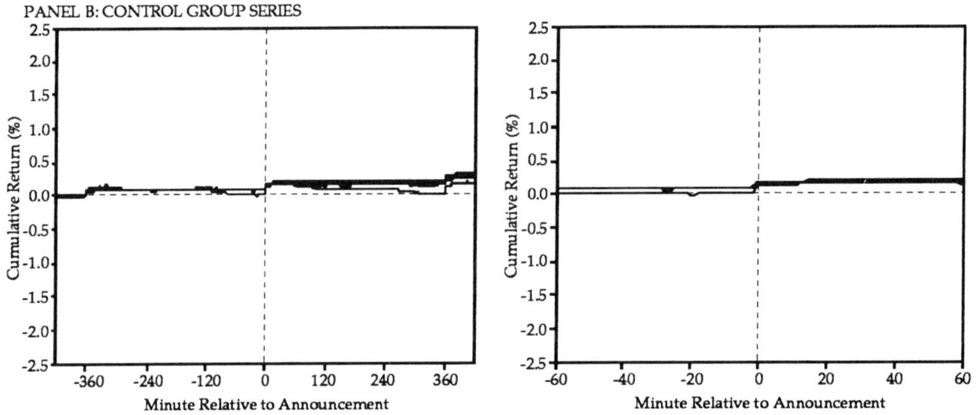

PANEL C: ANNOUNCEMENT MINUS CONTROL

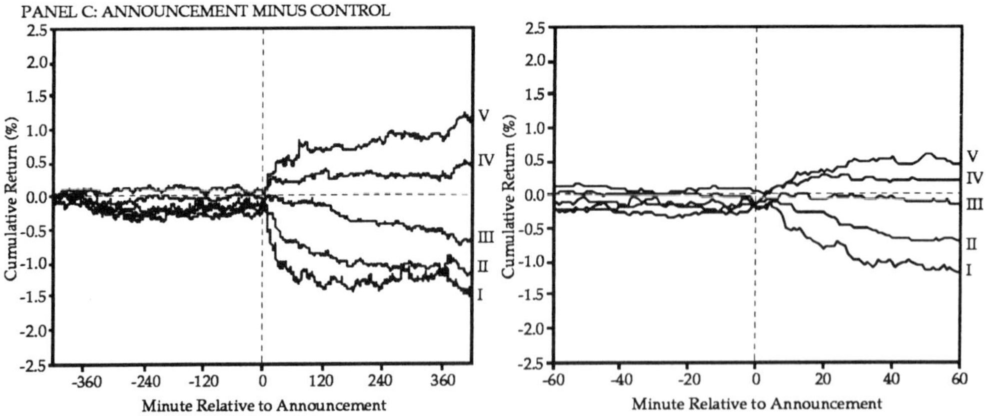

EXHIBIT 5-17 CONTINUED
CUMULATIVE RETURNS:
CALENDAR TIME FOR FIRST/LAST HALF HOURS SUBSAMPLE

PANEL A: ANNOUNCEMENT EFFECT SERIES

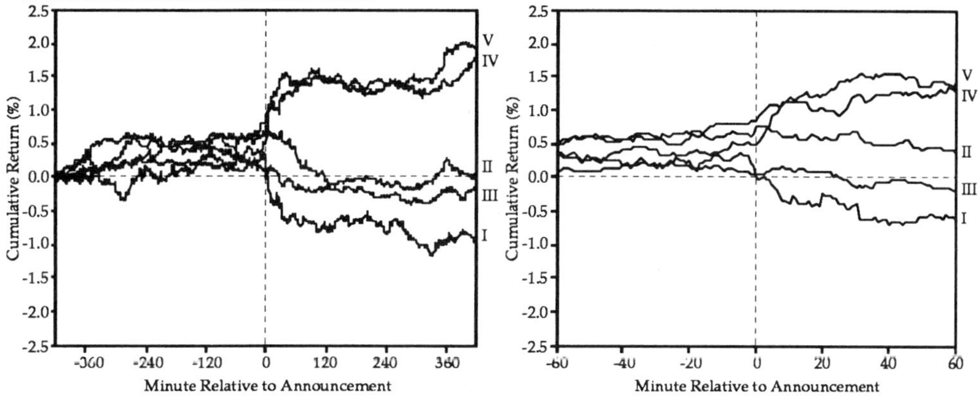

PANEL B: CONTROL GROUP SERIES

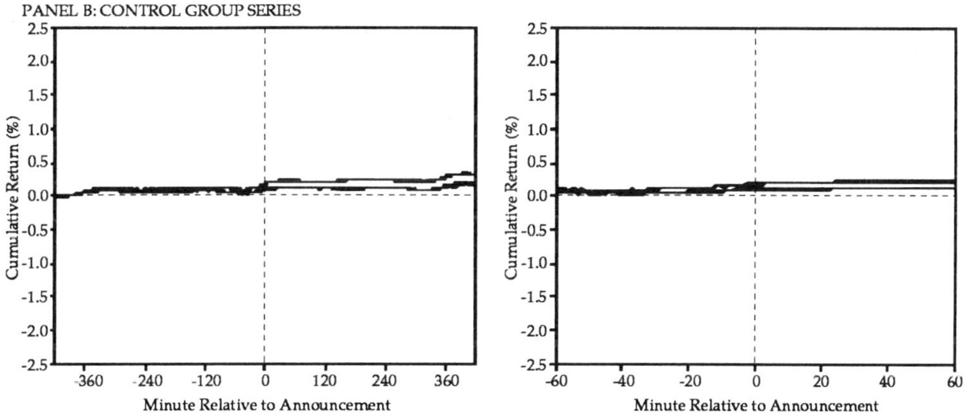

PANEL C: ANNOUNCEMENT MINUS CONTROL

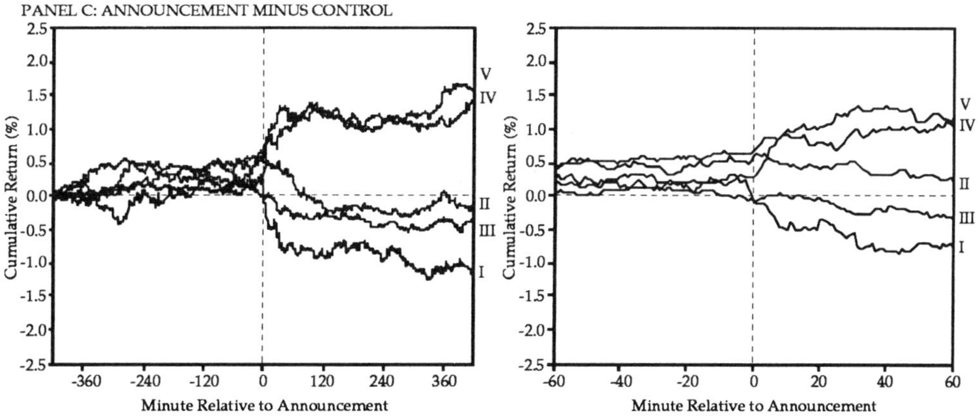

EXHIBIT 5-17 CONTINUED
CUMULATIVE RETURNS:
CALENDAR TIME FOR 10:30 TO 3:30 SUBSAMPLE

PANEL A: ANNOUNCEMENT EFFECT SERIES

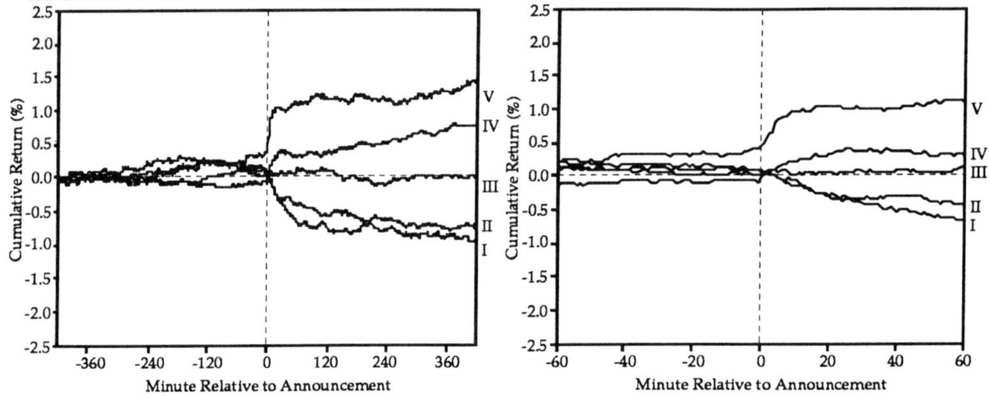

PANEL B: CONTROL GROUP SERIES

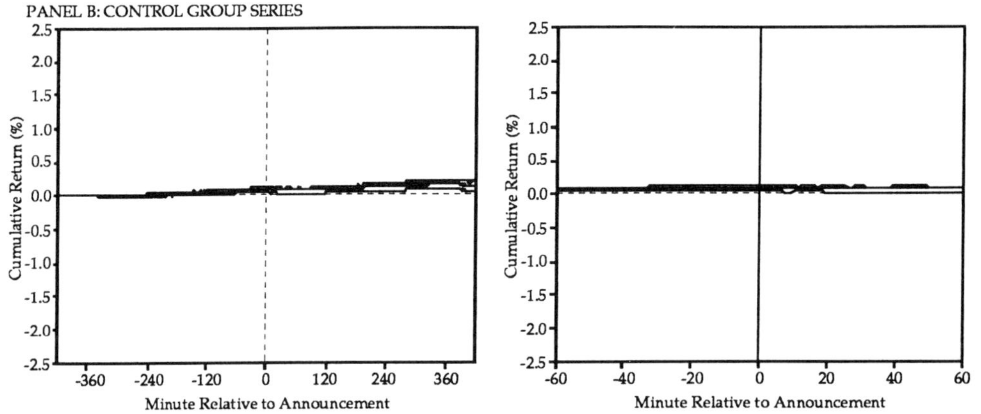

PANEL C: ANNOUNCEMENT MINUS CONTROL

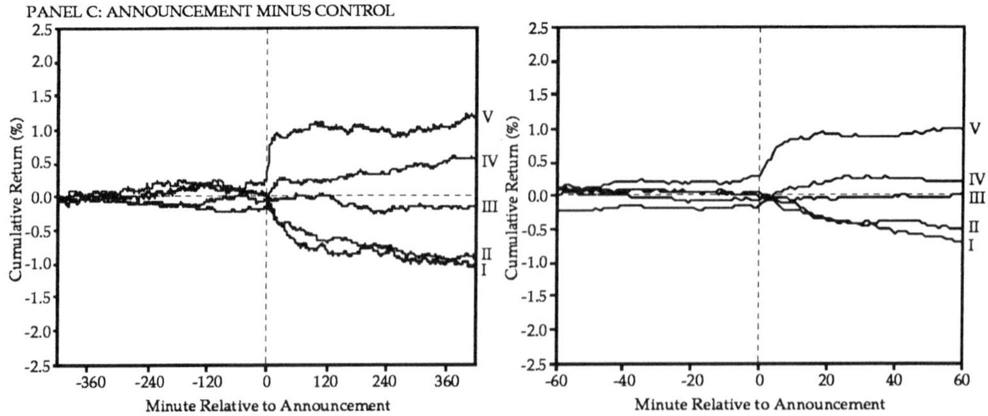

Chapter 6
Speed of Adjustment of Financial Series to Earnings Releases

6.1: Introduction and Overview

The speed of adjustment (SOA) of the capital market to an information release is of interest to a diverse set of persons, including security analysts, corporate management, regulators, and researchers. This chapter presents SOA results for four financial series at the time of earnings releases. Section 6.2 of this chapter outlines alternative approaches used to measure speed of adjustment. A step-by-step outline of the SOA measurement method we use is in Section 6.3. Distribution evidence on the speed of adjustment for the four series examined is presented in Section 6.4. The median SOA measures we report for the full sample are: absolute cumulative returns (adjust by the 9th transaction), security return variability (10th transaction), trading frequency (8th transaction), and trading volume (4th transaction).

6.2: Alternative Approaches to Measuring Speed of Adjustment

This section outlines alternative approaches to measuring the speed of adjustment based on a statistical analysis of release and nonrelease periods.[1] Our objective in measuring SOA, relating to an information release, is to estimate the number of transactions taken before the capital market returns to "normal" activity. Normal activity refers to how the market would behave in the absence of the information event of interest. Since this is not observable, estimation of SOA involves both a specification of what constitutes normal market activity (a comparison benchmark), and a procedure to determine whether market activity surrounding an announcement is different from the benchmark.

The existing approaches can be classified according to three criteria:

a. whether an individual information release or a more aggregate sample approach is used.
b. whether a parametric or non-parametric approach is used to specify the benchmark.
c. whether a local or global search procedure is used to determine if market activity surrounding an announcement departs from the chosen benchmark.

Individual vs. aggregate information release analysis

The most granular approach to measuring SOA is at the individual release level—see Hillmer and Yu [1979] for an example. This approach en-

[1] Appendix B provides more examples of this approach and two alternative approaches—a trading rule approach and a path to assumed full adjustment time approach.

ables probing the determinants of SOA using the maximum number of information releases available. The other end of the spectrum measures SOA at the aggregate sample level—see Patell and Wolfson [1984] for an example. An aggregate sample approach will diversify the measurement error in more granular approaches, but reduces the number of observations available to probe the determinants of SOA. This chapter focuses on estimating SOA at the individual release level, in part due to the limited prior research at this level.

Parametric and non-parametric approaches

One approach to specifying the appropriate benchmark for market activity, in the absence of an information event, is to characterize the probability distribution governing the market activity metric being employed (e.g., security return variability, trading volume, etc.). For example, Hillmer and Yu [1979] assume that short term price changes (over 10, 20, 30 and 60 minute intervals) are independently normally distributed with constant mean and variance in the absence of an information event (estimated from non-announcement periods). Based on this assumption, they are able to employ a cumulative sum procedure. They exploit the properties of the normal distribution to estimate if, and for how long, the process of price change departs from the benchmark distribution around an earnings announcement. Similarly, Defeo [1986] assumes normality and independence for the benchmark distribution to estimate SOA intervals using daily data surrounding earnings announcements.

The advantage of the parametric approach to specifying the appropriate comparison benchmark is to provide more powerful SOA estimates so long as the assumed parametric form is accurate. However, as the evidence presented in Chapter 4 and elsewhere indicates, when transaction level data are used the assumptions of normality and independence are highly questionable. As a result, much previous research (e.g., Patell and Wolfson [1984] and Jennings and Starks [1985]) has employed non-parametric benchmark procedures in estimating transaction level SOA. Typically this involves using an empirical distribution generated from non-announcement period transaction data to act as the benchmark for comparison. In this way, the particular characteristics of transaction level data can be captured without an appeal to precise parametric assumptions. A non-parametric approach is used in Chapters 5 and 6 of this monograph.

Local versus global procedures for comparison with benchmark

Once a benchmark has been chosen (parametric or non-parametric), a procedure is required to compare market activity around an announcement to the benchmark. Most prior research has employed a "local" procedure for determining whether activity surrounding an announcement departs from the benchmark. This simply involves beginning at the time of the announcement and expanding the estimated SOA until the activity with the SOA period is no longer significantly different from the benchmark distribution. For instance, Hillmer and Yu [1979] employ a local approach based on their parametric assumptions. Similarly, Patell and Wolfson [1984] and Jennings and Starks [1985] both employ a local search procedure based on a non-parametric (empirically generated) benchmark.

An advantage of the local procedure is its reasonably light computing demands (relative to a global procedure—see below). However, a disadvantage is that it will tend to underestimate the period of adjustment. This will be true if market adjustment is spread out over a period of transactions/time with the announcement effect decaying with time. It will also be true if there is some initial delay to adjustment. For example, if several transactions/minutes elapse before market activity is affected by an announcement, the local approach will underestimate the SOA interval.

An alternative approach is to conduct a global search (over a pre-specified interval) for the appropriate SOA estimate. This involves computing market activity (security return variability, trading volume, etc.) for each potential interval in the chosen window, and then choosing that interval which best reflects a departure from the benchmark. For example, Defeo [1986] employs a global procedure using daily data to estimate the number of days surrounding earnings announcements over which returns differ from the comparison benchmark. A global approach is also used in this monograph.

The global procedure overcomes the underestimation problem of the local approach since it considers all possible SOA intervals in the chosen window. However, it potentially suffers from overestimation of the SOA interval when an announcement has little or no effect on market activity.

6.3: Steps in Speed of Adjustment Measurement Method

We measure SOA associated with each announcement in our sample using a global non-parametric approach. Our estimates are made only in transaction time since at short intervals (of one trading minute, for example) calendar time analysis results in many minutes with no transactions. Our procedure involves several steps (illustrated using the trading volume series):

STEP ONE: For each earnings announcement, compute the number of shares traded per transaction (Xt) for each transaction in the [-1T, +60T] period. Convert the series into the cumulative number of shares traded, beginning with transaction -1T.

STEP TWO: Using the actual earnings announcement time of day, develop a comparable (control group) cumulative series to that in Step One for each trading day, in that calendar year, that is not within one trading day of an earnings release. For example, if firm AA releases earnings at 10:59 A.M. of the announcement day, we construct a [-1T, +60T] window around 10:59 A.M.

on each non-announcement day during the year for AA. These non-announcement windows constitute the control benchmark distribution used for comparison.

STEP THREE: Compute the p value of each transaction interval in the [-1T, +60T] window surrounding transaction 0T. This involves considering 132 intervals, from [-1T, 0T], . . . , [-1T, +60T] through [0T, 0T], . . . , [0T, +60T]. For each interval, the p value was determined by comparing the cumulative volume for the announcement series with the control distribution of cumulative volumes for the same transaction interval. (As a result, this step involved constructing 132 control group distributions.) The p value was computed as the relative frequency with which the announcement series exceeded the control group series distribution for that particular transaction interval.

STEP FOUR: Identify the highest p value obtained from Step Three. The transaction interval associated with this p value represents the SOA interval. The right hand term in the interval represents the estimated SOA (in number of transactions) following the earnings announcement.

STEP FIVE: Repeat Steps one to four using the [0T, +60T] period. Select the highest p value in the [0T, +60T] period for each earnings announcement.

STEP SIX: The SOA measure will be the end transaction with the highest p value from Step four for the [-1T, +60T] interval and Step five for the [0T, +60T] interval.

The rationale for including both the [-1T, +60T] and [0T, +60T] intervals is to reduce the sensitivity of the findings to mismeasurement of the announcement time or anticipation of its release time. The results in Chapter 5 are consistent with any mismeasurement/anticipation being relatively minor. Results were also examined using the event window [-20T, +60T] in Step One, without any substantive change in the conclusions drawn in this chapter.

The intuition underlying the SOA measure used in this monograph is: "Does adding an extra transaction or additional set of transactions up to +60T increase the statistical significance of the difference between the earnings announcement series and the control series?" Our control series will explicitly incorporate systematic intraday patterns in each series into the estimation of the SOA to each earnings release.

As noted in Section 6.2, our global search procedure potentially overestimates the SOA when there is little or no significant reaction to an announcement. This occurs because, even in the absence of a significant reaction, our procedure continues to pick out a SOA estimate. However, with no reaction to the announcement, each of the transactions following 0T will have an approximately equal chance of being selected, resulting in an average SOA of around 30 transactions. Thus, even if a subsample of announcements experiences a significant and rapid reaction, our full sample average (or distribution) may be "stretched out" by the inclusion of announcements with no significant reaction. (As mentioned in Section 6.2, this is the opposite of what would occur if a local search procedure had been used.)

In addition, it may not be appropriate to restrict attention to the subsample of announcements that has a significant reaction in the transaction or two following the announcement since this presupposes a particular response pattern to the announcement. (For example, this approach would exclude cases where the response does not begin, or is weak, until a few transactions following the announcement.) As a consequence, we provide SOA results for the full sample, and for a subsample based on the p value for each SOA (from Step 4 of our procedure).

Note that all SOA measures we report are computed at the individual earnings release level. There is potentially a high level of noise when measuring SOA at this level.

6.4: Distribution Statistics for Speed of Adjustment

SOA measures for the following four financial series are examined in this section:

- Absolute cumulative return. The cumulative return over the horizon interval is computed and then its absolute value taken. Use of the absolute value facilitates cross-sectional analysis of the variables that may explain differences in SOA across the sample.
- Security return variability—mean of the absolute value of each security price change. (We use this measure rather than absolute rate of return to reduce the impact of the discrete nature of transaction prices on the SOA measure.)
- Trading frequency—time (in trading minutes) between transactions.
- Trading volume—number of shares traded per transaction.

Plots of the SOA distribution for these four financial series are presented in Figures 6-1 to 6-8. For each series we present two plots, one for the full sample, the other for the three subsamples examined in Chapter 5—(a) earnings releases made outside trading hours, (b) earnings releases made at the start or end of trading (first and last half hours of trading), and (c) earnings releases made between 10:30 A.M. and 3:30 P.M. The SOA measure plotted in each figure is the end point (X) in the [-1T, +XT] or [0T, +XT] interval. Summary distribution statistics (.1, .3, .5, .7, and .9 deciles) underlying these figures are in columns (2) to (5) of Exhibit 6-1, while columns (6) to (9) report the number of trading minutes that correspond to the adjustment periods in columns (2) to (5).

Several patterns are common across Figures 6-1 to 6-8. First, all the SOA distributions are highly skewed. The median SOA values for the full sample are:

Absolute cumulative returns	9th transaction
Security return variability	10th transaction
Trading frequency	8th transaction
Trading volume	4th transaction

These median SOA values are all substantially less than the midpoint in the [-1T, +60T] interval.

The highest percentage of announcements in each full sample (i.e., the modes) have an end point of 0T in the [-1T, +60T] interval. This is consistent with a greater than expected number of observations having a rapid speed of adjustment to the earnings release.

The analysis in Exhibit 6-1 was repeated using only observations with a p-value greater than .95 for transaction 0. There was no major change in the inferences drawn in this chapter—Exhibit 6-2. For example, the median SOA values for the full sample and the subsample with a p-value greater than .95 are:

	Full Sample	Subsample Significant (p≥ .95 at Transaction 0)
Absolute cumulative returns	9th transaction	8th transaction
Security return variability	10th transaction	9th transaction
Trading frequency	8th transaction	7th transaction
Trading volume	4th transaction	7th transaction

Results for the three earnings release partitions (outside releases, start/end releases, and 10:30 A.M. to 3:30 P.M.) likewise show few major differences between the full sample in Exhibit 6-1 and the subsample in Exhibit 6-2. There is little evidence that our SOA median estimate for the full sample has been substantially "stretched out" by the inclusion of announcements with no significant reaction. (As with most results in this chapter, however, it may well be that our failure to observe this "stretch out" says more about the noise level in our individual information release SOA measures than about the use of a global search procedure for a sample including a subset of information releases with no significant reaction.)

The correlations between SOA measures across the four financial series are relatively low. Pearson correlations between pairwise combinations of the four series for the full sample of 1732 observations are:

	Security Return Variability	Trading Frequency	Trading Volume
Ab. (Cumulative Security Returns)	0.21	0.08	0.08
Security Return Variability		-0.03	0.07
Trading Frequency			0.02

Several explanations for these low correlations appear possible. One explanation is that each financial series captures a relatively independent dimension of capital market behavior. A second explanation is that the SOA measures have a low "information signal to noise" ratio at the individual information release level.

6.5: Explaining Speed of Adjustment Differences Across Earnings Releases

The SOA distributions in Figures 6-1 to 6-8 show sizable dispersion. This section probes the ability of several variables to explain the observed dispersion in our SOA measures. The analytical literature provides little explicit guidance on the determinants of SOA for the four financial series of interest. The three variables we examine (based, in part, on prior research—see, for example, Woodruff and Senchack [1988]) are:

- AB(UE): absolute value of the unexpected earnings measure used in Chapter 5. The absolute value is taken to facilitate the regression analysis. The coefficient on unexpected earnings may take a different sign depending on whether unexpected earnings are positive or negative; the use of absolute value avoids this problem.
- LOG(FS): log of firm size, where firm size is measured by market capitalization at the start of the year of the earnings release.
- LOG(TF): log of trading frequency, where trading frequency is measured by the number of transactions for the year of the earnings release.

Exhibit 6-3 reports results for the following multiple regression:

$$SOA_{i,t} = \alpha + \beta_1 \cdot AB(UE_{i,t}) + \beta_2 \cdot LOG(FS_{i,t}) + \beta_3 \cdot LOG(TF_{i,t}) + u_{i,t}$$

where $SOA_{i,t}$ is the speed of adjustment measure of the ith firm in quarter t. The results in Exhibit 6-3 show that these three variables have close to zero explanatory power in the linear multiple regression. The R^2 in Exhibit 6-3 ranges from a low of 0.00 to a high of 0.04.[2] The t-statistics on the β_1, β_2 and β_3 coefficients rarely reach conventional benchmarks for statistical significance.

Several additional tests were conducted to examine the sensitivity of our results to alternative specifications. One set of tests examined the effect of grouping our $SOA_{i,t}$ measures into portfolios prior to estimating the multiple regression. Grouping typically will increase the R^2 (in the limit, with 2 portfolios, the R^2 usually will be 1.00), but need not necessarily increase the efficiency of the β_1, β_2 and β_3 estimates. Exhibit 6-4 reports results for portfolios of size 1 (1732 observations), 5 (346 observations), 10 (173 observations) and 50 (34 observations). On balance, the results provide little support for differences in the $SOA_{i,t}$ measures being explained by the unexpected earnings, firm size and trading frequency variables. The mean of each portfolio variable is used in computing the regression results in Exhibit 6-4. There was little change in the results when the median of the observations underlying each portfolio variable was used.

Regression results were also examined for the subset of $SOA_{i,t}$ measures that were significantly different from the control group at the .05 level (823 of

---

[2] The explanatory power (R^2) of the regression in Exhibit 6-3 for the subsample with p-values greater than .95 at transaction 0 is similarly low:

	R^2 for Full Sample	**R^2 for Releases with ($p \geq .95$) at Transaction 0**
Absolute cumulative returns	0.00	0.00
Security return variability	0.01	0.00
Trading frequency	0.00	0.02
Trading volume	0.00	0.02

the 1732 observations). Inferences drawn from Exhibits 6-3 and 6-4 were not affected by this sample selection change.

Summary

The $SOA_{i,t}$ measures reported in this chapter probably contain a high degree of "noise". The steps taken to compute each $SOA_{i,t}$ were developed to recognize systematic patterns in intraday data documented in Chapter 4. It is likely that even after controlling for these patterns, there is still a sizable component of intraday behavior that is related to institutional aspects that currently we do not understand.

EXHIBIT 6-1
DISTRIBUTION STATISTICS FOR SPEED OF ADJUSTMENT (SOA) AT THE INDIVIDUAL EARNINGS RELEASE LEVEL*: FULL SAMPLE

	NUMBER OF TRANSACTIONS				NUMBER OF TRADING MINUTES			
	ABS. CUM. RET.	SEC. PRICE VARIAB.	TRAD. FREQ.	TRAD. VOL.	ABS. CUM. RET.	SEC. PRICE VARIAB.	TRAD. FREQ.	TRAD. VOL.
(1)	(2)	(3)	(4)	(5)	(6)	(7)	(8)	(9)
A. TOTAL SAMPLE								
.1 Decile	0	0	1	0	13	13	5	7
.3 "	4	3	3	1	44	48	21	26
.5 "	9	10	8	4	115	130	57	74
.7 "	22	28	20	16	287	344	162	227
.9 "	48	54	51	45	792	1034	633	752
B. OUTSIDE TRADING HOURS								
.1 Decile	0	0	0	0	13	14	5	7
.3 "	4	3	3	1	48	49	23	29
.5 "	9	10	9	4	121	135	60	77
.7 "	23	29	21	17	302	366	170	236
.9 "	49	54	51	47	813	1027	671	790
C. FIRST/LAST HALF HOURS								
.1 Decile	1	0	1	0	11	13	4	4
.3 "	5	4	3	1	35	40	15	17
.5 "	12	12	6	5	84	84	40	58
.7 "	24	28	17	19	247	277	88	198
.9 "	50	55	47	40	740	1029	431	751
D. 10:30 TO 3:30								
.1 Decile	0	0	1	0	11	14	5	7
.3 "	3	3	3	1	47	58	24	29
.5 "	7	9	8	4	126	158	68	86
.7 "	18	24	18	15	279	339	194	235
.9 "	45	51	48	44	776	1045	684	835

* SOA is measured by the ending transaction in the [-1T, +60T] or [0T, +60T] intervals for which the cumulative series is most significantly different from the control series.

EXHIBIT 6-2
DISTRIBUTION STATISTICS FOR SPEED OF ADJUSTMENT (SOA) AT THE INDIVIDUAL EARNINGS RELEASE LEVEL: FULL SAMPLE*: SUBSAMPLE WITH ANNOUNCEMENTS WITH P-VALUE ≥ 0.95

	NUMBER OF TRANSACTIONS				NUMBER OF TRADING MINUTES			
	ABS. CUM. RET.	SEC. PRICE VARIAB.	TRAD. FREQ.	TRAD. VOL.	ABS. CUM. RET.	SEC. PRICE VARIAB.	TRAD. FREQ.	TRAD. VOL.
(1)	(2)	(3)	(4)	(5)	(6)	(7)	(8)	(9)
A. TOTAL SAMPLE								
.1 Decile	1	0	1	0	11	13	3	13
.3 "	4	3	3	1	41	45	10	43
.5 "	8	9	7	7	101	121	27	97
.7 "	21	20	16	19	285	309	68	277
.9 "	47	50	42	44	730	1110	247	807
B. OUTSIDE TRADING HOURS								
.1 Decile	1	0	1	0	23	13	4	14
.3 "	6	0	4	1	53	32	14	32
.5 "	15	7	9	6	123	69	31	80
.7 "	31	28	25	24	413	299	80	309
.9 "	49	50	49	51	777	1034	387	781
C. FIRST/LAST HALF HOURS								
.1 Decile	1	2	1	0	16	19	3	9
.3 "	6	5	3	5	40	41	7	32
.5 "	16	13	6	13	89	84	18	61
.7 "	28	25	13	27	236	220	45	198
.9 "	53	50	41	42	631	816	100	525
D. 10:30 TO 3:30								
.1 Decile	0	1	1	0	8	10	3	13
.3 "	3	4	3	1	36	61	10	46
.5 "	6	9	7	6	98	149	27	111
.7 "	16	19	13	17	257	324	71	272
.9 "	43	50	36	42	690	1190	243	880

* SOA is measured by the ending transaction in the [-1T, +60T] or [0T, +60T] intervals for which the cumulative series is most significantly different from the control series.

EXHIBIT 6-3
SPEED OF ADJUSTMENT:
ASSOCIATION WITH UNEXPECTED EARNINGS, FIRM SIZE AND TRADING FREQUENCY FOR FULL SAMPLE AND THREE SUBSAMPLES

SAMPLE/FINANCIAL SERIES	AB.(UNEXP. EARN.)		LOG(FIRM SIZE)		LOG(TRD. FREQ.)		
	β_1	$t(\beta_1)$	β_2	$t(\beta_2)$	β_3	$t(\beta_3)$	R^2
(1)	(2)	(3)	(4)	(5)	(6)	(7)	(8)
A. TOTAL SAMPLE							
Ab. Cum. Return	–20.50	–1.74	–0.287	–0.74	1.08	1.86	0.00
Absol. Return	–6.79	–0.52	–0.640	–1.48	1.90	2.95	0.01
Trad. Freq.	–4.65	–0.38	0.497	1.24	0.70	1.18	0.00
Trad. Vol.	21.20	1.80	0.584	1.50	–0.89	–1.54	0.00
B. OUTSIDE TRADING HOURS							
Ab. Cum. Return	–26.32	–1.73	0.667	0.88	0.75	0.65	0.01
Absol. Return	–10.67	–0.62	0.091	0.11	1.00	0.77	0.00
Trad. Freq.	–0.47	–0.03	1.957	2.47	–0.93	–0.78	0.01
Trad. Vol.	9.49	0.62	0.266	0.35	0.94	0.82	0.00
C. FIRST/LAST HALF HOURS							
Ab. Cum. Return	–40.99	–0.96	–0.103	–0.08	2.05	1.13	0.02
Absol. Return	33.90	0.72	–2.745	–1.98	4.70	2.34	0.03
Trad. Freq.	19.26	0.45	0.895	0.71	3.06	1.68	0.04
Trad. Vol.	–27.81	–0.69	1.976	1.67	–3.24	–1.89	0.02
D. 10:30 TO 3:30							
Ab. Cum. Return	–5.68	–0.24	–0.943	–1.95	0.63	0.87	0.00
Absol. Return	–2.07	–0.08	–0.723	–1.35	1.84	2.30	0.01
Trad. Freq.	–18.49	–0.76	–0.380	–0.77	0.74	1.00	0.00
Trad. Vol.	1.14	2.07	0.018	1.65	–0.01	–0.45	0.01

* Regression is:
$SOA = \alpha + \beta_1 . AB(UE) + \beta_2 . LOG(FS) + \beta_3 . LOG(TF)$

EXHIBIT 6-4
SPEED OF ADJUSTMENT:
ASSOCIATION WITH UNEXPECTED EARNINGS, FIRM SIZE AND TRADING FREQUENCY: EFFECT OF GROUPING OF OBSERVATIONS FOR FULL SAMPLE

FINANCIAL SERIES/ # OF OBSERVATIONS IN EACH PORTFOLIO	AB.(UNEXP. EARN.)		LOG(FIRM SIZE)		LOG(TRD. FREQ.)		
	β_1	$t(\beta_1)$	β_2	$t(\beta_2)$	β_3	$t(\beta_3)$	R^2
(1)	(2)	(3)	(4)	(5)	(6)	(7)	(8)
A. AB. CUM. RET.							
1	–20.50	–1.74	–0.287	–0.74	1.08	1.86	0.00
5	–21.55	–1.63	–0.541	–0.69	2.65	2.15	0.02
10	–11.59	–0.65	0.390	0.34	3.68	2.17	0.06
50	33.78	1.60	5.110	2.51	0.81	0.28	0.41
B. ABSOL. RET.							
1	–6.79	–0.52	–0.640	–1.48	1.90	2.95	0.01
5	–2.48	–0.17	–0.063	–0.07	1.94	1.43	0.01
10	1.81	0.09	0.201	0.16	2.23	1.17	0.02
50	29.51	0.86	3.958	1.20	–1.05	–0.22	0.09
C. TRAD. FREQ.							
1	–4.65	–0.38	0.497	1.24	0.70	1.18	0.00
5	–1.35	–0.10	1.136	1.38	–0.31	–0.24	0.01
10	–1.15	–0.06	–0.117	–0.09	2.55	1.36	0.02
50	33.42	1.05	5.097	1.66	–0.92	–0.21	0.18
D. TRAD. VOL.							
1	21.20	1.80	0.584	1.50	–0.89	–1.54	0.00
5	28.79	2.18	1.150	1.47	–0.53	–0.43	0.02
10	39.15	2.19	1.230	1.08	–0.57	–0.34	0.03
50	31.79	1.32	1.692	0.73	–3.42	–1.03	0.09

* Regression is:
$SOA = \alpha + \beta_1 . AB(UE) + \beta_2 . LOG(FS) + \beta_3 . LOG(TF)$

FIGURE 6-1
ABSOLUTE CUMULATIVE RETURNS:
DISTRIBUTION OF SPEED OF ADJUSTMENT FOR FULL SAMPLE

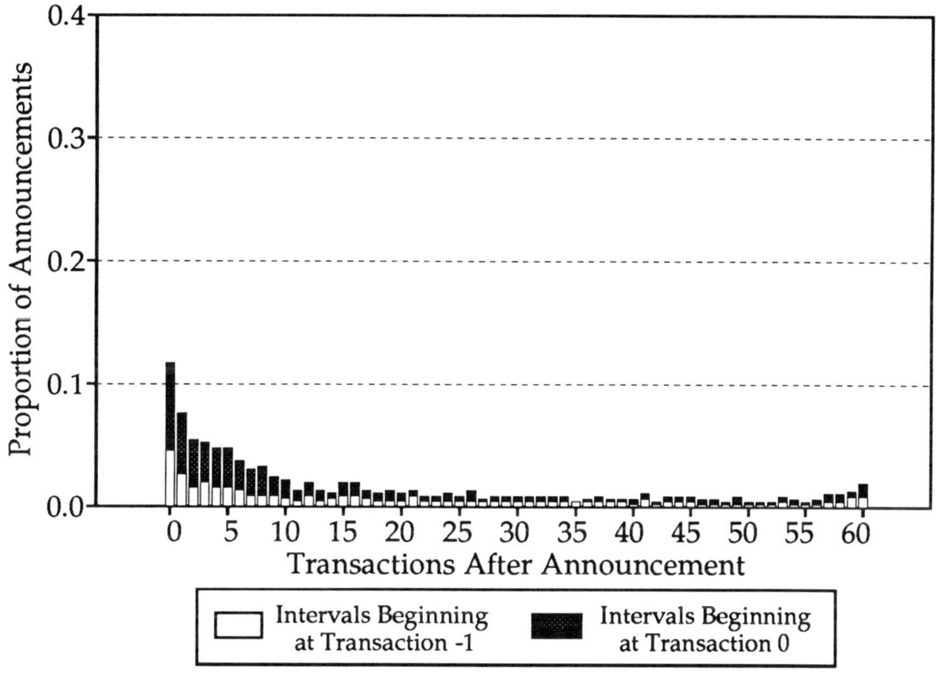

FIGURE 6-2
ABSOLUTE CUMULATIVE RETURNS:
DISTRIBUTION OF SPEED OF ADJUSTMENT FOR SUBSAMPLES

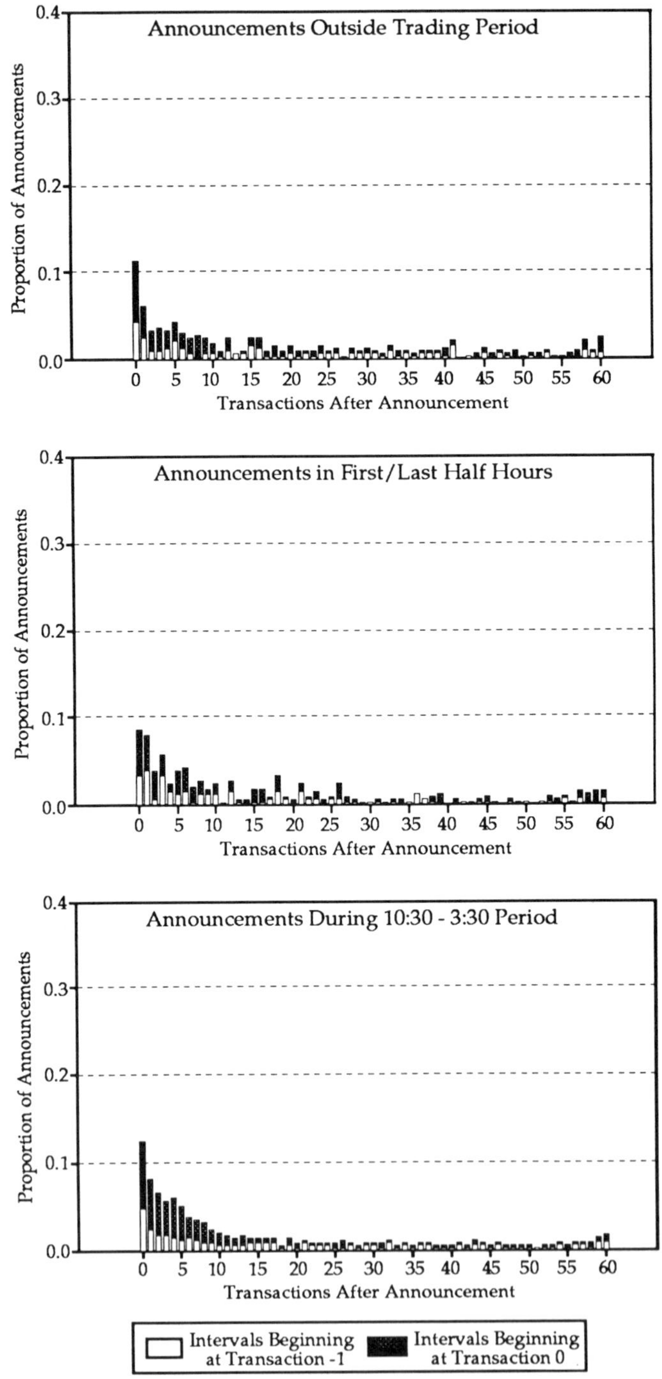

FIGURE 6-3
SECURITY RETURN VARIABILITY:
DISTRIBUTION OF SPEED OF ADJUSTMENT FOR FULL SAMPLE

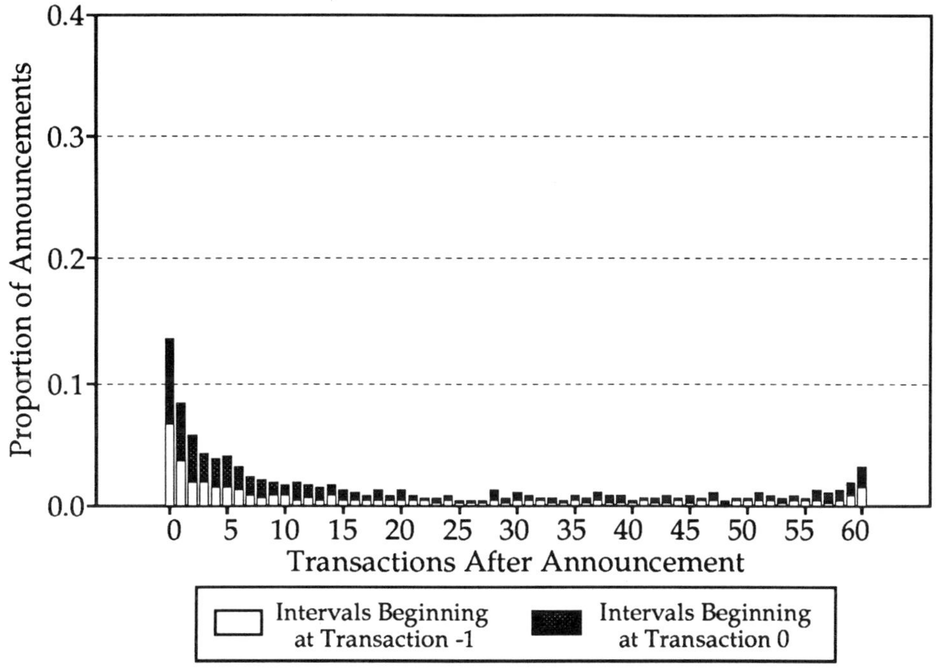

FIGURE 6-4
SECURITY RETURN VARIABILITY:
DISTRIBUTION OF SPEED OF ADJUSTMENT FOR SUBSAMPLES

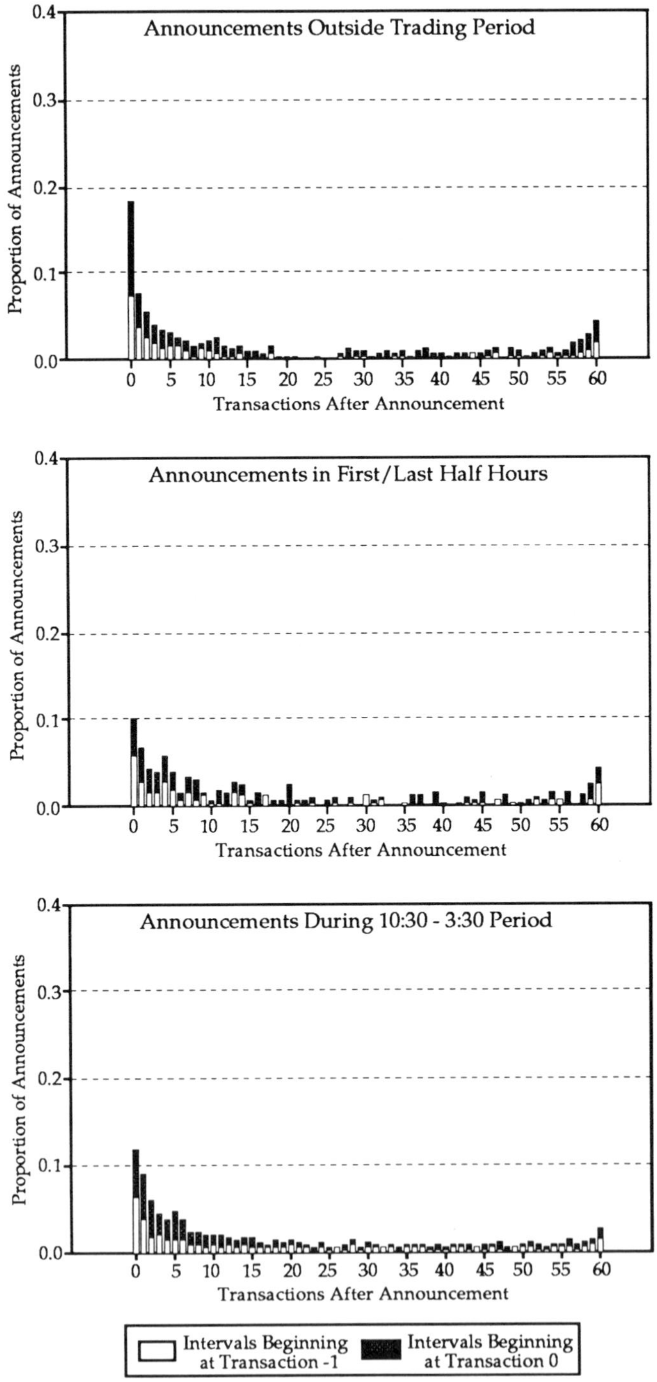

FIGURE 6-5
TRADING FREQUENCY (TIME BETWEEN SUCCESSIVE TRANSACTIONS): DISTRIBUTION OF SPEED OF ADJUSTMENT FOR FULL SAMPLE

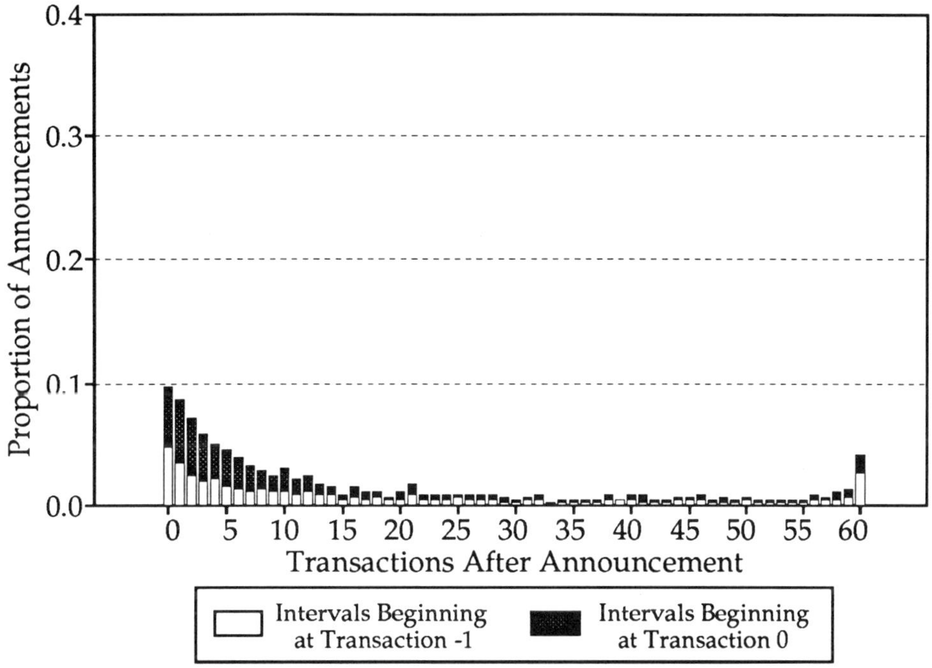

FIGURE 6-6
TRADING FREQUENCY (TIME BETWEEN SUCCESSIVE TRANSACTIONS): DISTRIBUTION OF SPEED OF ADJUSTMENT FOR SUBSAMPLES

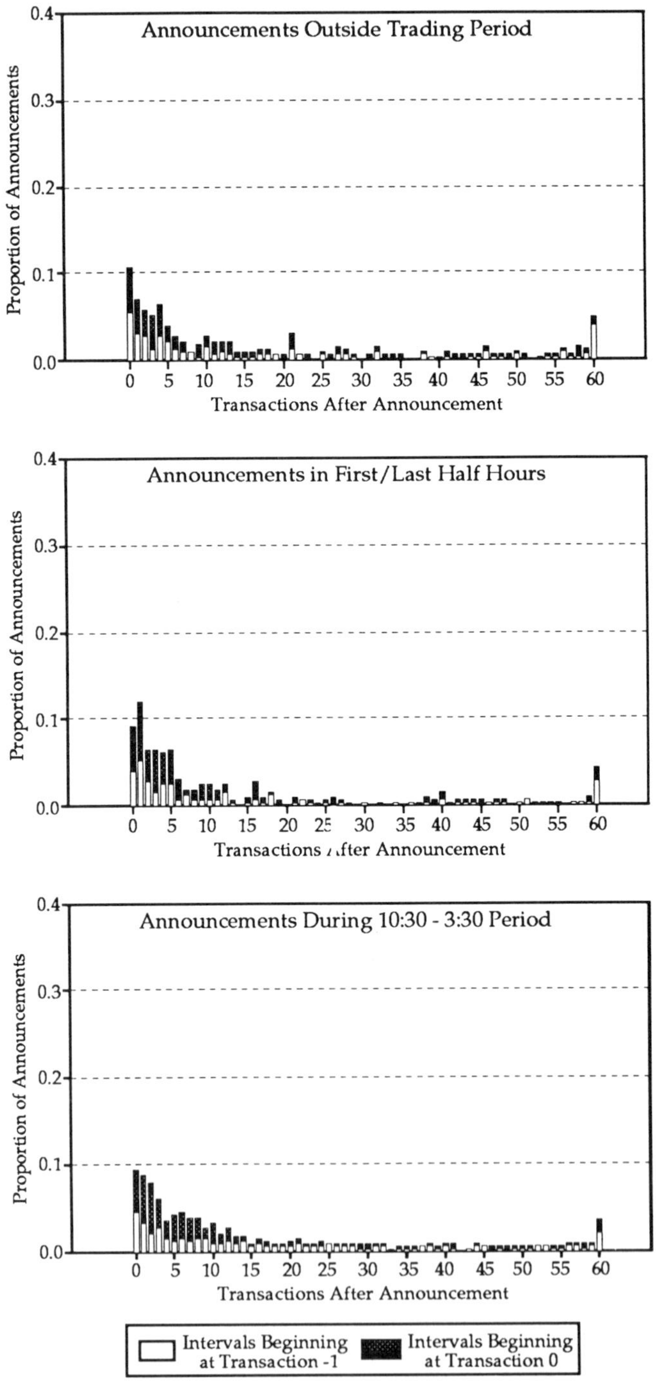

FIGURE 6-7
TRADING VOLUME (NUMBER OF SHARES TRADED PER TRANSACTION): DISTRIBUTION OF SPEED OF ADJUSTMENT FOR FULL SAMPLE

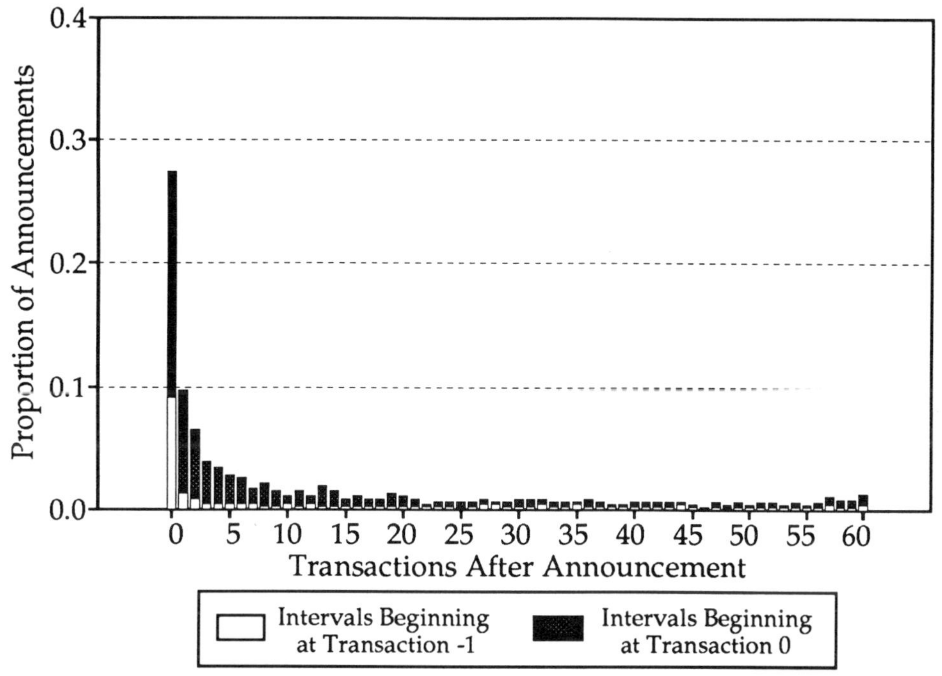

FIGURE 6-8
TRADING VOLUME (NUMBER OF SHARES TRADED PER TRANSACTION): DISTRIBUTION OF SPEED OF ADJUSTMENT FOR SUBSAMPLES

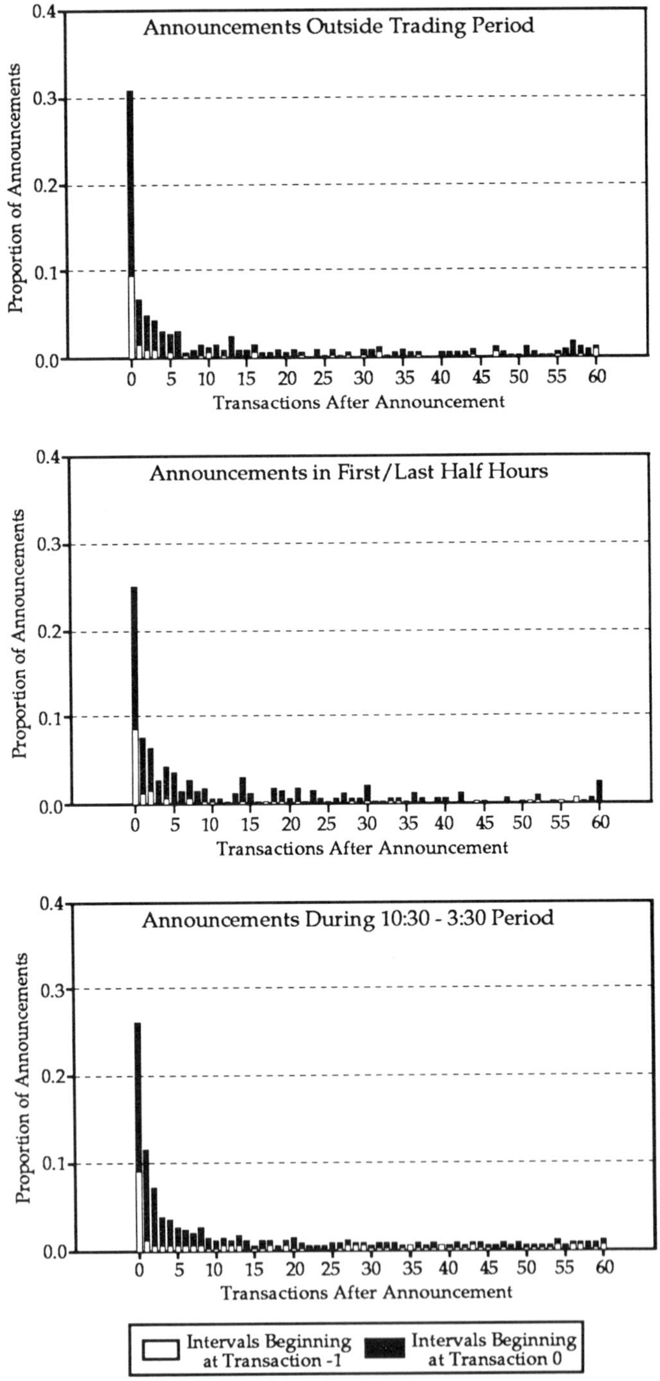

Appendix A
Research on Intraday Properties of Capital Market Variables

This appendix reviews the literature on intraday properties of the capital market variables examined in this monograph. An exhaustive listing of individual contributions is not presented. Our aim is to highlight the major findings in this literature. A broad set of explanations has been proposed for the observed systematic intraday patterns in the variables discussed. However, there has been limited progress in documenting that one or more of the proposed explanations has predictive ability. Indeed, progress to date has been mostly reporting how proposed explanations are inconsistent with the patterns reported in the literature.

A.1: Transaction Time Analysis

Chapter 4 presented results for four transaction time variables—mean security returns, variability of security returns, trading frequency and trading volume. Exhibit A-1 presents annotated bibliographies of key studies in the literature relating to these four variables.

A. Mean Security Returns

One finding in many studies is that the opening transactions on Mondays have negative mean returns while for other trading days the opening transactions have positive mean returns. Harris [1986] reports results for all NYSE stocks from December 1981 to January 1983. The mean returns for the first 8 transactions at the start of trading on Mondays are negative while the mean returns of the first 8 transactions for Tuesdays to Fridays are all positive. Further evidence on this pattern in opening return behavior is in Freedman and Terry [1988]. They report mean returns on Mondays and other days for the first 13 transactions for two samples:

(a) a sample of NYSE stocks simultaneously listed on the London Stock exchange (LSE), and

(b) a sample of 97 NYSE stocks not listed on the LSE.

The (b) sample was chosen to match the characteristics of firms in the (a) sample. The LSE is still open when trading on the NYSE opens. Freedman and Terry examined whether the availability of information on transaction prices on the LSE affects the pattern of opening returns on the NYSE. The time-period covered was 1980-85. The same start-of-day pattern in the sequence of mean returns in successive transactions is reported for both the (a) and (b) samples. The conclusion was that "the rate at which information is incorporated into stock prices at the beginning of the day on the NYSE is similar for LSE listed and non LSE listed stocks" (p. 7).

Many studies report the last transaction of the day has a positive mean return. Harris [1989] presents results based on a transaction by transaction record for 1617 NYSE common stocks for the December 1, 1981 to January 31, 1983 period. The last transaction is positive 84.1 percent of the time for the full sample. For the sub-sample with the last trade in the final 5 minutes of trading (42 percent of the cases), the percentage of positive observations increases to 98.7 percent. The evidence published to date reports that the "end of day" effect for the NYSE is concentrated in the last transaction, e.g., Wood, McInish and Ord [1985], Harris [1986] and Terry [1988]. McInish and Wood [1990b] analyze "end of the day" returns for stocks listed on the Toronto Stock Exchange. The data comprise a complete record of every transaction on the Toronto Stock Exchange for February 1987. Like the NYSE, evidence of high mean returns at the "end of the day" was reported.

One explanation for Monday's opening return being negative is an "abnormally high" closing price on Friday; the opening trade on Monday is a "correction" of the Friday close. Data consistent with this argument would be a negative correlation between the return for the last transaction on Friday and the return from the Friday close to Monday open. Harris [1989] does not find significant evidence of such a negative correlation for a sample of NYSE stocks between December 1981 and January 1983. Terry [1986] likewise finds little support for this "data errors" explanation for the systematic patterns at the start and end of the day.

Harris [1989] hypothesizes that "if ask prices are more common at day-end than earlier, mean day-end price changes would be positive" (p. 11). Terry [1986] also outlines this hypothesis and provides a rationale for an increase in trades at the ask price at day end. He argues that this increase is caused by liquidity traders (as opposed to information traders):

> The end of the day effect arises because. . .liquidity traders tend to submit more buy orders than sell orders at the end of the day. Thus, the last price tends to be above the "true" equilibrium price, causing the observed end of day return to be abnormally high (p. 13).

McInish and Wood [1990b] provide a test of this hypothesis using data from the Toronto Stock Exchange. The time period was twenty trading days in February 1987. They found that:

> The proportion of trades at the ask is significantly higher for a last trade occurring during the last ten minutes of trading [minutes 382-391] than either for other trades or for a last trade occurring in minutes 1-376 (p. 8).

The generalizability of the Toronto Stock Exchange results to other markets or other time periods is yet to be examined. The factors causing an increase in the percentage of day-end transaction prices that are at the ask price also are yet to be examined. One problem in probing the hypothesis that the increase arises from the activities of liquidity traders is that liquidity traders and information traders are not readily identifiable groups; nor need the two groups be mutually exclusive.

Several individual investor related explanations for the end of day increase in mean returns have been proposed. Miller [1988a] posits that investors at the end of the day "lighten their short positions but not their long positions". Both psychological and economic motivations are offered for this behavior:

- Psychological—"short positions have traditionally been considered riskier and carrying such a position interferes more with sleep and general feeling of well being" (p. 15).
- Economic—"long positions are on average money makers and short positions money losers. A short term trader who believes he is skilled at intraday trading would be more likely to close out his short position near the close, producing an upward bias" (pp. 15-16).

This explanation has been offered more as an ex post rationalization rather than as a testable proposition. Individual investor based explanations potentially can be empirically investigated. Research in experimental economics offers the ability to examine how individual investor behavior aggregates into observable market variables. One finding from several experimental economics studies is that the end of session trade price change is consistently positive in multi-trading session markets—see Forsythe, Palfrey and Plott [1982] and Plott and Sunder [1988].

B. Variability of Security Returns

There is little published evidence on intraday differences in the variability of transaction-by-transaction security returns. The most extensive evidence is based on the opening and closing transactions of successive trading days. For example, Amihud and Mendelson [1987] report that the variance of open-to-open security returns on successive trading days is higher than the variance of close-to-close security returns on successive trading days for 29 out of 30 Dow-Jones industrial stocks. Extensions of this research are in Amihud and Mendelson [1989, 1991], Stoll and Whaley [1990] and Amihud, Mendelson and Murgia [1990].

Two of the possible explanations for the higher variance of security returns at the opening of trading vis-a-vis the close of trading are:

(a) differences in trading mechanisms (the opening trade uses an auction regime versus a dealer regime for subsequent transactions).

(b) the long period of no trading which precedes the opening transaction.

Amihud and Mendelson [1991] use data from the Tokyo Stock Exchange (TSE) to probe these two explanations. The TSE has separate morning and afternoon trading sessions, with each opening using an auction regime. They report that while the TSE morning open-to-open returns are more volatile than the close-to-close returns, the afternoon open-to-open returns have "the same volatility as the close-to-close returns of the morning and afternoon sessions" (p. 19). They conclude, after additional tests, that "the culprit in the high volatility of daily open-to-open returns is the preceding non-trading period rather than the clearing transaction mechanism itself" (p. 20). One unresolved issue with this conclusion is that it leaves unexplained the systematic intraday variation in security return variability during the trading period. These systematic patterns include the U-shaped pattern in hourly security return variability and the increase in variability in the last minute of trading volume.

C. Trading Frequency

There is limited published evidence on intraday differences in the frequency of transactions at the transaction-by-transaction level. Garbade and Lieber [1977] report evidence on the time between transactions for two stocks (IBM and Potlatch) in September 1975. They report that the time between successive transactions of both IBM and Potlatch is not independent. However, when "only those transactions separated by some minimum interval of time" are considered, they were not able to "reject the hypothesis that they were independent events" (p. 168). Garbade and Lieber argue that part of the transaction-to-transaction dependence was due to floor brokers splitting single orders into two or more transactions. Evidence on average trading frequency in transaction time is in Holthausen, Leftwich and Mayers [1990]. They report that for a sample of 109 NYSE stocks "the average time between trades for the benchmark period [one without large-block transactions] is 30.07 minutes" (p. 95). Stoll and Whaley [1990] report that "considerable time elapses before stocks actually begin trading in a given day. In 1986, for example, the average number of minutes between the official opening of the exchange and the opening transaction in a stock was 15.48 minutes... Trading typically stops well before the exchange closes. An average of 19.94 minutes elapsed between the last trade and the close of the market in 1986" (p. 48).

D. Trading Volume

Wood, McInish and Ord [1985], Amihud and Mendelson [1987] and Stoll and Whaley [1990] all report evidence on the average number of shares traded for the opening transaction. Wood et al report that, for a sample of NYSE stocks in the September 1971 to February 1972 and calendar 1982 periods, "the size [average number of shares per trade] of overnight trades is more than 150 percent greater than [other] intraday trades." Amihud and Mendelson [1987] report opening trading volume statistics for the 30 Dow Jones stocks from February 8, 1982 to February 18, 1983. The ratio of the mean volume of the opening transaction to the mean volume of the closing transaction for each stock was computed. The range of this ratio was from 1.4 to 22.1 with a mean of 8.4. Amihud and Mendelson also report that "the volume on the opening transaction constituted on average 5.6 percent of the total NYSE daily volume in the sampled stocks" (p. 539). Note that under the NYSE institutional framework, the first transaction of the day (conducted using an auction regime) is an aggregation of orders that have accumulated since the previous close of trading. Stoll and Whaley [1990] report that "in the period 1982 through 1986, daily dollar volume nearly tripled, and opening volume as a fraction of daily volume fell from an average of 15.37 percent to an average of 10.59 percent" (p. 50).

A.2: Calendar Time Analysis

Chapter 4 presented results for four calendar time variables—mean security returns, variability of security returns, trading frequency, and trading volume. Exhibit A-2 presents annotated bibliographies of key studies in the literature relating to these four variables.

A. Mean Security Returns

A consistent finding across many studies is that intraday mean returns differ systematically over the trading day. An illustrative study is Jain and Joh [1988], which reports evidence on hourly mean returns on Standard and Poor's 500 stock index. During the 1979-83 time period studied, the NYSE was open for trading from 10:00 A.M. to 4:00 P.M. Jain and Joh report mean returns for 6 separate hourly trading periods. The mean return for the first hour of trading on Monday is negative; it is the most negative return for any of the 30 trading hours examined. Mean returns in the last hour of trading are positive on every trading day of the week.

Start of day returns on Mondays are consistently negative for NYSE stocks while start of day returns on Tuesdays to Fridays are consistently positive. This systematic pattern is observed over an extended time period and an extended number of companies in several studies. For example, Harris [1986] examines "a time-ordered record of every common stock transaction made at the NYSE for the fourteen months between December 1, 1981 and January 31, 1983" (p. 101). He reports that "significant weekday differences in intraday returns accrue during the first 45 minutes after the market opens. On Monday mornings, prices drop, while on the other weekday mornings, they rise" (p. 99).

Mean returns at the "end of the day" for NYSE stocks are consistently positive. For example, Wood, McInish and Ord [1985] report that the last trading minute has a "very high return" for samples of NYSE stocks in both the 1971-72 and 1982 time periods.

B. Variability of Security Returns

Many studies have reported a U-shaped pattern in variability of security returns over the trading day. For example, Wood, McInish and Ord [1985] report results for an equally weighted index of NYSE common stocks from September 1971 to February 1972 and calendar year 1982. High standard deviations are observed for a longer calendar time period at the start of the day (at least the first 20 trading minutes) than at the end of the day (concentrated in at most the last two trading minutes). Foster and Viswanathan [1988] also find a U-shaped pattern for 798 NYSE stocks over the January 1985 to December 1986 period. They report that the decline in the variance of hourly price changes after the start of the day and the increase toward the end of the day are steeper for less actively traded firms than for more actively traded firms. Lockwood and Linn [1990] likewise report that "return volatility falls from the opening hour until early afternoon and rises thereafter" (p. 591).

Gerety and Mulherin [1991] report that the first hour of trading has the highest variance for the Dow Jones price index vis-a-vis successive hours of trading over a 40 year period. They argue that this finding is inconsistent with the hypothesis that trading leads to higher variances due to noise associated with mispricing of securities.

C. Trading Frequency

There is relatively little research on calendar time intraday patterns in trading frequency. McInish and Wood [1991a] find a U-shaped pattern in hourly trading frequency. They report the first hour of trading has the highest trading frequency (in contrast to our results in Chapter 4 where the last hour of trading has the highest trading frequency).

D. Trading Volume

The consistent finding in the literature is a U-shaped pattern in trading volume over the trading day. For example, Jain and Joh [1988] report a U-shaped pattern in relative trading volume during each weekly trading day for the 1978-84 period. The average hourly trading volume for stocks in Standard and Poor's 500 index declines monotonically until the 4th trading hour and then increases again in the 5th and 6th hours. The average relative trading volume in the first hour of trading is over 50 percent more than the average hourly volume for the other five hours of trading.

Choe, McInish and Wood [1991b] examine the relative proportion of block trades (defined as trades of 20,000 shares or more) and nonblock trades (defined as trades of less than 10,000 shares) for all NYSE stocks in 1988 and 1990. They find that the "ratio of block to nonblock trades increases from the first to the second [thirty minute trading] period, declines through the period ending at 3:30 P.M. and increases for the last thirty-minute period. There are substantially fewer block trades on Mondays, but no other day-of-the-week effects are noted" (p. 6).

A.3: Systematic Patterns in Time-Series Dependencies of Security Returns

Studies of serial correlation in intraday price series have attracted considerable attention, in part due to their being one of the earliest sources of evidence inconsistent with the random walk theory of stock prices.

Niederhoffer and Osborne [1966] examined "the correspondence between the movements of ticker prices and the predictions of the random walk hypothesis" (p. 898). Data for six stocks in the Dow Jones Index for 22 trading days in October 1964 were examined. The percentage of observations in the –, 0, + categories for the returns in successive transaction sequences was:

		ΔP_t			
		–	0	+	TOTAL
ΔP_{t-1}	–	2.96%	11.43%	9.32%	23.71%
	0	11.98	29.79	11.14	52.91
	+	8.67	11.76	2.95	23.38
	TOTAL	23.61	52.98	23.41	100.00

There is strong evidence of negative first-order serial correlation in successive price changes in these percentages. For example, the authors report that "most of the non-zero changes in price were opposite in direction to the preceding non-zero change" (p. 900). Hausman, Lo and MacKinlay [1991] likewise report a "tendency towards price reversals from one transaction to the next" for the transaction data of 10 randomly chosen stocks in 1988.

One factor proposed to explain the observed negative serial correlation in successive price changes is the role of the specialist on the NYSE and the existence of limit orders and market orders. Limit orders set a limit on the price at which a buy or sell can be executed while a market order permits a trade to be at the "best price" existing on the market. Niederhoffer and Osborne [1966] argue as follows:

> The ability of customers to place orders at restricted prices as well as at current prices is an essential feature of market making on the New York Stock Exchange...Consider now what happens when a sequence of random buy and sell orders (without a preponderance of either), arrives at the post of the specialist. In the short run, the limit orders on the book will act as a barrier to continued price movement in either direction. Until all limit orders at the highest bid and the lowest offer are executed, transaction prices will fluctuate up and down between the bid and the offer in accordance with random arrival of the market orders... The pattern of numerous reversals displayed by the data...is just what one might expect from the current system of trading on the Exchange (p. 905).

Hausman, Lo and MacKinlay [1991] likewise report a "tendency towards price reversals from one transaction to the next" for the transaction data of 10 randomly chosen stocks in 1988.

Most published results focus on first-order serial correlation in successive price changes. Evidence on autocorrelations at higher lags is in Hasbrouck and Ho [1987]. The sample was all transactions for stocks on the NYSE for 42 trading days (March-April 1985). The mean autocorrelations are:

		Percentiles		
Lag	**Mean Autocorrelation**	**25%**	**50%**	**75%**
1	–0.264	–0.319	–0.249	–0.155
2	0.007	–0.002	0.006	0.036
3	0.008	–0.002	0.011	0.036
4	0.003	–0.020	0.003	0.027
5	0.003	–0.019	0.005	0.034

The positive autocorrelation patterns at lags 2 to 5 were reported to be statistically significant, albeit small in magnitude. Hasbrouck and Ho suggest two explanations for this finding: "positive dependences in order arrival" and "lagged adjustments in quotes" (p. 104).

Patell and Wolfson [1984] also present evidence of intraday dependencies in security returns. They focus on transaction-to-transaction non-zero price changes for a sample of 96 firms in the 1976-77 period. The relative frequencies of reversals and continuations in intraday stock price changes were:

Interval	Observations	Percent of Reversals	Percent of Continuations
Consecutive changes	434,327	69.07%	30.93%
One hour	75,076	56.80	43.20
Two hours	32,251	54.70	45.30
Three hours	16,227	50.53	49.47

Returns computed over longer intervals exhibit less evidence of a reversal pattern than do returns computed over shorter intervals.

Amihud and Mendelson [1987] focus specifically on autocorrelation patterns for daily returns for an "open to open" series and a "close to close" series. The mean first order autocorrelation coefficient and the percentage of firms with negative and positive autocorrelations are:

Daily Returns	Mean	% Negative	% Positive
Open to Open	–0.0635	76.7%	23.3%
Close to Close	+0.0464	20.0%	80.0%

Based on subsequent research on the Tokyo Stock Exchange (see Section A.1 of this Appendix for discussion of Amihud and Mendelson [1991]), they attribute these differences in autocorrelation behavior to the long period of no trading which precedes the opening transaction.

Several studies have reported evidence of variation in daily serial correlation patterns at different intraday times. Richardson and Smith [1988] examine autocorrelation evidence for daily returns of the 30 Dow-Jones Industrials over the 1980-84 period. Seven daily return series were examined: "Returns are measured each hour but from day to day. Thus for example the 11:00 A.M. return measures the return from 11:00 A.M. the previous day" (p. 16). Richardson and Smith report "implied autocorrelations" for each stock. The percentages of these 30 companies with negative and positive autocorrelations are:

Daily Returns Measurement	% Negative	% Positive
10 A.M. to 10 A.M.	83.3%	16.7%
11 A.M. to 11 A.M.	50.0	50.0
12 P.M. to 12 P.M.	23.3	76.7
1 P.M. to 1 P.M.	20.0	80.0
2 P.M. to 2 P.M.	10.0	90.0
3 P.M. to 3 P.M.	0.0	100.0
4 P.M. to 4 P.M.	6.7	93.3

Rejections of the random walk model are most marked at the beginning and in the afternoon trading hours (especially with the 2 P.M., 3 P.M. and 4 P.M. series). Negative autocorrelations predominate at the beginning of the day while positive autocorrelations predominate at the end of the day. Smith and Richardson argue that these "results are at least partially driven by market microstructure effects" since it "would be especially difficult to develop a model of fundamental factors alone which affect daily returns" (p. 20) in the manner observed in the data.

Froot and Gammill [1990] examine the predictability of short-run (successive 15 minute periods) returns on the S & P 500 index from 1983 to 1989. They find that predictability has declined over this period. Froot and Gammill hypothesize that their result is most likely due to the "improved efficiency with which market-wide information is impounded into the prices of individual stocks. This improvement appears to stem from the recent ability of portfolio trading to exploit positive serial correlation in index returns and from the facilitating role played by the stock index futures in disseminating market-wide information" (pp. 24-5).

EXHIBIT A-1
ANNOTATED BIBLIOGRAPHY OF STUDIES ON TRANSACTION TIME INTRADAY PROPERTIES OF CAPITAL MARKET VARIABLES

STUDY	DATA BASE	FINDINGS
A. MEAN SECURITY RETURNS		
Harris [1986]	• All NYSE stocks • Dec 1981-Jan 1983	• Mean returns for first 8 transactions on Mondays negative; positive for first 8 transactions on each of Tuesday to Friday • Mean return for last transaction highly positive
Terry [1986]	• 30 Dow Jones stocks Jan 1980-Dec 1984 • All ASE stocks Jan 1983-Dec 1983	• High positive mean return for last transaction observed across all days of week, days of the month, months, years and days surrounding holidays • Entire mean return over 1980-1984 period for 30 Dow-Jones industrials accrued between the last two transactions of each day
Freedman and Terry [1988]	• All NYSE stocks Jan 1980-Dec 1985 • 97 stocks listed on both NYSE and London Stock Exchange (LSE)	• No significant difference between opening prices of the LSE listed and non-LSE listed stocks • Mean returns negative for first 10 transactions on Mondays • Mean returns positive for first 7 transactions on all other days
Harris [1989]	• All NYSE stocks Dec 1981-Jan 1983 • All ASE stocks Mar 1985-Apr 1985	• Large mean price change on last daily NYSE transaction • Larger mean price change for sub-sample with last trade in last five minutes of trading day • An increase in the frequency of ask prices occurs at day-end
McInish and Wood [1990b]	• All Toronto Stock Exchange (TSE) stocks • Feb 1987	• Positive mean returns occur not just for last transaction but for other transactions near the end of the day

EXHIBIT A-1 CONTINUED

STUDY	DATA BASE	FINDINGS
B. VARIABILITY OF SECURITY RETURNS		
Amihud and Mendelson [1987]	• Dow Jones industrials on NYSE • Feb 1982-Feb 1983	• Variance of open-to-open security returns is higher than the close-to-close return variance
Stoll and Whaley [1990]	• All NYSE common stocks • Jan 1982-Dec 1986	• "Open-to-open variance is about 12 percent higher than close-to-close variance" • "Volatility ratio for high-volume stocks significantly exceeds... low-volume stocks" • "Daytime volatility is 5.4 times as large as overnight volatility"
Amihud and Mendelson [1991]	• 150 Tokyo Stock Exchange stocks (most actively traded) • Jul 1987-Jun 1988	• "Daily [morning] open-to-open returns more volatile" than afternoon open-to-open returns and both morning and afternoon close-to-close returns
C. TRADING FREQUENCY		
Garbade and Lieber [1977]	• 2 NYSE stocks • September 1975	• Transaction-by-transaction data are not independent • Transactions separated by "some minimum interval of time" are independent
Holthausen, Leftwich and Mayers [1990]	• 109 NYSE stocks • Dec 1982-Jan 1984	• "The average time between trades for the benchmark period is 30.07 minutes"
Stoll and Whaley [1990]	• All NYSE common stocks • Jan 1982-Dec 1986	• "Average delay between exchange open and the first trade of the day was 15.48 minutes" • "Average time between last trade and the exchange close was 19.94 minutes"
D. TRADING VOLUME		
Wood, McInish Ord [1985]	• 946 NYSE stocks Sept 1971-Feb 1972 • 1,138 NYSE stocks Jan 1982-Dec 1982	• Size of overnight trades is more than 150% greater than intraday trades

EXHIBIT A-1 CONTINUED

STUDY	DATA BASE	FINDINGS
Amihud and Mendelson [1987]	• 30 Dow Jones industrials on NYSE • Feb 1982-Feb 1983	• Volume on opening transaction averages 8.4 times the volume on closing transaction
Harris [1989]	• All NYSE stocks Dec 1981-Jan 1983	• Size of last transaction, relative to average during day, "increases, the later in the day the last transaction occurs"
Stoll and Whaley [1990]	• All NYSE common stocks • Jan 1982-Dec 1986	• In 1986, proportion of daily volume that occurs at the open is 32% for the smallest daily volume decile and 5.3% for the largest daily volume decile

EXHIBIT A-2
ANNOTATED BIBLIOGRAPHY OF STUDIES ON CALENDAR TIME INTRADAY PROPERTIES OF CAPITAL MARKET SERIES

STUDY	DATA BASE	FINDINGS
A:MEAN SECURITY RETURNS		
Garbade and Sekaran [1981]	• 5 NYSE stocks • Aug 1973-Sep 1975	• No evidence that opening transactions behave differently from subsequent transactions
McInish and Wood [1984]	• 959 NYSE stocks • Sep 1971-Feb 1972	• Significant cross-dependence in mean returns for last 60 minutes of one day and first 60 minutes of next day
McInish and Wood [1985b]	• 958 NYSE stocks • Sep 1971-Feb 1972 • Minute by minute returns tape provided by NYSE	• Interday returns negative for Monday and positive for Friday • Day of week effects are most pronounced for actively traded stocks
Wood, McInish and Ord [1985]	• 946 NYSE stocks Sep 1971-Feb 1972 • 1,138 NYSE stocks for Jan 1982-Dec 1982 • Fitch data	• High mean returns at the beginning and end of trading day • Last trading minute has "very high return"
Harris [1986]	• All NYSE stocks • Dec 1981-Jan 1983 • Fitch data	• Mean returns for Monday negative across all 10 firm size deciles • Only half of the negative Monday close-to-close return accrues between Friday close and Monday open
Smirlock and Starks [1986]	• Dow Jones Index • Hourly values • 1963-1984	• Weekend effect "changed over time; it has been 'moving' up in time... Over the post-1974 period, trading period returns on Monday were positive, although opening hour returns are negative"
Jain and Jo [1988]	• S & P 500 Index • Hourly mean returns 1978-1984	• Monday first hour negative mean return. Last trading hour of each day has positive mean return. Fifth trading hour of each day has the lowest average mean return

EXHIBIT A-2 CONTINUED

STUDY	DATA BASE	FINDINGS
McInish and Wood [1990b]	• All Toronto stock Exchange (TSE) stocks • Feb 1987	• Mean returns at start (minutes 1-15) and end (minutes 387-391) of the trading day are higher than mean returns in the middle periods (minutes 16-386)
McInish and Wood [1991a]	• All NYSE stocks • 1980-1984	• Monday 1st trading hour negative mean return • Last trading hour of each day positive mean return. Fifth trading hour of each day has the lowest average mean return
B. VARIABILITY OF SECURITY RETURNS		
McInish, Ord and Wood [1985]	• All NYSE stocks • Sep 1971-Feb 1972	• Variance of security returns is invariant to the length of time between trades
Wood, McInish and Ord [1985]	• 946 NYSE stocks Sep 1971-Feb 1972 • 1,138 NYSE stocks Jan 1982-Dec 1982	• "Unusually high standard deviations of returns are found at the beginning and the end of the trading day"
French and Roll [1986]	• All NYSE and ASE stocks • Jan 1963-Dec 1982	• "Per hour security return variance about 70 times larger during a trading hour than during a weekend non-trading hour"
McInish and Wood [1987]	• 1,200 NYSE stocks • Jan 1980-Dec 1984	• Return variability during the first 30 minutes is higher than during minutes 31-356" • Variance of returns is lower for stocks listed on both London Stock Exchange and NYSE
Foster and Viswanathan [1988]	• 798 NYSE stocks • Jan 1985-Dec 1986	• U-shaped relationship in variance of price changes by hour of day • Drop at start of day and increase at the end are steeper for less active firms than for more active firms
Lockwood and Linn [1990]	• Opening, closing intraday hourly values of Dow Jones index • Jan 1964-Feb 1989	• Return volatility falls from the opening hour until early afternoon and rises thereafter

EXHIBIT A-2 CONTINUED

STUDY	DATA BASE	FINDINGS
McInish and Wood [1990a]	• 1,400 NYSE stocks • Jan 1980-Dec 1984	• High variability of security returns at beginning and end of trading day occurs in 1980, 1981, 1983 and 1984 • Variability of minute by minute returns has U-shaped pattern when plotted against time of day
McInish and Wood [1990b]	• All Toronto stock Exchange (TSE) stocks • Feb 1987	• Standard deviation of returns has U-shaped pattern when plotted against time of day
McInish and Wood [1991a]	• All NYSE stocks • Jan 1980-Dec 1984	• Opening hour of each trading day has highest variability of security returns • U-shaped patterns on all days except Friday
C. TRADING FREQUENCY		
McInish and Wood [1991a]	• All NYSE stocks • Jan 1980-Dec 1984	• U-shaped pattern • Largest number of trades during the first trading hour, followed by the 2nd, last, 5th, 3rd, and 4th hours
D. TRADING VOLUME		
Foster and Viswanathan [1988]	• 798 NYSE stocks • Jan 1985-Dec 1986	• Volume is U-shaped: high at the start, lower during the day and increases towards the end • Less active firms show a more pronounced U-shaped pattern than more active firms
Jain and Joh [1988]	• S & P 500 Index • Hourly mean returns • 1978-1984	• Volume is U-shaped • Average first hour volume 50% more than the average hourly volume during the day • Average trading volume declines monotonically until the 4th hour but increases again in 5th and 6th hours

EXHIBIT A-2 CONTINUED

STUDY	DATA BASE	FINDINGS
Choe, McInish and Wood [1991b]	• All NYSE stocks • 1988, 1990	• Ratio of block to nonblock increases from first to the second [thirty minute trading] period, declines to period ending 3:30 P.M. and increases in last thirty minute period • Substantially fewer block trades on Mondays
McInish and Wood [1991a]	• All NYSE stocks • Jan 1980-Dec 1984	• Volume is high at the beginning and end of the trading day relative to other times • Variability of volume by hour of the day results primarily from changes in the number of trades • Opening trading hour has highest average number of shares traded per transaction on each trading day • Monday has lowest average number of shares traded per transaction

Appendix B
Research on Intraday Capital Market Information Content

This Appendix discusses how experimental design issues examined in this monograph have been addressed in other studies that have used intraday data.

B.1: Content of Studies

Exhibits B-1 and B-2 summarize the growing number of information content studies that use intraday data:

- Exhibit B-1 summarizes studies on information releases made by companies, e.g., dividends, earnings, and earnings forecasts.
- Exhibit B-2 summarizes studies on information generated by capital market events, e.g., a block trade.

Several early studies focused on the security return series and extended information content issues previously researched using daily, weekly or monthly return data—see Patell and Wolfson [1984] and Jennings and Starks [1985]. For example, Patell and Wolfson [1984] examined the association between security returns and the sign of the unexpected earnings signal at the time of the earnings release. This study extended the prior literature, in part by its more rigorous tests of speed of adjustment using intraday security return data.

Recent studies have used a broader range of financial variables to expand the issues examined. These issues include:

- The behavior of individual capital market participants at the time of information releases. For example, Lee, Mucklow and Ready [1991] report how earnings releases are associated with increases in the bid-ask spread that specialists quote and in the depth of their quotations.
- The effect of information releases on trading size and trading frequency. For example, Cready [1988], Cready and Mynatt [1991] and Lee [1991a] examine several transaction size series to gain insight into the behavior of different classes of investors at the time of earnings releases.

B.2: Data Bases Available

Three main sources of intraday data have been used in existing studies: Fitch, the Institute for the Study of Security Markets, and CBOE.[1]

---

[1] Hasbrouck [1990] and Bronfman [1991a] use other sources of intraday data. Hasbrouck [1990] uses "transactions and quotes for all NYSE, AMEX and NASDAQ issues [that] were collected by a firm under contract" (p. 29). Bronfman [1991a] uses intraday data directly provided by the NYSE—"The data used in this study includes all orders entered into the NYSE's SuperDOT, not only off-floor from a brokerage house, but also from booths of the member firms on the exchange floor, or by the specialist directly. SuperDOT is an electronic order routing system that 'enables member firms to quickly and efficiently transmit market and limit orders in all NYSE-listed securities directly to the specialist post where the securities are traded or to the member firm's booth.'" (p.2).

1. *Francis Emory Fitch, Inc. (Fitch).* This source reports the security price, trading volume, and time of day of each transaction for all NYSE listed securities. Information content studies using Fitch data include Dann, Mayers and Raab [1977], Jennings and Starks [1985], Barclay and Litzenberger [1988], Cready [1988], Woodruff and Senchack [1988], Holthausen, Leftwich and Mayers [1990], Cready and Mynatt [1991], Watts [1991], Francis, Pagach and Stephan [1992] and this monograph. Fitch is a commercial organization that sells data to brokerage firms and other customers.

2. *Institute for the Study of Security Markets* (ISSM). This source reports trade (transaction) and quotation data for all equity issues on the NYSE, Amex, and regional exchanges, and for some over-the-counter (OTC) issues:

- Trade data—"the record contains the time to the second, the price, the volume, originating exchange, condition codes, correction codes, stop codes, print indicator, sellers day and bankruptcy indicator."
- Quotation data—"the record contains bid and ask prices timed to the second, the originating exchange, bid and ask size (market depth), condition codes and market maker (for third-market quotes)."

ISSM is a non-profit education foundation "established for the purpose of providing transactions security price data to academic institutions for research purposes" (ISSM [1991, p. 1]). Information content studies using the ISSM data base include Lee [1991a], Lee, Mucklow and Ready [1991], Lee, Ready and Seguin [1991] and Mucklow [1991].

3. *Chicago Board Options Exchange (CBOE)/Berkeley.* Stock prices are recorded (i) each time a new bid or ask price is quoted for any put or call option written on a particular stock, or (ii) each time a put or call option transaction occurs. Only stocks with options traded on the CBOE are included. This data base does not include a complete transaction record for equity securities. For any one stock, there may be transactions occurring without any change in bid or ask quotations for puts or calls. Similarly, stock transactions may occur without any put or call transactions also occurring. Patell and Wolfson [1984] use this data base in a study of the speed of adjustment of security prices to earnings and dividend announcements.

The ISSM data base is being used with increasing frequency (relative to the Fitch and CBOE data bases) in current research. Charles Lee of The University of Michigan (in unpublished notes) lists the following strengths of the ISSM data.

(i) ISSM is a consolidated tape. Trades on all exchanges (NYSE, Amex, and regional exchanges) are recorded in chronological order.

(ii) ISSM reports both trade (transaction) data and every quote revision (bid-ask price and number of shares available at each) issued by NYSE and regional specialists.

(iii) ISSM reports extensive "condition code" information. For example, trading halts are marked on the ISSM tape with special quote indicators, as are trades which are reported late or out of sequence, non-firm quotes during fast trading or trades transacted at a premium or discount because of unusual settlement conditions (same day delivery, for example).

(iv) All trades and quotes on the ISSM data base are reported to the second.

All three of the above intraday data bases do not capture the full set of transactions for all publicly traded stocks. For example, for stocks cross-listed on exchanges outside the United States, transactions on non-United States based exchanges are not included on the Fitch, ISSM or CBOE data bases. Similarly, transactions made outside all organized exchanges are excluded from all three data bases.

The Fitch data base is the only data base available for the whole period examined in this monograph (1980-1985). The ISSM data base reports trade and quote data since 1983, although for the 1983-1987 period there are "some missing days in each year".

B.3: Incorporating Intraday Regularities into the Experimental Design

Systematic intraday regularities have been documented in each of the financial series examined in this monograph (see Chapter 4 and Appendix A):

- mean security returns
- variability of security returns
- trading frequency
- trading volume

The approaches adopted in existing intraday information content studies to incorporate these regularities into the experimental design include[2]:

Approach 1: Exclude observations or periods believed to be non-homogeneous. For example, Jennings and Starks [1985], Barclay and Litzenberger [1988], Lee [1991a] and Lee, Mucklow and Ready [1991] exclude from their sample all information releases made outside trading hours on the presumption that they might behave differently from releases made during trading hours.[3] Cready [1988] excludes the first five minutes of trading "because at the beginning of each trading day orders are frequently grouped and executed as one or several large transactions. This exclusion removes the potential inflating effect of such transactions on mean transaction sizes" (p. 9).

---

[2] Systematic intraday regularities have also been documented in other financial series. For example, McInish and Wood [1991b] report that bid-ask "spreads are shown to have a U-shaped time-of-day component" (p. 25). Brock and Kleidon [1990] likewise report a U-shaped intraday pattern in bid-ask spreads.

[3] For example, Barclay and Litzenberger [1988] note: "to avoid problems from mixing intraday and overnight returns, the intraday analysis uses only those announcements that occurred within the trading day" (p. 81).

Approach 2: Separately examine subsamples in which the regularities may have different implications for the experimental design or the inferences drawn. Patell and Wolfson [1982] examine security returns for (i) earnings releases made during trading, and (ii) earnings releases made after trading. They report the percentage of price decreases for (i) and (ii) separately for six time periods—all one-hour periods, all two-hour periods, open to close, 10:00-11:00 A.M., 11:00 A.M.-12:00 P.M., and close to open. The choice of the separate sub-samples is a key aspect of this approach. For example, the evidence presented in Chapter 4 and Appendix A suggests that trading behavior in the opening and closing minutes is different than at other times of the day.

Approach 3: Incorporate any systematic patterns in intraday variables via a companion portfolio approach. This approach controls for any systematic patterns without any explicit recognition of them. Patell and Wolfson [1984] adopt this approach when comparing announcement period returns with non-announcement period returns: "we compare the announcement period returns to those of control samples constructed by matching five of the firm's non-announcement days to each disclosure date and implementing the strategy at exactly the same time as the actual earnings or dividend release. The non-announcement dates are selected at random after excluding the day of and the day following the Broad Tape release date for all earnings, dividend, and forecast announcements listed in the Wall Street Journal Index." (p. 232).

Lee, Mucklow and Ready [1991] use a companion portfolio approach in their study of bid-ask spreads and depth at the time of earnings releases—"to eliminate the effect of systematic patterns during the day, the medians are calculated separately by firm for each of the 13 half-hour trading periods". This approach was adopted because "the levels of spread and depth exhibit pronounced intraday patterns" (p. 13).

Approach 4: Examine whether the results are sensitive to alternative inclusion/exclusion rules. Holthausen, Leftwich and Mayers [1990], in a study of block trades, report that they "replicated the results after eliminating blocks that occurred in the first hour of trading, and after excluding trades not taking place on the same day as the block. These sample restrictions eliminate 7.7 percent of the sample and have no impact on the qualitative conclusions reached." (p. 75).

This monograph uses several approaches to incorporate intraday regularities into the experimental design. One approach is to construct subsamples that differ sizably in the effect that intraday systematic patterns have on the earnings announcement series being examined. Chapter 5 presents results for announcements made (a) outside trading hours, (b) in the first or last 30 minutes of trading, and (c) in the 10:30 A.M. to 3:30 P.M. period. A second approach is to use a companion portfolio that is matched with an earnings release portfolio using the minute of the earnings announcement to align the companion portfolio in transaction and calendar time. We use the companion portfolio in the development of the significance tests (see Appendix 5.A).

B.4: Speed of Adjustment

Three main approaches have been used to examine the speed of adjustment of capital market variables to information releases:

1. Statistical analysis of release and non release periods,
2. Trading rule approach, and
3. Path to assumed full adjustment time approach.

1. Statistical Analysis of Release and Non-Release Periods

The benchmark used in several papers to analyze the speed of adjustment is based on the statistical properties of the series in periods where the information item of interest is not released. The three main classes of approach are:

(A) cumulative sum approach,
(B) price reversal approach, and
(C) extreme value approach.

CUMULATIVE SUM (CUM SUM) APPROACH: Hillmer and Yu [1979] use a cum-sum approach to test for changes in the mean or variance of security returns at the time of information releases. Returns from a prior period are used to estimate the mean and variance of each of two series—security returns and the frequency of transactions. The authors adapt tests, proposed for detecting parameter changes in a time-series, to obtain "an unbiased estimate of the disturbance interval" (p. 325). The cum-sum tests employed by Hillmer and Yu implicitly assume that consecutive price changes are independently and identically distributed. The evidence outlined in Appendix B and Chapter 4 is inconsistent with this assumption.

PRICE REVERSAL TEST: The evidence of serial correlation in successive price changes (see Chapter 4 and Appendix A) forms the basis of the price reversal test used in Patell and Wolfson [1984], Jennings and Starks [1985] and Woodruff and Senchack [1988]. This test examines the time period during which the reversal pattern in successive price changes is interrupted at the time of an information release. Only the sign (not the magnitude) of price changes is used in this analysis. A period in which there is no release of the information item of interest is used to develop a distribution of successive price changes.

EXTREME VALUE TEST: This test uses a period with no releases of the information item of interest to determine the distribution of returns under the null hypothesis (against which observations in the experimental period can be compared to see how many are extreme). This distribution is then used to determine how many observations are "extreme" in the period when the information items of interest are released. Papers reporting results with this test include Patell and Wolfson [1984] and Jennings and Starks [1985].

2. Trading Rule Approach

This approach examines the returns from hypothetical investment strategies designed to exploit information in the release of interest. The longer the time period during which an investment strategy earns abnormal returns, the slower the speed of adjustment of security prices to the release. The computation of these "abnormal returns" is affected by assumptions made in several areas including:

- Assumptions about when an investor could react to a release. Three classes of parties can be distinguished:
  (i) floor traders,
  (ii) specialists, and
  (iii) external investors (i.e., investors with no organized links to floor traders or specialists).

Classes (i) and (ii) can react more quickly than (iii). Grier and Albin [1973] argue that "fifteen minutes is generally accepted as the minimum time interval needed by an outsider to react to the tapes and effect his own transactions" (p. 427).

- Assumptions about transactions costs incurred. This will differ according to whether the long or short position is taken by a floor trader, specialist, or external investor. Even for external investors, sizable differences in transactions costs can exist.

Grier and Albin [1973] hypothesize a systematic price-reversal pattern surrounding a large block trade; i.e., the stock price change from the block trade to the end of day is likely to be the reverse of the stock price change from the start of day to the block trade. A trading rule designed to exploit this hypothesized price reversal was reported to earn abnormal returns. The methodology underlying this trading rule was debated in Reback [1974] and Grier [1974]. Further analysis of trading strategies associated with block sales is in Dann, Mayers and Raab [1977]. The data were all transactions from August 1968 to December 1969 for a set of stocks with large block transactions. The authors report that "the use of intra-day prices yields results consistent with the weak form of the efficient markets hypothesis" (p.3).

Patell and Wolfson [1984] report results of trading strategies designed to exploit information in earnings releases. They find that "the 30 minute period beginning at the minute of the announcement exhibits a significant positive return (approximately one quarter of one percent) that is four to five times larger than those in surrounding periods. The average 30 minute return beginning five minutes later is considerably smaller (approximately one tenth of one percent)" (p. 235). These authors note that their "trading rules are extremely simple and may seriously understate the potential returns to more sophisticated trading." (p. 232).

3. Path to Assumed Full Adjustment Time Approach

This approach assumes the capital market fully adjusts to an information release by a designated end-time (in either calendar time or transaction time). The focus is on the path of adjustment to this designated end-time. The earlier the adjustment occurs prior to the designated end-time, the more rapid is the inferred speed of adjustment.

The most frequently designated end-times chosen for analysis are either:

(a) the end of trading on the day of the information release, or

(b) the end of trading on the first trading day subsequent to the information release day.

Dann, Mayers and Raab [1977] adopt (a) in their analysis of how quickly security returns become unbiased estimates of the closing price on the day a block trade occurs. They report:

> Prices are still not fully adjusted ten minutes after the occurrence of the block. That is, the first price at least ten minutes after the block is, on average, significantly below its closing price (p. 20).

Woodruff and Senchack [1988] adopt (b) in their study of earnings releases.

The choice of the "fully adjusted" end-time involves several considerations. Too short a time will result in part of the adjustment being excluded. Too long a period increases the probability that other information releases subsequent to the release of interest will affect the behavior of the capital market variable being examined.

Two interpretation issues arise with this approach to examining the speed of adjustment. First, how should one interpret adjustments greater than 100 percent? Any time a post-release price exceeds the "fully adjusted" price, an adjustment greater than 100 percent is computed. Should this number be interpreted as the market having a short-run over-reaction to the release? Second, how should one interpret security returns with the opposite sign to that of the return from the release time to the full-adjustment time? Should this opposite sign be interpreted as short-run mis-adjustment?

EXHIBIT B-1
INTRADAY INFORMATION CONTENT STUDIES: INFORMATION RELEASES BY COMPANIES

STUDY	INFORMATION RELEASES/ SAMPLE EXAMINED	DATA BASE/ FINANCIAL SERIES EXAMINED	FINDINGS
Hillmer and Yu [1979]	• 5 individual company releases • 1977-78	Fitch data base 1. Security returns 2. Transaction frequency	• Illustration of how speed of adjustment can be operationalized
Patell and Wolfson [1982]	• 571 earnings and dividend releases of 96 companies with CBOE options • 1976-77	CBOE/Berkeley data base 1. Security returns	• Good news more likely to be released in trading periods • Bad news more likely to be released after close of trading
Patell and Wolfson [1984]	• 571 earnings and dividend releases of 96 companies with CBOE options • 1976-77	CBOE/Berkeley data base 1. Security returns	• Earnings releases induce more activity than dividends • Initial price reaction to releases evidenced in first pair of price changes
Jennings and Starks [1985]	• 418 earnings releases of NYSE companies with options or in S & P 500 • 1981-82	Fitch data base 1. Security returns	• Earnings reports with high unexpected good news have adjustment process that begins before and extends beyond adjustment process of earnings reports with high unexpected bad news
Barclay and Litzenberger [1988]	• 218 new issues of common equity and 85 new issues of long-term debt • NYSE or ASE companies • 1981-83	Fitch data base 1. Security returns 2. Trading volume 3. Transaction frequency 4. Transaction size	• During first 15 minutes following new equity announcements, an abnormally large number of transactions, high trading volume, and a -1.3% average return
Cready [1988]	• 727 earnings releases from 386 firms • 1981-82	Fitch data base 1. Transaction size 2. Number of transactions	• Above-average stock trade size in earnings announcement days 0, +1, +2
Woodruff and Senchack [1988]	• 325 earnings releases • 1980	Fitch data base 1. Security returns 2. Trading volume 3. Transaction frequency 4. Transaction size	• Rapid price adjustment "within first few hours" • More rapid adjustment for unexpected favorable earnings than for unexpected unfavorable earnings

EXHIBIT B-1 CONTINUED

STUDY	INFORMATION RELEASES/ SAMPLE EXAMINED	DATA BASE/ FINANCIAL SERIES EXAMINED	FINDINGS
Cready and Mynatt [1991]	• 563 earnings releases from 320 firms • 1981-1983	Fitch data base 1. Security returns 2. Trading volume 3. Number of transactions	• "An increase in the number of transactions, weaker evidence of an increase in volume of shares traded, and the absence of any sizable price response at annual dates"
Lee [1991a]	• 607 earnings releases from 230 firms • Jan 1988-Dec 1988	ISSM data base 1.Trading volume 2. Buy (sell) imbalance	• Large trades have rapid speed of adjustment • Small trades (less than $10,000) have persistent period of unusually high buying activity
Lee, Mucklow and Ready [1991]	• 607 earnings releases from 230 firms • Jan 1988-Dec 1988	ISSM data base 1. Bid/ask spread 2. Depth of quote 3. Elasticity of market liquidity	• "Increases in quoted spread and decreases in the quoted depth"
Watts [1991]	• 393 quarterly earnings releases by 140 NYSE firms • 1979-88	Fitch data base 1. Security returns	• "Unexpected component of earnings releases made after markets are closed... larger than [for] earnings releases made during trading"
Francis, Pagach and Stephan [1992]	• 558 annual earnings releases by Compustat firms • 1982-86	Fitch data base 1. Security returns 2. Trading volume	• "No evidence that investors react to over-night announcements in their opening trades"

EXHIBIT B-2
INTRADAY INFORMATION CONTENT STUDIES: INFORMATION GENERATED BY CAPITAL MARKET EVENTS

STUDY	INFORMATION RELEASE SAMPLE EXAMINED	DATA BASE/ FINANCIAL SERIES EXAMINED	FINDINGS
Grier and Albin [1973]	• 166 large block transactions	• No details 1. Security returns	• Security returns exhibit reversal pattern at time of block transactions
Dann, Mayers and Raab [1977]	• 2129 large block transactions (50,000 shares or more) • 1968-69	Fitch data base 1. Security returns	• Within 15 minutes of block transaction, prices are unbiased estimate of closing price of day
Holthausen, Leftwich and Mayers [1990]	• 109 NYSE firms • Dec 1982-Jan 1984	Fitch data base 1. Security returns 2. Trading volume 3. Transaction frequency	• "Prices adjust within at most three trades" • "Most of price effect of block trades is permanent, and related to block size"
King, Pownall and Waymire [1990]	• 189 trading halts • Aug 1988-Oct 1988	• Daily Halts Log of NYSE	• The greater the absolute return during a halt, the greater the number of specialist indicator quotes during a halt
Lee, Ready and Seguin [1991]	• 852 halts by NYSE firms • 1988	ISSM data base 1. Security returns 2. Trading volume	• "Initiation of a trading halt increases both trading volume and price volatility"

Appendix C
Firms in Sample

4 DIGIT INDUSTRY SIC CODE	INDUSTRY/ FIRM NAME AND SYMBOL	DATA AVAILABLE
1011	*IRON ORES*	
	CLEVELAND-CLIFFS IRON (CLF)	1980-1985
	HANNA MINING (HNM)	1980-1985
1044	*SILVER ORES*	
	CALLAHAN MINING (CMN)	1981-1985
	HECLA MINING (HL)	1980-1985
	SUNSHINE MINING (SSC)	1980-1985
2032	*CANNED SPECIALITIES*	
	CAMPBELL SOUP (C0)	1980-1985
	GERBER PRODUCTS (GEB)	1980-1985
2041	*FLOUR/GRAIN MILLING*	
	GENERAL MILLS (GIS)	1980-1981
	PILLSBURY (PSY)	1980-1985
	CONAGRA (CAG)	1980-1985
	INTERNATIONAL MULTIFOODS (IMC)	1980-1985
	ARCHER-DANIELS-MIDLAND (ADM)	1980-1981
2043	*CEREAL BREAKFAST FOOD*	
	GENERAL MILLS (GIS)	1982-1985
	KELLOGG (K)	1980-1985
	QUAKER OATS (OAT)	1980-1985
2046	*CORN WET MILLING*	
	CPC INTERNATIONAL (CPC)	1980-1985
	STALEY (A.E.) MFG (STA)	1980-1985
2111	*CIGARETTES*	
	AMERICAN BRANDS (AMB)	1980-1985
	PHILIP MORRIS (MO)	1980-1985
	REYNOLDS R.J. (RJR)	1980-1985
	LIGGET GROUP (LGT)	1980-1985
2421	*SAWMILLS*	
	PACIFIC LUMBER (PL)	1980-1985
	EVANS PRODUCTS (EVY)	1980-1985
	LOUISIANA PACIFIC (LPX)	1980-1985
	POPE & TALBOT (POP)	1980-1985
	WEYERHAEUSER (WY)	1980-1985
	POTLATCH (PCH)	1980-1985
	BOISE CASCADE (BCC)	1980-1985
2621	*PAPER MILLS*	
	UNION CORP (UCO)	1980-1981
	CROWN ZELLERBACH (ZB)	1980-1985
	FORT HOWARD PAPER (FHP)	1980-1985
	GREAT NORTHERN NEKOOSA (GNN)	1980-1981
	HAMMERMILL PAPER (HML)	1980-1985
	INTERNATIONAL PAPER (IP)	1980-1985

4 DIGIT INDUSTRY SIC CODE	INDUSTRY/ FIRM NAME AND SYMBOL	DATA AVAILABLE
	JAMES RIVER CORP OF VIRGINIA (JR)	1980-1985
	KIMBERLY-CLARK (KMB)	1980-1985
	MEAD CORP (MEA)	1980-1985
	ST REGIS CORP (SRT)	1980-1985
	SOUTHWEST FOREST INDUSTRIES (SWF)	1980-1985
	WESTVACO (W)	1980-1985
	SCOTT PAPER (SPP)	1980-1985
3011	*TIRES & INNER TUBES*	
	CARLISLE CORP (CSL)	1980-1985
	COOPER TIRE & RUBBER (CTB)	1980-1985
	FIRESTONE TIRE & RUBBER (FIR)	1980-1985
	GOODRICH (B.F.)	1980-1985
	GOODYEAR TIRE & RUBBER (GT)	1980-1985
	UNIROYAL (R)	1980-1985
	ARMSTRONG RUBBER (ARM)	1980-1985
	BANDAG (BDG)	1980-1985
	MOHAWK RUBBER (MWK)	1980-1985
3221	*GLASS CONTAINERS*	
	BROCKWAY (BRK)	1980-1985
	KERR GLASS MANUFACTURING (KFM)	1980-1985
	DORSEY CORP (DSY)	1980-1981
	ANCHOR HOCKING (ARH)	1980-1985
	BALL CORP (BLL)	1980-1985
	OWENS - ILLINOIS (OI)	1980-1985
3241	*CEMENT*	
	GIANT PORTLAND & MASONRY (GPO)	1980-1985
	IDEAL BASIC INDUSTRIES (IDL)	1980-1985
	KAISER CEMENT (KCC)	1980-1985
	PUERTO RICAN CEMENT (PRN)	1980-1985
	SOUTHDOWN (SDW)	1980-1985
	ALPHA PORTLAND (SGI)	1980-1981
	GENERAL PORTLAND (GPT)	1980-1981
	PENN DIXIE (PDI)	1980-1980
3621	*MOTORS & GENERATORS*	
	EX-CELL-O CORP (XLO)	1980-1985
	EMERSON ELECTRIC (EMR)	1980-1985
	GENERAL ELECTRIC (GE)	1980-1985
	NORTH AMERICAN PHILIPS (NPH)	1980-1985
	WESTINGHOUSE ELECTRIC (WX)	1980-1985
	AMETEX (AME)	1980-1985
	BALDOR ELECTRIC (BEZ)	1980-1985
3634	*ELECTRICAL HOUSEWARES*	
	McGRAW - EDISON (MGR)	1980-1985
	NATIONAL PRESTO INDUSTRIES (NPK)	1981-1985
	ALLEGHANY CORP (Y)	1982-1985
	SUNBEAM (SMB)	1980-1981

4 DIGIT INDUSTRY SIC CODE	INDUSTRY/ FIRM NAME AND SYMBOL	DATA AVAILABLE
3673	*TRANSMITTING TUBES*	
	SCIENTIFIC - ATLANTA (SFA)	1980-1985
	VARIAN ASSOCIATES (VAR)	1980-1985
3711	*MOTOR VEHICLES*	
	CHRYSLER CORP (C)	1980-1985
	FORD MOTOR (F)	1980-1985
	GENERAL MOTORS (GM)	1980-1985
	AMERICAN MOTORS (AMO)	1980-1985
	WHITE MOTOR (WH)	1980-1980
3721	*AIRCRAFT*	
	UNITED TECHNOLOGIES (UTX)	1980-1981
	CESSNA AIRCRAFT (CEA)	1980-1985
	FAIRCHILD INDUSTRIES (FEN)	1980-1985
	GENERAL DYNAMICS (GD)	1980-1985
	GRUMMAN CORP (GQ)	1980-1985
	McDONNELL DOUGLAS (MD)	1980-1985
	NORTHROP (NOC)	1980-1985
	LOCKHEED (LK)	1980-1985
	BOEING (BA)	1980-1985
	BEECH AIRCRAFT (BCX)	1980-1980
4712	*FREIGHT FORWARDING*	
	TRANSWAY INTERNATIONAL (TNW)	1980-1985
	EMERY AIR FREIGHT (EAF)	1980-1985
	AIRBORNE FREIGHT (ABF)	1980-1985
4953	*REFUSE SYSTEMS*	
	BROWNING - FERRIS INDUSTRIES (BFI)	1980-1985
	SCA SERVICES (SCV)	1980-1984
	WASTE MANAGEMENT (WMX)	1980-1985
6411	*INSURANCE AGENTS*	
	CORROON & BLACK (CBL)	1980-1985
	MARSH & McLENNAN (MMC)	1980-1985

REFERENCES

Admati, A. R., and P. Pfleiderer, "A Theory of Intraday Patterns: Volume and Price Variability," *The Review of Financial Studies* (1988, Volume 1, Number 1): 3-40.

———, "Divide and Conquer: A Theory of Intraday and Day-of-the-Week Mean Effects," *The Review of Financial Studies* (1989, Volume 2, Number 2): 189-223.

Amihud, Y., and H. Mendelson, "Trading Mechanisms and Stock Returns: An Empirical Investigation," *The Journal of Finance* (July 1987): 533-53.

———, "Market Microstructure and Price Discovery on the Tokyo Stock Exchange," *Japan and the World Economy* 1 (1989): 341-70.

———, "Volatility, Efficiency and Trading: Evidence from the Japanese Stock Market," *The Journal of Finance* (December 1991): 1765-89.

———, ———, and M. Murgia, "Stock Market Microstructure and Return Volatility: Evidence from Italy," *Journal of Banking and Finance* (August 1990): 423-40.

Ball, R., and P. Brown, "An Empirical Evaluation of Accounting Income Numbers," *Journal of Accounting Research* (Autumn 1968): 159-78.

Bamber, L. S., "The Information Content of Annual Earnings Releases: A Trading Volume Approach," *Journal of Accounting Research* (Spring 1986): 40-56.

Barclay, M. J., and R. H. Litzenberger, "Announcement Effects of New Equity Issues and the Use of Intraday Price Data," *Journal of Financial Economics* (May 1988): 71-99.

———, J. B. Warner, and R. H. Litzenberger, "Private Information, Trading Volume and Stock Return Variances," (Working Paper, University of Rochester, 1989).

Barth, M. E., "Relative Measurement Errors Among Alternative Pension Asset and Liability Measures," *The Accounting Review* (July 1991): 433-63.

Beaver, W. H., "The Information Content of Annual Earnings Announcements," *Journal of Accounting Research* (Supplement 1968): 67-92.

Berkowitz, S. A., D. E. Logue, and E. A. Noser, "The Total Cost of Transactions on the NYSE," *The Journal of Finance* (March 1988): 97-112.

Bernard, V. L., "Stock Price Reactions to Earnings Announcements: A Summary of Recent Anomalous Evidence and Possible Explanations," (Working Paper, Harvard University, 1991).

Blume, M. "Order Imbalances and Stock Price Movements on October 19 and 20, 1987," (Working Paper, Wharton School - University of Pennsylvania, 1988).

Brock, W. A., and A. W. Kleidon, "Exogenous Demand Shocks and Trading Volume: A Model of Intraday Bids and Asks," (Research Paper No. 1034, Stanford University, 1990).

Bronfman, C., "The Informational Content of Frequently Changing Intraday Prices: Framework for an Empirical Analysis," (Working Paper, University of Arizona, 1989).

———, "Order Placement Decisions and Trading Strategies in the Securities Markets: An Empirical and Theoretical Investigation," (Working Paper, University of Arizona, 1991a).

———, "From Trades to Orders on the NYSE: Pitfalls in Inference Using Transactions Data," (Working Paper, University of Arizona, 1991b).

Choe, H., T. H. McInish, and R. A. Wood, "Market Microstructure Effects on the Measurement of the Impact of Block Trades,"(Working Paper, Memphis State University, 1991a).

———, "An Investigation of Block Versus Non-Block Intraday Trading Patterns," (Working Paper, Memphis State University, 1991b).

Cohen, K. J., S. F. Maier, R. A. Schwartz, and D. K. Whitcomb, *The Microstructure of Securities Markets* (Prentice-Hall: Englewood Cliffs, N.J., 1986).

Cready, W. M., "Information Value and Investor Wealth: The Case of Earnings Announcements," *Journal of Accounting Research* (Spring 1988): 1-27.

———, "Dividend Policy, Investor Clienteles, and Mean Transaction Size," (Working Paper, University of North Carolina at Chapel Hill, 1989).

———, and P.G. Mynatt, "The Information Content of Annual Reports: A Price and Trading Response Analysis," *The Accounting Review* (April 1991): 291-312.

———, and R. Ramanan, "Detecting Trading Responses Using Transactions-Based Research Designs: A Simulation Analysis," (Working Paper, Texas A & M University, 1991).

Damodaran, A., "The Weekend Effect in Information Releases: A Study of Earnings and Dividend Announcements," *The Review of Financial Studies* (1989, Volume 2, Number 4): 607-23.

Dann, L.Y., D. Mayers, and R. J. Raab, "Trading Rules, Large Blocks and the Speed of Price Adjustment," *Journal of Financial Economics* (January 1977): 3-22.

Defeo, V. J., "An Empirical Investigation of the Speed of the Market Reaction to Earnings Announcements," *Journal of Accounting Research* (Autumn 1986): 349-63.

Dyl, E. A., and E. D. Maberly, "A Possible Explanation of the Weekend Effect," *Financial Analysts Journal* (May-June 1988): 83-4.

Easley, D., and M. O'Hara, "Price, Trade Size, and Information in Securities Markets," *Journal of Financial Economics* (September 1987): 69-90.

Flannery, M. J., and A. A. Protopapadakis, "From T-Bills to Common Stocks: Investigating the Generality of Intra-Week Return Seasonality," *The Journal of Finance* (June 1988): 431-50.

Forsythe, R., T.R. Palfrey, and C. R. Plott, "Asset Valuation in an Experimental Market," *Econometrica* (May 1982): 537-67.

Foster, F. D., and S. Viswanathan, "Variations in Volumes, Spreads and Variances," (Working Paper, Duke University, 1988).

———, "A Theory of the Interday Variations in Volume, Variance and Trading Costs in Securities Markets," *Review of Financial Studies* (1990, Volume 3, Number 4): 593-624.

Francis, J., D. Pagach, and J. Stephan, "The Stock Market Response to Earnings Announcements Released During Trading Versus Nontrading Periods" (Working Paper, University of Chicago, 1992).

Freedman, R., and E. Terry, "Overnight Information and Opening Prices on the New York Stock Exchange," (Working Paper, Stanford University, 1988).

French, K. R., and R. Roll, "Stock Return Variances: The Arrival of Information and the Reaction of Traders," *Journal of Financial Economics* (September 1986): 5-26.

Froot, K., and J. Gammill, "New Trading Practices and Short-Run Market Efficiency," (Working Paper, MIT, 1990).

Garbade, K., and Z. Lieber, "On the Independence of Transactions on the New York Stock Exchange," *Journal of Banking and Finance* (October 1977): 151-72.

———, and C. P. Sekaran, "Opening Prices on the New York Stock Exchange," *Journal of Banking and Finance* (September 1981): 345-55.

Garman, M. B., "Market Microstructure," *Journal of Financial Economics* (June 1976): 257-75.

Gerety, M. S., and J. H. Mulherin, "Price Formation on Stock Exchanges: The Evolution of Trading Within the Day," (Working Paper, Office of Economic Analysis, U.S. Securities and Exchange Commission, 1991).

Grier, P. C., "Reply to Robert Reback's Comment," *The Journal of Business* (October 1974): 566-67.

———, and P. S. Albin, "Nonrandom Price Changes in Association with Trading in Large Blocks," *The Journal of Business* (July 1973): 425-33.

Griffin, P. A., and S. J. R. Wallach, "Latin American Lending by Major U.S. Banks: The Effects of Disclosures About Nonaccrual Loans and Loan Loss Provisions," (Working Paper, University of California at Davis, October 1988).

Harris, L. E., "A Transaction Data Study of Weekly and Intradaily Patterns in Stock Returns," *Journal of Financial Economics* (May 1986): 99-117.

———, "A Day-End Transaction Price Anomaly," *Journal of Financial and Quantitative Analysis* (March 1989): 29-45.

———, *Liquidity, Trading Rules, and Electronic Trading Systems* (New York University Salomon Center, Monograph Series in Finance and Economics; New York, 1990).

———, G. Sofianos, and J. E. Shapiro, "Program Trading and Intraday Volatility" (Working Paper, New York Stock Exchange, 1990).

Hasbrouck, J., "Trades, Quotes, Inventories and Information," (Working Paper, New York University, 1987).

———, "Assessing The Quality of a Security Market," (Working Paper, New York University, 1990).

———, and T. S. Y. Ho, "Order Arrival, Quote Behavior, and the Return-Generating Process," *The Journal of Finance* (September 1987): 1035-47.

Hausman, J. A., A. W. Lo, and A. C. MacKinlay, "An Ordered Probit Analysis of Transaction Stock Prices," (Working Paper, MIT, 1991).

Hillmer, S. C., and P. L. Yu, "The Market Speed of Adjustment to New Information," *Journal of Financial Economics* (December 1979): 321-45.

Holthausen, R. W., R. W. Leftwich, and D. Mayers, "Large-Block Transactions, the Speed of Response, and Temporary and Permanent Stock-Price Effects," *Journal of Financial Economics* (July 1990): 71-95.

Institute For the Study of Security Markets (ISSM), *Database Description* (Memphis State University, 1991).

Jain, P.C., "Response of Hourly Stock Prices and Trading Volume to Economic News," *The Journal of Business* (April 1988): 219-31.

———, and G. Joh, "The Dependence Between Hourly Prices and Trading Volume," *Journal of Financial and Quantitative Analysis* (September 1988): 269-83.

Jennings, R., and L. Starks, "Information Content and the Speed of Stock Price Adjustment," *Journal of Accounting Research* (Spring 1985): 336-50.

Kaul, G., and N. Nimalendran, "Price Reversals: Bid-Ask Errors or Market Overreaction?" (Working Paper, University of Michigan, 1991).

Keim, D. B., "Trading Patterns, Bid-Ask Spreads, and Estimated Security Returns," *Journal of Financial Economics* (November 1989): 75-97.

King, R., G. Pownall, and G. Waymire, "Corporate Disclosure and Price Discovery Associated With NYSE Temporary Trading Halts," (Working Paper, Washington University, 1990).

Kleidon, A. W., "Arbitrage, Nontrading, and Stale Prices: October 1987," (Working Paper, Stanford University, 1990) —forthcoming in *Journal of Business.*

———, and R. E. Whaley, "One Market? Stocks, Futures and Options During October 1987," (Working Paper, Stanford University 1990) —forthcoming in *Journal of Business.*

Kyle, A. S., "Continuous Auctions and Insider Trading," *Econometrica* (November 1985): 1315-35.

Lakonishok, J., and E. Maberly, "The Weekend Effect: Trading Patterns of Individual and Institutional Investors," *The Journal of Finance* (March, 1990): 231-43.

Lease, R. C., R. W. Masulis, and J. R. Page, "An Investigation of Market Microstructure Impacts on Event Study Returns," (Working Paper, University of Utah, 1991).

Lee, C. M. C., "Information Dissemination and the Small Trader: An Intraday Analysis of the Small Trader Response to Earnings Announcements," (Working Paper, University of Michigan, 1991a).

———, "Discussion of 'Corporate Disclosure and Price Discovery Associated with NYSE Temporary Trading Halts'," (Working Paper, University of Michigan, 1991b).

———, and M. J. Ready, "Inferring Trade Direction from Intraday Data," *The Journal of Finance* (June 1991): 733-46.

———, B. Mucklow, and M. J. Ready, "Spreads, Depths and the Impact of Earnings Information: An Intraday Analysis," (Working Paper, University of Michigan, 1991).

———, M. Ready, and P. J. Seguin, "Volume, Volatility and NYSE Trading Halts" (Working Paper, University of Michigan, 1991).

Lev, B., "On the Usefulness of Earnings and Earnings Research: Lessons and Directions from Two Decades of Empirical Research," *Journal of Accounting Research* (Supplement, 1989): 153-92.

Lo, A. W., and A. C. MacKinlay, "An Econometric Analysis of Nonsynchronous Trading," *Journal of Econometrics* (July/August 1990): 181-211.

Lockwood, L. J., and S. C. Linn, "An Examination of Stock Market Return Volatility During Overnight and Intraday Periods, 1964-1989," *The Journal of Finance* (June 1990): 591-601.

———, and T. H. McInish, "Tests of Stability For Variances and Means of Overnight/Intraday Returns During Bull and Bear Markets," *Journal of Banking and Finance* (December, 1990): 1243-53.

McInish, T. H., and R. A. Wood, "Proxies for Nonsynchronous Trading," *The Financial Review* (May 1983): 206-13.

———, "Intertemporal Differences in Movements of Minute-to-Minute Stock Returns," *The Financial Review* (November 1984): 359-71.

———, "A New Approach to Controlling For Thin Trading," *The Journal of Financial Research* (Spring 1985a): 69-75.

———, "Intraday and Overnight Returns and Day-of-the-Week Effects," *The Journal of Financial Research* (Summer 1985b): 119-26.

———, "Adjusting for Beta Bias: An Assessment of Alternate Techniques: A Note," *The Journal of Finance* (March 1986): 277-86.

———, "A Transactions Data Analysis of the Variability of Common Stock Returns During 1980-1984," *Journal of Banking and Finance* (March 1990a): 99-112.

———, "An Analysis of Transactions Data for the Toronto Stock Exchange" *Journal of Banking and Finance* (August 1990b): 441-58.

———, "Hourly Returns, Volume, Trade Size and Number of Trades," *Journal of Financial Research* (Winter 1991): 303-15.

———, "Stock Return Variances: Trading Versus Nontrading Periods," (Working Paper, University of Texas at Arlington, 1987).

———, "Market Frictions, Market Microstructure, Imperfect Decision Making and Autocorrelation of Portfolio Returns," (Working Paper, University of Texas, 1988).

———, "An Analysis of Intraday Patterns in Bid/Ask Spreads for NYSE Stocks," (Working Paper, Memphis State University, 1991b).

———, J. K. Ord, and R. A. Wood, "A Transactions Data Test of the Calendar Time and Transactions Time Models," (Working Paper, University of Texas at Arlington, January 1985).

McMillan, H., "The Effects of S&P500 Futures Market Circuit Breakers on Liquidity and Price Discovery," (Working Paper, Office of Economic Analysis, U.S. Securities and Exchange Commission, 1990).

———, and J. Overdahl, "NYSE Rule 80A: An Evaluation of its Effects on Trading Costs and Intermarket Linkages," (Working Paper, Office of Economic Analysis, U.S. Securities and Exchange Commission, 1991).

Madhavan, A., and S. Smidt, "A Bayesian Model of Intraday Specialist Pricing," (Working Paper, Wharton School, 1991)

Miller, E. M., "Explaining Intraday and Overnight Price Behavior," (Working Paper, University of New Orleans, 1988a).

———, "Why a Weekend Effect?" *Journal of Portfolio Management* (Summer 1988b): 43-8.

Morse, D., and B. Mucklow, "Autocorrelations of Daily Returns Without Bid/Ask Spreads and Price Discreteness," (Working Paper, University of Oregon, 1991).

Mucklow, B., "Market Microstructure: An Examination of the Effects On Intraday Event Studies," (Working Paper, University of Wisconsin, 1991).

Neal, R., "Program Trading on the NYSE: A Descriptive Analysis and Estimates of the Intraday Impact on Stock Returns," (Working Paper, University of Washington, 1990).

New York Stock Exchange, *Fact Book* (New York: New York Stock Exchange, Inc., 1985, 1986, 1987 editions).

Niederhoffer, V., and M.F.M. Osborne, "Market Making and Reversal on the Stock Exchange," *Journal of the American Statistical Association* (December 1966): 897-916.

Oldfield, G. S., and R. J. Rogalski, "A Theory of Common Stock Returns Over Trading and Non-Trading Periods," *The Journal of Finance* (June 1980): 729-51.

———, ———, and R. A. Jarrow, "An Autoregressive Jump Process for Common Stock Returns," *Journal of Financial Economics* (December 1977): 389-413.

Ord, J. K., T. H. McInish, and R. A. Wood, "Trade-to-Trade Beta Estimation: Methodology and Deficiencies," (Working Paper, Pennsylvania State University, 1984).

Patell, J. M., and M. A. Wolfson, "Good News, Bad News, and the Intraday Timing of Corporate Disclosures," *The Accounting Review* (July 1982): 509-27.

———, "The Intraday Speed of Adjustment of Stock Prices to Earnings and Dividend Announcements," *Journal of Financial Economics* (June 1984): 223-52.

Petersen, M., and S. Umlauf, "An Empirical Examination of the Intraday Behavior of the NYSE Specialist," (Working Paper, University of Chicago, 1990).

Peterson, D. R., "A Transaction Data Study of Day-of-the-Week and Intraday Patterns in Option Returns," *The Journal of Financial Research* (Summer 1990): 117-31.

Pincus, M., and L. Starks, "An Empirical Investigation of Differential Intraday Speed of Stock Price Adjustment to Annual Earnings Announcements," (Working Paper, Washington University, 1987).

Plott, C. R., and S. Sunder, "Rational Expectations and the Aggregation of Diverse Information in Laboratory Security Markets," *Econometrica* (September 1988): 1085-1118.

Porter, D. C., "The Probability of a Trade at the Ask: An Examination of Interday and Intraday Behavior," (Working Paper, Marquette University, 1989).

Reback, R., "Nonrandom Price Changes in Association with Trading in Large Blocks: A Comment," *The Journal of Business* (October 1974): 564-65.

Richardson, M., and T. Smith, "On Tests for Serial Dependency of Returns," (Working Paper, Stanford University, 1988).

Rogalski, R. J., "New Findings Regarding Day of the Week Returns Over Trading and Non-Trading Periods," *The Journal of Finance* (December 1984): 1603-14.

Roll, R. , "The International Crash of October, 1987," (Working Paper, UCLA, 1988).

Santoni, G. J., "The October Crash: Some Evidence on the Cascade Theory," *Federal Reserve Bank of St.Louis* (May/June 1988): 18-33.

Schwartz, R. A., *Equity Markets: Structure, Trading, and Performance* (Harper & Row: New York, 1988).

———, *Reshaping the Equity Markets: A Guide for the 1990s* (Harper Business: New York, 1991).

Skinner, D. J., "Stock Returns, Trading Volume, and Bid/Ask Spreads Around Earnings Announcements: Evidence from the NASDAQ National Market System," (Working Paper, University of Michigan, June 1991).

Smirlock, M., and L. Starks, "Day-of-the-Week and Intraday Effects in Stock Returns," *Journal of Financial Economics* (September 1986): 197-210.

———, "An Empirical Analysis of the Stock Price-Volume Relationship," *Journal of Banking and Finance* (March, 1988): 31-41.

Stephan, J. A., and R. Whaley, "Intraday Price Change and Trading Volume Relations in the Stock and Stock Option Markets," *The Journal of Finance* (March 1990): 191-220.

Stoll, H. R., *The Stock Exchange Specialist System: An Economic Analysis* (New York University Salomon Center, Monograph Series in Finance and Economics; New York, 1985).

———, "Inferring the Components of the Bid-Ask Spread: Theory and Empirical Tests," *The Journal of Finance* (March 1989): 115-34.

———, and R. E. Whaley, "Stock Market Structure and Volatility," *Review of Financial Studies* (1990, Volume 3, Number 1): 37-71.

Terry, E., "End of the Day Returns and the Bid-Ask Spread," (Working Paper, Stanford University, August, 1986).

———, "Essays in Financial Economics," (Working Paper, Stanford University, 1988).

Watts, S. G., "Market Microstructure and the Timing of Earnings Releases: An Empirical Investigation" (Working Paper, University of British Columbia, 1991).

Wood, R. A., and T. H. McInish, "Bias From Nonsynchronous Trading in Tests of the Levhari-Levy Hypothesis," *The Review of Economics and Statistics* (May 1984): 346-51.

———, ———, and J. K. Ord, "An Investigation of Transactions Data for NYSE Stocks" *The Journal of Finance* (July 1985): 723-39.

Woodruff, C. S., and A. J. Senchack, "Intradaily Price-Volume Adjustments of NYSE Stocks to Unexpected Earnings," *The Journal of Finance* (June 1988): 467-91.